CANTICLES
I
(MMXVII)

ESSENTIAL POETS SERIES 247

Canada Council **Conseil des Arts**
for the Arts **du Canada**

ONTARIO ARTS COUNCIL
CONSEIL DES ARTS DE L'ONTARIO

an Ontario government agency
un organisme du gouvernement de l'Ontario

Guernica Editions Inc. acknowledges the support of the Canada Council
for the Arts and the Ontario Arts Council. The Ontario Arts Council
is an agency of the Government of Ontario.

We acknowledge the financial support of the Government of Canada.
Nous reconnaissons l'appui financier du gouvernement du Canada.

GEORGE ELLIOTT CLARKE

CANTICLES

I
(MMXVII)

GUERNICA
EDITIONS
TORONTO • BUFFALO • LANCASTER (U.K.)
2017

Michael Mirolla, editor
David Moratto, cover and interior design
Cover font, interior drop caps: Bill Clarke Caps
Guernica Editions Inc.
1569 Heritage Way, Oakville, (ON), Canada L6M 2Z7
2250 Military Road, Tonawanda, N.Y. 14150-6000 U.S.A.
www.guernicaeditions.com

Distributors:
University of Toronto Press Distribution
5201 Dufferin Street, Toronto (ON), Canada M3H 5T8
Gazelle Book Services, White Cross Mills
High Town, Lancaster LA1 4XS U.K.

First edition.
Printed in Canada.

Legal Deposit—First Quarter
Library of Congress Catalog Card Number: 2016952740
Library and Archives Canada Cataloguing in Publication

Clarke, George Elliott, 1960-, author
Canticles I : (mmxvii). -- First edition.

(Essential poets series ; 247)
Includes bibliographical references and index.

Issued in print and electronic formats.
ISBN 978-1-77183-190-1 (paperback).--ISBN 978-1-77183-191-8
(epub).--ISBN 978-1-77183-193-2 (mobi)

I. Title. II. Series: Essential poets series ; 247

PS8555.L3748C37 2017   C811'.54   C2016-905974-X   C2016-905975-8

It will be rewritten
by black pamphleteers, History will be revised....
— Derek Walcott, *Omeros*.

The beautiful would be an essential quality of their freedom.
— Herbert Marcuse, *An Essay on Liberation*.

For Geraldine Elizabeth Clarke (1939–2000)
& William Lloyd Clarke (1935–2005):
Adepts, Believers, African Baptists.

& For Burnley Allan "Rocky" Jones (1941–2013):
Africadian Revolutionary, Radical, Rebel.

INTRODUCTORY (II)

Once poetry was a form of government.
— Pain Not Bread, *"Long Ago (An Introduction to Du Fu)"*.

～⁓

Herein commences the *second* half of *Canticles I*, namely, *Canticles I (MMXVII)*, which chases *Canticles I (MMXVI)*. Hereby I maintain a dialogue with the dead, both the once actually existing and the present, evidently fanciful, to dramatize a partisan *History*, one showcasing genocidal *Imperialism* and criminal *Slavery and Justice*-seeking rebels and *enragés*.

Because *Canticles I (MMXVI)* prefaces this work, I need not iterate here the original introduction. However, if this intro *is your* induction to *Canticles I*, I repeat that *Canticles* is a lyric-structured epic. The subject of the second half of this Testament I continues to be *History*, with the pertinent biases as proclaimed above. Testament II (to be published later) will issue rereadings of scriptures pertinent to the emergent African Diaspora in the Americas. Testament III (also to appear later) will chronicle the creation of the African Baptist Association churches of Nova Scotia by 1853.

My method? Oulipo, elliptical, and serendipitous. Upon meditating on a collection of words, phrases, images, and/or lines, a 'voice' would begin to order the disparate materials into a 'confessional' narrative. Usually, I did not know beforehand the identity of the subject. However, I would soon realize that my speaker was Nat Turner or Alexandre Dumas, *fils*; or Jeanne Duval or Malcolm X (as Detroit Red); or Sojourner Truth or Colette. Once the new piece was scribed, I'd find a space for it — chronologically — in the developing whole. Once I blundered into century XX, I knew I should include Holocaust testimony, plus the brazen voice of Mao Zedong. Thus, my process traces *Whimsy* more than *History*: I take the print keyboard as a *Ouija* board. I construct a collage of accidental inspirations.

My 'constraints' here were 1) to draft no piece in Toronto, Ontario, and 2) always to write in black ink (usually *via* a fountain pen). Hence, *Canticles* is a species of travel writing in black-and-white. I pray that the reader will find some extra pleasure in connecting a poem, say, 'by' Ntshingwayo kaMahole in one space with a poem written about him in another, possibly years—and/or an ocean—apart. My wish is to layer events and actors—as palimpsests and mirrors—to present *History* as an echo chamber.

That enough illumination? *Fine!* Now, sojourn (further, deeper) amid shadowy *History*....

George Elliott Clarke
Ottawa (Ontario) 17 *avril* / *Nisan* mmxvi
& Marburg—Mainz (Germany) 12 *décembre* mmxvi
& Montréal (Québec) 24 *décembre* mmxvi

THE BOOK OF ORIGINS

Raced Traces

[The Continuation of
CANTICLES I MMXXVI]

Ma mémoire a sa ceinture de cadavres.
— Aimé Césaire, *Cahier d'un retour au pays natal*

"Prophet" Nat Turner
on his Southampton Insurrection (1831)

I.

A raven splashed the primal sign.
Its beak leaked drool,
scarlet spittle,
burgundying a branch,

so that freakish streaks imaged
The Holy Family—
Babe Jesus, Mama Mary, Papa Joe—
as clear Red Indian.

Shortly, I watched tea leaves erect
a transcendent bric-a-brac*—
an upright black cross in a white china cup.

Next, I witnessed seagulls
turn to ashes in a volcano's vent
while its lake vanished in steam,
and dormancy yielded to instant fire,

and, next, I saw black horses shivered in flames,
tumbling to silver bones.

These symbols—hieroglyphs—
provoked my brain as distinctly
as bells barking—untimely—

and hyenas chiming in.

---

* Cf. Gaudi.

II.

You have my *Historic Diary*—
black-lace ink looping white-face pages—

and so you know I did dream
of inseminating a blonde ballerina,

while parental applause
kept time with our galloping bed.

Yes, if not for my *Prophetic Mission*,
I'd've fucked even the wrinkled white wives
and gunked my throat with way too much white wine.

III.

When the *Liberation*—
not "ruction"—
got going,
I tutored my lads—
"No *Fornication*, no *Intoxication*:
Only kill and slaughter and massacre."

Disobeying, fellers yanked out dogging cocks
to hound and sound any blanching bitch,

but also acted piggish, slurping every drip
and drop of firewater.

IV.

Yes, I did rip free Whitehead's—
misty pantaloons—
as see-through as breathing*—

to know her delicious sprawling,
her gold hair slopping over my copper chest.

I steeled myself against her silkiness;
stayed no more an affable, natty Negro;

knifed open her milk breasts;
sucked their brilliant scarlet;

suddenly, my lurching, drooling penis
felt as nauseatin as a stallion's.

Yessum, I smashed her brains to mincemeat;
stilled her bleating....

[**Hull-Gatineau (Québec)** 25 *janvier* **mmxv**]

---

* Cf. Styron.

Nat Turner Confessing All

By Thomas Grey

Sunlight singed dour air lapis-lazuli;
unhinged that atmosphere; dingy
Apartheid angels — salt-n-pepper shades — winged,

muscling aside clouds.
That ghoulish light slashed corn
so blood gooped out;
whole crops stooped down,

swaddled in red crud;
crimson *cum* slathered wheat.

But I didn't flinch at such wonders.

Naturally, magnolia undulated under beings
as translucent as moonlight.
Cherubs fluttered about a vacated crucifix:

They flaunted black capes and strummed harps
strung with serpents.

My conspirators? Various arsonists —
whose dream — or predilection —

was to leave vile Virginia,
a cache of ashes;

to scuttle — or slit open — white chits,
but perpetrate coal-cellar *Coitus* —
black dicks brimming *blancmange* quim.

(Me? I only hustled to fit my mitts
round leather-backed Bibles.)

My comrades were as heartless
as emptied brandy bottles;

they were grotesquely excited,
going shoeless over grass—
thanking God for letting em manhandle (mangle)
any snow-flanked missy.

(My wench splayed amid a sea of wheat.
Her legs jerked, arcing.

"Dew" silvered that camel-toe
impressing her pantaloons.

I eyed a supine statue—
out-thrust tits, oozing cooze,
medallions of pink blotches
spotting her thighs and bloomers.

To be biblically self-damning—
to stop the gold tears scudding from her dark, almond eyes,
I dropped a fence post; thudded her blonde skull.)

Our cabal of killers—
boasted a gargantuan orangutang—
Hark—
whose moustache brushed gainst
least a dozen bleached teats,

while his nostrils burnt gainst a throat,
and his eyeballs slurped the blush of a slap.
His cock rooted like a spade.

His culling of Mrs. Travis was
quite uncalled for—
to pick-axe her sickly lungs....

But such is *Revolt!* We mutilated mansions
and punched holes in pallid *Virginity*
(formerly as disagreeable as vinegar)
in our scourging excursions.

Eventually, a shot blew off Hark's top hat;
the next chiselled open his "Me, first" brains.

(Wet clay frothed—slicked—his saddle.)
Our *Insurrection?*

Pigmentation
en route to *Fermentation*—

our fundamental *Firmament.*

[**Peterborough (Ontario)** *6 avril* / *Nisan* **mmxv**]

Rum: A Metaphysical Disquisition

I.

*R*um* leaks everywhere like a honkytonk skank—
expressly humid
at crux of her pincer hips.

Heck! White *Rum* gleams a lachrymose patina,
so this personable milk
mirrors tin-coloured cream.

If black ink spells out a crow's *Grief,*
white *Rum* distills white *Poetry—*
vers blanc.

If I study *Political Economy* spiritually,
I admit *Nothing* is unpolluted or untainted—
except white *Rum—*
a molten salt,
a napalm tonic.

Still, I prefer dark *Rum—*
barbed-wire perforating the throat.

II.

Let no *State* impose a *cordon sanitaire,*
strangling our *Rum* islands,
for, the full-bore torrent of this *Lubricant*
spurs on laggard *Savages'*
unaccustomed staggering:

---

* Masters, "The Spooniad": "If rum must be / ... the medium to release / From ...
slavery, / Then give me rum."

If they're not drunk,
our throats are cut.

III.

To imbibe any rum is to leverage
licorice-tint slaves liquidated
to compose the most caustic, bleached sugar.

Each dawn comes branded, hot, as searing as alcohol.
Each dusk whiplashes in, tobacco-tinted.

The sorority of Carib isles
plot comparably despicable pastures,

but *History*—to be honest—
indoctrinates Caucasians in *Piracy*,
not the plough.

IV.

Sugar is *White Gold*
enslaving *Black Gold*

via lacerating machetes—
or macerating machetes—

flashing back painfully Barbados' urine-gold sun.

(In dull, barbarian *Thought*,
sugar means king-size icing,
period.

So, no Euro, philosophical issue
tallies its cost in black nigger bile,
that imported—but homemade—*Venom*.)

V.

Label each bottle, *"Black Labour*
stabled by *White Government,"*

the hold of a pale chrome liquid—
gun-metal livid—
a nectar as glossy as formaldehyde—

and as muddling and befuddling as opium.

VI.

I shy from the shacks adjacent
to my mansion,
the cantankerous calypsos of blackie drunks,
reeling in their Royal-backed and Royal-backing ghettoes.

Like staccato shadows,
they stoop in my cane,
defecate, urinate, copulate,
begetting more kindred beggars,

Kindergarten bastards,* crapulent.

VII.

I am a *preux chevalier.***

Imperial *scriptoria* insists that fecal tasks—
to go unbungled—
need be handled in blackface.

---

* If ya don't catch a nigger by the toe
And then cut off his head,
He'll have a white lady on *his* say-so,
And sleigh her in his bed....
** French: Gallant knight.

My workforce — servants — slaves
induce raw sugar
to produce
gum-gooey syrup,
coffee-dark tea,
honey-churned puddings,
pear-tint porridge,
charcoal-chocolate cakes,
and noggin grog,

to seduce Europe's cosmopolitan palate
(infallibly greedy).

Our *Commerce* exudes pig-sty stench —
a smell of dung mashed up with olives
and sardines.

Too, black maidens suck down spunk
like slippery sugar —

and caterwaul for gowns of sapphire calico
plus trinkets of gaudy brass.

Cataclysms shadow *Orgasms.*

VII.

But gilded sugar is as gourmet as the sun —
that belligerent *Brightness* —
and helps us tamper with wine
and maybe tamp down *Insurrection.*

My *Rum* is awash with *Radiance* —
that sweet, glistening *Clarity.*

I let *Whiteness* shiver into my coffee;
I scalpel a slice of *Rum* cake.

I do fantasize an outrageous disemboweling;
my *Blood*—

my dreamy, white-sauce lineage—

distilled to *Soot*—

or skulls bunched—
hanging, dangling, *ensemble*—
for vultures' lunches—
or for a murder of ravens* to munch,
tearing into carnation lips, cornflower eyes, conch-tint ears....

Yes, I fear my suited, servile *Calibans*
will prove—soon or late—suitable cannibals....

—*George Elliott Clarke, B.A., LL.B.***
Proprietor, Stepney Plantation,
Parish of St. George,
Barbados, W.I., 1832

[**Berlin (Germany) 9 & 10** *mars* **mmxiii**]

---

* Or: An assassination of poets.
** Cf. *The Journal of the Barbados Museum & Historical Society: Pupils of the Charterhouse.*
No lie.

An Introduction to the Late Revolution in "Haiti"

By Abraham Lincoln (1834)

Sugar Eden is Saint-Domingue:

Alps of albescent sweetness—
pyramids of paradisal sunlight—
sail daily to Nantes and Bordeaux,

or did so

when 60% of the *métropole*'s shipping
triangulated oozing-chancred slaves,
avalanching sugar, *delirium-tremens* rum.

C'est vrai:
The recompense for *les nègres*,
was sour cod, teaspooned brandy,
cockroach-shat-upon flour,

and aches, wounds, *Pain*.

Anyway, sugar slushes veins, arteries....

Cane must be crushed, flushed with water
(or bled out), dried,
to conjure sugar.

So *les ésclaves*—
"black gold"—
mustered—
alchemized "white gold"—

sugar, rum—

and toted white planters

mustard-gold profits.

Those black "Zombies" who proved zealots—
sucked teeth—
needled planters *via* cut-eye and tart tongues—

got nicely mowed down by muskets,
gutted by cannon gusts.

Their witch doctors urged on *Reaction*,
chanting,
in contraband, Congo lingo,
"We swear to dig apart the whites!
We'll die if we can't knife em all!"

Quarrels exploded into *Revolution*

immediately when ox-cart courier,
Bookman
(ironically, "ill-literate," to spite his name),

launched white-skin-peeling, white-folk-repealing killings
at "Bwa Kayiman,"

urged on by his murderous Muse,
the green-eyed, maple-syrup-hued *Bacchante*—
Cécile Fatiman.

This jungle woman speechified,
"Machetes, chop every crucifix into kindling!
France's paleface god only loves our tears!"

Next, hog gore plastered black faces,
jabbering,
"*Liberty* or *Damnation*!"

In seven days, Bookman's "Hubbub"
gobbled up 2,000 plantations
and gobbled down 1,000 masters,
crimsoning lily-white sugar.

Once these insurgent slaughters were stanched
and Bookman guillotined,

traipsed along twelve years of *War*,
thanks to Toussaint L'Ouverture,
tricked out as a general,
killing off Caucasian *commandantes*,

while the pack of maddog ex-slaves—
roiled anti-royalists—

pounced on shock-troops of three Empires—
French, Spanish, British—
wolfed em down and spat out epaulettes.

(It was they who broke Napoléon
and bust his *Treasury*,
so he hawked Louisiana cheap.)

1800 dawned,
and Napoléon dispatched
bro-in-law Le Clerc,
heading 40,000 Marines—
FORTY-THOUSAND Marines—
to shackle Saint-Domingue anew.

"The Cleric" started out "gangbusters,"
warping black bodies *via* iron and steel,
conjuring worms to bleach nigger flesh.

Le Clerc so addled L'Ouverture,
the jigaboo general indulged curlicued, *Peace* overtures.

But, once aboard ship and afforded *Calvados*,
got clapped in chains and frog-marched to Jura,
to end, upchucking blood, in an icy cell.

There the Negro *Ruction* would've stalled,
or gone to ground—
ground-down by Parisian cannon—
save Dessalines dubbed himself commander,

and that dark-complected Atilla only wept
whenever he didn't slay enough French.

"The Cleric" struggled to stave off Dessalines,
but black soil now yanked down white skins—
due to the gravity
that's Yellow Fever.

Plus, Dessalines' troops were sage guerrillas;
nay, sanguinary gorillas—
Maroons high up in the hills,
but low-down at any *Killing*:

Scathin with machetes
and shootin off (captured) bullets,
these ghouls disembowled the howling French—
fricassee-ing em
(so bodies resembled stewed chicken and white sauce)—
come *Fracas* after *Fracas*.

Those whom Dessalines didn't pepper or squash,
damn mosquitoes chewed up:

Frenchmen flopped, face-down, jaundiced:
Even Le Clerc went belly-up—
turned "yellah"-bellied (pardon the pun).

Rochambeau disembarked, voted *White Terror*
the antidote to *Black Murdering*:

He gave up *Humanity*.

He loosed human-flesh-lovin dogs,
to bite and chomp and rip
enemy, ebony hides.
But the diabolical tactic was damnably tricky:
The canines found white flesh just as swank!

Stymied in this drastic *Gothicism*,
Rochambeau aped Robespierre's *Sadism*:

Trapped blacks got burned alive,

or flung, screaming, into ditches
muffling shovels quick covered up,

or shot down into graves
they'd been forced to dig.

Yet, by 1803, 80% of Rochambeau's musketeers
added up to zero,
totalled by machete, musket, or mosquito.*

Soon, Jean-Jacques Dessalines
(nominal antithesis to Rousseau)
decided undead planters
looked best stuck headfirst in quicksand,
or pitched into stake-bottomed pits.

So, his emancipated brutes ran amok,
macheteing every *blanco* skull.

This *Black Terror* erased ledgers of black ink.

By 1807, Brits started stoppin
any Euro and Yankee vessel
thought to be ferrying black loot

(i.e., Afro'd galoots),

---

* 100% of the dying felt an unpatriotic hatred for Napoléon: Yes? No?

and repatriating captives
to Africa—

either to St. Helena or Sierra Leone.

Humanitarian? Politic!

Brits sought to cancel
the cancer *Insurrection*,
an *Ebola*
that could bleed scarlet
th'Anglican Caribbean,

if fresh Africans set polished hoe*
and household blade and gun
contra King James Version Christians....

Nevertheless, liquidating fires leapt swift from "Haiti"

to char Charles's Louisiana,
and torch Turner's Virginia:

This conflagration—
Liberty—
erased plantations with gold flame;
blazes swamped capitals and citadels;

and in the ensuing sluice of smoke,

Europe's marble heroes, now dingy,

all toppled hard,

with a backward, crashing thud.

[Helsinki (Finland) 27 *juin* mmxiii]

---

* Cf. Austin Chesterfield Clarke.

A Russian Aristocrat Complains of Pushkin

That quadroon poetaster, Pushkin,
talks over unrivalled, undiluted Dante?

His verses, spicy and sassy —
peppered vodka —
lisp sparkling expletives,
spill vintage *Farce*.

Thus, our rose-blushed sweethearts rush to Pushkin:
Any room he graces,
soon boasts a glamorous gathering of snow,
and he appears an emperor
harassed by his *Harem*.

Apparently, to parrot poetry is to flirt
(to expound two pounding hearts,
then pound four thighs together).

In her sly glances, a woman cries for *F—king?*
And subversive *Blackness?*

Pushkin's cunning, Kushite darkness,
cons em, is Don-Juan seductive.

The pimp purrs honey —
that should sear like acid the Czar's ears.
This abhorrent darky's a mandarin of *Whoring*.

His pen perpetrates *Penetration*!
(He'd shovel his stylus
into the Czarina's inkwell;
jet a dusky inkling.)

But that eve-tinted bull can,
one dawn, be put down,
if a dauntless matador appears—
aiming to streak a black hide burgundy.

[Southampton (Bermuda) 28 *mars* mmxii]

A Prospect of Bahia (January 1835)

By Vitório Sule

I.

Their Christ is a great poet for the dead.
And the Pope is Christ's whining echo.

Priests gulp our coins like fish trying to breathe
Sweat. Salvador cathedrals are wedding-cakes of garbage.

A shindig of flies:
Smacked down angels sport maggot wings.

Then again, blasphemers inspire boondoggles of *Prayer*—
as silly as trophy cups brimming with urine.

II.

Black people, do not act timid as moonlight!
No! Put our ivory foes to death—

like pages washed out by black ink!
Wash away the dry-bleached-feces faces

in an ebony tsunami.
Treat each pallid pup as small, squirming prey,

splattering its body as easily as a vase.
Act festive, immodest butchers!

III.

I'm no aqueous poet —
pure tears and ink,

nor do I acquiesce
to any vacillation amid the cemetery

in which we find ourselves.
Yes, our oppressors are even our ancestors:

Lust fathers *Hybridity*.
To overthrow em all,

we must be as astonishing as thunder.
Our *Opprobrium* opposes *Equilibrium*.

IV.

Ramadan is nigh. Now! Now —
ruddy baroquely dictator Satan's "Christians"!

Aye, that *Evil* must be expunged:
Lest every black phallus signal a minus sign....

[**Puumala [Finland]** *9 août* **mmxii**]

The Liberation of Bahia Has Begun! (1835)

By Vitório Sule

Rip fresh holes in the thronged slavemasters.
Scythe em in a swath.

After the hissing of our machetes,
as our oppressors crumple,
they'll hear murmurs of grass.

Hammer down windows, doors!
Trample wan widows, whores!

Wet mauve ochres white plaster.

Slice off each white stump of cock;
slash the tits off every ivory bitch.

If you crave *Liberty*!

(*Justice* is a kiss, a touch.
But *Liberation* is much more:

An orgy, palpable.)

Remember:
Mountains are mere ruins to tunnelling worms.

[Vicenza (Italy) **23** *septembre* **mmxii**]

At Pompey Square

I.

A ghostly haunt—
pace 1834—
here's where Pompey sued
most miserly *Charity*—

the right to remain
(a slave)
on Exuma (isle)—

in the throes of tolerable *Governance*;

so as not to get carted off
to Barbados' worse-off
fens and glens;

to suffer that despairing *Arrival*

and again th'Atlantic,
that salty brightness,
that tidal *Enemy*.

Better to scramble to Nassau—
assault

bedraggled straggler after straggler, i.e.,
the scraggly haired, craggy mugged loyalist slaves,

and then appeal to the regnant *Vanity*

(i.e. pay unmatched compliments
to the "matchless"—ahem—Governor),

to burrow into his caved-in *Conscience*,

so he offsets th'oppressive ills
of *Thirst* and hunch-backed *Stooping*....

II.

Succeeding, Pompey got to affix
a branding X
to his *Article of Emancipation* —

parchment almost as robust as gold,

to erase in this plangent ink
his once face-value as currency.

But first had he to be
a sterling hero —

an African John Ball —

his cracked breath breaking even Creole
lexicons —

as he framed the Caribbean
as the Mediterranean's mirror,

wherein Greece also strives
to no more be Turkish slaves.

III.

Pompey purveyed the disturbing *Villain* —
i.e., a *Freedom Fighter*;

risked ending as a row of black coffins,
all his tribe, silenced as bastard laureates.

IV.

Soon anchors an exodus of privileged eyes
at The Bahamas' Governor's palaced municipality—
London—

to condemn that white ruler's acquiescence
to darkies as obstinate as drunks.

"Won't he plummet into plaster dust?
Set the Empire withering anew?"

But Pompey's corpus of ink x's
imperialist, corporatist alabaster;

his freed physique marks his signature
cancelling a blighting *Bureaucracy*—

Anglican
(anti-angelic),

hurling out snow—
a storm-burst of papers—

signifying malignant ligatures, *Indenture*,
malicious, calligraphic ligatures,

the stuff of laws—

shackles spiked to walls.

[**Nassau (The Bahamas) 25** *août* **mmxiv**]

Audubon's Observations (1835)

Sired at Saint-Domingue (now Haiti),
but France-reared, I've quit Europe

for *Illumination* amid mud—
the putrid gangrene of the bayou.

Louisiana seethes with black-green wastes.
Poets amble among graves—

statues of sunflowers—
in spongy, mosquito-fogged boneyards,

where palm tree shadows imitate
spindly spider legs.

Rainbow-feathered songbirds—
brabble through over-sufficient *Greenery*;

their whooping shadows swoop
over the Utopian muck.

Mists brighten the murk,
so I can do heartless shooting,

sculpt loosed gore, flustered feathers,
as my bullets arrow,

cutting down fugitive,
winged gentry.

I park on a square of beach,
thin out each squawk and trill.

Next, my brush elaborates
avian spectres,

the translucent remains,
suddenly superior

to their flitting lives.
Some creatures sustain

a gleaming scalpel —
while ichor streams, steaming,

just so I can sow anatomies
in-situ tissue,

the jolts of silenced, muffled feathers.
Art is worth

the reek of entrails.
Bird-tracking Latin becomes *Poetry* —

a quill bleeding stains.
I pluck and supply

rare-bird flesh
to appreciative priests,

who like to imagine my felled fowl
screeching in a book.

Each painting is a glossy construction —
a strategic *Deletion*.

So plaintive, avian wings —
flout the whiteness —

the pristine clarity —
of the manuscript.

My birds constitute air-borne coral reefs,
aviaries wafted — frozen — by *Art*, or *Torture*.

[**Coral Harbour (The Bahamas) 22** *août* **mmxiv**]

Audubon's Observations: Gloss

I.

Caustic bullets churn, upturn, flesh,
feathery, light as heather:
Decisive decimation unfurls,

until wraiths with claws —
a griffin-like family —
become red mire,

or fill sooty ditches
as grandiose dung
as exaggerated as *Porn.*

The dying birds prove
no one dwells in lilies.
The litter of plumes —

the prurient blush —
settles on fringes of branches
like talons gripping butterflies.

(Arrows nail down their coffins,
where the sparrows got skewered —
like impaled, skinny, miniature swine.)

II.

Flustered, I lumbered out of Haiti —
to Paris —
a baroque pelican

(model for Baudelaire's "Le Cygne" —
the laughing-stock of guttersnipes —
and symbolizing Negresses,

otherwise negated by snow)....
How to find *Lustre?*
Well, ruthless, *Art* opens eyes — like butchers' surgery.

[Coral Harbour (The Bahamas) 22 *août* mmxiv]

32

Pushkin Acts Byronic[*]

Vigorous wallowing in vodka —
plush swallows of the honey'd heat —
coax Pushkin to his nightly "dump" —

pumping *cum* in his drunk slut's *chatte*,
that bitch well-thumped on a pillow,
her tush braying like a trumpet.

Geez, the gouts of vodka that poet
deprives all the other depraved
of, at the Court, that *salon* of booze.

Strumpets with peppermint skin
nosh on Pushkin's chocolate mint,
while he slobbers down their brine,

and then books, deposits, scrams,
so *les belles dames* spy the white lie
of his silhouette,

not as dark as his actual, demon self.
Soon, a fresh punk sweetens his sheets,
laps his chrome-plated spunk.

(The taste of vodka is licorice made snow.)
Her belly gets plastered with tears
as pasty as glue.

Nyet!
Her belly is beset with spew
the colour of anis, milky.

[Cambridge (Massachusetts) 27 *novembre* mmxiii]

---

[*] Russian poet Alexander Pushkin (1799–1837) was a long-distance acolyte of British
poet George Gordon, Lord Byron (1788–1824)

The Death of Alexander Pushkin

When d'Anthès discharges his pistol —
a conflagration flashes forth —
to flush out my flesh.
A ball rips my guts.

I suffer a stained-glass, Russian Orthodox *Murder* —
to steel my glassy wife's *Honour*
from being broken up by gossips' crunching jaws.

If only d'Anthès had suffered my bullet's inhuman bluntness,
had savoured a goring by an untethered bull!
I'd watch his eyes discandy to ingots of coal.

Instead, he unloosed a lightning bolt from his nozzle;
a spear-point I couldn't dodge.

The bullet struck home like notes
in a barbaric elegy.
I'm smeared, smutched, smucked.

The bullet is like hooves dragging me down,
tumbling me under a stallion's tonnage,
so I am Pushkin *and* cadaver.

The bullet is as crippling to my sight
as are my eyelids.
My lips warble a scarlet harmonica.

I'd be a world-class poet —
and shine among the poets —
because I crave *Justice* —
which is the Negro's gold —
just as *Hunger* craves fat.

But now Pushkin—I—am "out-of-print."*
Let my corpus play my clone, *if* it's mint.

[**Tulum (Mexico)** 2 & 3 *septembre* **mmxv**]

_____

* P.Z.: Victorian bookseller terminology signifying the dead.

La Muerte de Alexander Pushkin*

Cuando *d'Anthès* dispara su pistola
una conflagración destella
para enjuagar mi carne.
Una bola rasga mis entrañas.

Sufro un *Homicidio* de cristal de colores, ruso ortodoxo,
para endurecer el *Honor* de mí esposa vidriosa de ser
roto por las mandíbulas crujientes del chisme.

¡Si tan solo *d'Anthès* había sufrido la franqueza
inhumana de mi bala, había saboreado la cornada por un
toro sin ataduras!
Yo miraría sus ojos derretirse en lingotes de carbón.

En vez, él soltó un rayo de su boquilla;
una punta de lanza que no podía esquivar.

La bala dio en el blanco como notas
en una elegía bárbara.
Estoy embarrado, manchado, enlomado.

La bala es como pezuñas arrastrándome hacia abajo,
tumbándome bajo el tonelaje de un semental,
así que soy Pushkin y cadáver.

La bala es tan lastimosa a mi vista
como son mis parparos.
Mis labios trinan una harmónica escarlata.

---

* Trans. James Eugene Lindsey.

Yo sería un poeta de clase mundial—
y brillaría de entere los poetas—
porque anhelo la *Justicia*—
la cual es el oro del Negro—
tal como el *Hambre* anhela la grasa.

Pero ahora Pushkin—yo—estoy "fuera-de-impresión"*
Deja que mi cuerpo tome el papel de mi clon, *Si* se quiere.

[Tulum (Mexico) 2 & 3 *septiembre* 2015]

---

* Terminología del librero del Victoriano que significa a los muertos.

A *Passage from* Les Cenelles:
Choix de poésies indigènes* *(1845)*

To have bad luck and good wine
is a kind of *Equality*—
or an unkind kind of *Inequality*—
suiting a poet's leisure—
his *métier,* in free measure,
at musing, loafing, wenching....

And I like women,
and I like one woman,
her eyes copying the blue-green** iridescence
of Maltese, Mediterranean waves,
and her moans frothing plush as sea-foam,
when we tipple and trip,
pale hip and brown hip,
intertwined tight,
mating polarities....

Okay, it is my bad luck to love her,
but our wine is good.

And wasn't the historical Jesus as Negroid,
as real black, *regal* black,
as Adam and Eve,
bo'n way down in Ethiopia (Eden)?

Lemme say, flat out, then,
the slavers are human beings.
Sure they are.
But they're human beings as callous as rhinos!

---

* This debut anthology of African-American poetry featured "Creole" poets from
Louisiana, whose choice tongue was French.
** Due to cyanobacterial scum.

It is an old system.
Slavery is a classical system.
It counts on abominations
not even numbered in Leviticus.

(Exceptin my belle, my gal,
most of the white ladies —
the massas' lasses —
slouch big-assed as whales.

And prop up the crackers' old churches,
those gutters —
not pews —
of pompous, shitty pigeons!)

But still I adore that *skupa**
whose god is her shape —
a grotto, a fissure —

pink coral within,
ivory coral without —

quite suitable for a Creole
in this Nouvelle-Orléans
of the finest, most fair sex

(sometimes *Free[d]*).

[Sliema (Malta) 21 & 22 *août mmxi*]

---

* Maltese: Loose woman (i.e., a *mal* tease).

*Declaration of the Independence of Liberia (1847)**

I.

P rohibited from Congressing to progress—
or to Preside over—
our America,
what we've constructed out our "Sambo" sweat—
and unacknowledged black tears—

and forbidden *Freedom* itself—

the right to vote *and* revolt—

those of us deliberately liberated
by Maryland, Virginia, Mississippi—
to disallow our continued breathing in their *States*—

(*ours*, really)—

have elected to ferry our cast-off *Caste*
back to homeland (anywhere) Africa,

to forge our own Puritanical
Pilgrimage,

cross gilded, piecemeal waves,
the unsleeping *Deep*,

under stratospheric slivers of cloud and/or sunbeams.

Aye, the Atlantic is a tunnel of sharks—
a funnel of sharks—

---

* Cf. Tolson, *Libretto.*

but we braved it,

having decamped from *Slavehood*,

to reach Africa's queer pastoral—
wretched, vine-and-palm-tree architecture,
the disease-inflicting jungle—

and hove to and repulse sinister whistles—
fluting spears—
the salutations of *Savages*....

II.

Took a crutch of rope and canvas
to push us off from U.S. *Hades*

with two-sided waves crashing ships' bows—
like spume, gloomy,
disputing our reputedly, *inalienable* liberties.

The sea brought blows, insults, spitting foam,

but our colonizing vessels,
embarking keels puffing up spray,
sails unflagging
(against Betsy Ross's rag),
forged a navy of statesmen
and church ladies—
poets and schoolmarms
(all us ex-house Negroes),
surging onward (upward, metaphorically),
splitting lily-bright waters,
to attain this land of palm wine and coconut

(ex-Canaan version of "milk and honey").

Even the coal-black waters, snow-tipped,
flaked into suds—
the U.S. stars, stripes, trailing us
like a disciplined line of ivory wolves,
snow-skinned sharks....

Though th'Atlantic pelted our convoy
with surge after surge,
we toasted Jesus, Lord of the waves
(plus Apollo, god of homecomings),
for our *Repatriation* to the Gold Coast,
with goblets of green-gold wine,
vinegary nectar of Africa.

III.

Exodus (exo-*d'eau*) accomplished,
having laved *Slavery*-soiled *Liberty*
with blood pungent as sweat,

and accepted *Salvation*
ex the *Republikkk* of *Bullwhip* and *Auction Block*,

we know no more *Tergiversation*.

Overseas (here) is unclouded.
Already, ready *Liberty* is ours:

We gusted up muskets, seized the right
to allocate our own plots,
tax ourselves to spirit up revenues,

and now even anti-republican Britain
registers Americo-Liberians as a *Nation*.

IV.

Yet, we're unwelcome in our *Liberia*.
The heathen *Peoples* sport visages
hard as lava,
and paleo-palaver too hot—
agog with *Hatred*—

and approach us as *sans-culottes* warriors—
glistening obsidian *objets*,
insidious,
due to the incineratin we accomplish
with fanged blades and banged-banged balls.

V. [Embargo'd]

(My sword divided one nigger's head.
His parted eyes died surprised
to spy each other individually
as the two halves of his skull
bumped down on his shoulders
and then thudded pon th'earth.
Yes, I was a foul pugilist—
skills honed in Gotham—
and so my thumbs pressed
into another opponent's eye sockets,
springing out his eyeballs.

That night, the Pagan Queen
was forced down for my *Pleasure*—
gun-butted to her knees—
her loin cloth lifted....

Yes, I took her like a bull
covering a cow's back:
Raucous was our rutting—
black Yank on black gook.)

VI.

Amid doddering winds and whining gulls,
Triumph visits us
the same way God partied with the First Puritans.

Slowly, th'ebony *Foe* filters backward
into impenetrable *Murk*,
their sable forest,
against which we'll draw a curtain of flames
and, before it, erect
white church walls.

VII.

When night scatters its bright seeds
above our mingled torches —
light of Christ and *Civilization* —
we toast both Chrysus, god of *Gold*,
and Ares, god of *War*.

Our girding weapons glint intermittently
as we spring up our stockade,
the scintillating and shushing sea behind us,
the witchily incantating wind before us;

then, after some damn good bayoneting,
we drive the *Natives* to a stiff margin,
introduce em to multitudinous smouldering —
until each of the thousand-plus corpses is ash.

VIII.

Grim is the knowledge that the indigenous *Powers*
are perishing,
while we ex-slaves wax empowered,

but so be it....

Therefore, I, Horatio Ignatius Tubman,
once of tyrannous Virginia,
decant my sanguine signature
upon this *Declaration of Independence*,

implanting Africa's first *Republic*

(and Earth's second-Negro republic
pace Haiti),

The Empire of Liberia —

the whitest blossom
(first fruit) —
most intoxicating perfume —

 of Afro-Saxon *Imperialism*!

[**Montréal (Québec)** 4 *mai* **mmxiv**]

Elizabeth Barrett Browning Recalls
Robert Browning's Wooing (ca. 1847)

Against my arid, rigid self—
my Arctic-glacial, unyielding *Purity*—
Mr. Browning broached himself, sibilant,
and undulant as a libertine.

I did act coy, fey, cold;
I was smoothly difficult,
exhibiting a dour façade.

I guyed up and down staircases,
always at a remove,
one gloved hand on a banister,
the other smothering my smile.

Looked I as unconquerable as *Heaven*.

Mon père feared I'd show fertile,
and gift my publicly spic-and-span spouse
"swarthy droplets,"
exposing the "sooty roots"
of our whitewash ancestry.

Better that I live—
a breathing, perfumed corpse
than that my offspring wreck
th'alabaster emporium
shielding our spurious *Genealogy*,

so swore *mon père*.

But Mr. Browning was resolute—
to have me dissolute;

and after much gallant stroking,
what had been a welter of ice—
mine heart, became a mine of gold.

(When he "Frenched", me, the feel of his tongue,
serpentine, thrusting, in my mouth,
had me fainting in thought of his other
intrusive *Member*,
coolly eeling into my drooling sex.)

Blushes—unexpected flowers—
pinked my skin, my face,
and *Vices* looked *Blessings*.

As Mr. Browning waltzed into our parlour,
and leaned over me at piano or at table,
our garb became more and more undone,
and we lounged, almost as one,
our thighs kissing upon *chaise longue* or settee....

O! The hazards of *Leisure*!

A thousand happy cups of brandy
I quaffed while his hot whispers
charred the air.

He presumed an apostolic *Authority*,
as I assumed supine *Submission*—
the discipline befitting a *Disciple*.

I felt myself swooning—
like the waves
before Christ's feet.

Now, I worried Mr. Browning might prefer
thin, quivering beauties—
their prosaic busts—
decorating every London theatre balcony—
that he'd choose one lovely, refreshingly young,

not my faded *Innocence*—

my dry, drab
I.

No: He eased and jollied my jangled nerves,
taught me that indoors should flaunt fire
and outdoors vaunt stars.

We jaunted about at dusk,
haunting the sun's gleaming, gold wake
as it trailed off, shining;

and so my own once-stale *"Opulence"*
inspired his vocal eyes.

"Silvery" was I—
because he was *Chivalry*.

Next, I fretted I was too albescent in breast,
too ivory in face,

for truly my father's warning was worrying:
My privy "Africanness,"
generated *via Generation*,
could yet blacken us all:

What if my babes proved darkies?

Again, Mr. Browning eased my spasms, shudders.
He pledged we'd wed—
and away to Italy,
to drowse our days amid the warm green there
that spites English frost;

and spurn the damnable looking-glass
by passing off any darkling chillun
as "Sicilian"

48

(just as Sicilians do).

Now, Londoners chastise
"unnatural Italy, Gomorrah Rome,"
but I canter Chianti out a wicker bottle,
letting redness gallop down my white throat,
while my Bobby laps my lips and tits
in most spirited consumption.

Here he's Brontë's swarthy Heathcliff,
and I'm as smug as a "fellatrix."

Immeasurable titters please us.

I am so constantly wet,
I must gush *vino blanco*.

I'm now as fond of groping
as I've been of opium.

[Baia Mare (Romania) 21 *septembre* mmxiii]

Bobby & Betty: Anatomy of a Marriage

I.

In bed, a typhoon's her physique.
To grapple her, he's Caliban.

Coitus is demolition,
not a handshake.

II.

It was a head-long, head-first battering:
Betty felt Bobby's rod splinter her *Virginity*,

then drive hard to her backbone.
But she sensed no lethal *Humiliation*.

No, she knew luxurious soiling
as Bobby manned her—

like a vulture pressing down a swan.
She'd never felt more exhilaratingly free,

heaving her humping rump
up and down the proud poet's dick.

She saw her unbound hair ramp
over his face, while her thighs romped,

shining, with a bitch's *Splendour*,
until "B. & B." were one seething cauldron,

moulded tight, their pelting, pivoting
flesh brewing indestructible *Bliss*.

III.

To wed her in church, maul her in bed,
is Bob's predilection—

to champion her gaping *Lust*,
stampeding the vixen to an orgy,

both his fists clenching her dugs,
so the poetess posts beastly snorts,

obeying every convulsive impulse
(no matter how simultaneously repulsive).

Later, she can lunch on sermons;
scrunch down in a pew, take punch

for wine. But, now, Bob will bound
and have her jounce as he pounds.

(*Happiness* ends with p-e-n-i-s.)
Betty sprawls, unmistakably spunked.

IV.

Anyway, Bob's fed up with serving-girls;
He's scarfed hordes of whorish waitresses,

for *Cheating* has been his *Discretion*....
To tongue a lady's teat—

her roseate nipple thrust out—
or to chafe her chafing sex—

is as unforgettably joyous as prevailing in a feud.
Yet, it's best to have a wife—

a pretty imbiber of rod —
an ingester of seed at every portal —

and then have her immortalize —
in sporting abstractions —

every jolting orgasm as
so-called *Sonnets from the Portuguese.*

[**Orillia (Ontario)** 5 *juillet* **mmxv**]

The Port of Bordeaux: Un aperçu

I.

5oo ex-fishing trawlers
unleashed from this *négrier* depot,

make it impossible
(unprofitable)
to advocate *Abolition*:

Dragoon soldiery—goons—instead,
to bayonet, cannonade, guillotine Negrory—

all the revolting Africans,
rather than free em.

II.

Bordeaux doesn't like *Slavery*'s sleaze
to sully tourist-ogled marble;
to stigmatize the patrician parliamentarians
whose grandfathers said "oui,"
with ovations upon ovations,
to treading-down human millions in the maritime *Trade*—

those thus chained down to ledgers
and accounting records,

apprised and assayed
by sobre—ice-eyed—attorneys
emptying

Methuselah, Balthazar, Jeroboam, Salmanazar—
really, all of the best Bordeaux—

to digest *Crime*, to piss it away.

[**Bordeaux** (**France**) 1 *septembre* **mmxiv**]

Follow Martin, Follow Moses!

By Daniele Manin*

I.

D amn all undammed Venice! —

unless the *Arsenalotti* hearken to, mirror,
the luminous, tumultuous *Arson* —

Revolution —

American, French, Haitian, and now
the Danish Caribbean, St. Croix —

before the dreary *Enlightenment* dims —
and no *Liberty* lives —
except on bullet subsistence.

1848, there is still such *Light* —

the insurgent *Lustre*
that eclipses stars.

---

* In 1848, Daniele Manin led a (temporarily) successful uprising against the
Austrians then controlling Venezia, Italia. He found inspiration in the slavery-
abolishing rebellions led by Moses Robert and Martin Williams, that same year, in
the Danish West Indies.

II.

Eye St. Croix—
the illuminating *Insurrection* of Moses Robert
and Martin Williams:

To bray conch-shells
and bash bells as alarm,
to marshall 8,000 slaves
to toss fire all about
Fort Frederik,
a spindly keep of kindling.

(Negresses brought dry cane leaves
to fuel the torching).

In that breakneck twilight,
cross the Atlantic,
there was turmoil of troops,
turbulent men ejaculating shot,
blasting off black gunpowder,

but also the seizure of dark rum and dark coffee,
an end to the wasting and fasting
of the blacks,

thanks to exquisite, comprehensive *Purging*.

When Moses and Martin were finally seized,
heads chopped,
their searing blood was its own light—
a rainbow fallen down to bones.

III.

Now here, where Austrian dogs bark
and Austrian bitches howl,
to gnaw on Venice's carcass,

I cry, "Viva San Marco!"

I want volcano-galled air—
just as in the Danish West Indies.

Liberty is never premature.

[**Strait of Gibraltar / Passio Per Formentera,** *6 décembre* **mmxii**]

Fai come Martin, fai come Moses!*

di Daniele Manin**

I.

Maledetta sia l'immaledetta Venezia! —

A meno che gli *Arsenalotti* porgano orecchio,
o si facciano specchio al luminoso, tumultuoso *Ardere* —

La *Rivoluzione* —

americana, francese, haitiana, e ora
la danese antillana, St. Croix —
prima che il lugubre *Illuminismo* s'offuschi
e nessuna *Libertà* viva —
se non nella sussistenza delle pallottole.

1848, esiste ancora quella *Luce* —
il *Lustro* insorgente
che eclissa le stelle.

II.

Osserva St. Croix —
l'illuminante *Insurrezione* di Moses Robert
e Martin Williams:

---

* Traduzione di Fausto Ciompi, Università di Pisa.
** Nel 1848, a Venezia, Daniele Manin capeggiò una (momentaneamente) vittoriosa
insurrezione contro gli Austriaci, ispirandosi alle rivolte anti-schiaviste guidate nello
stesso anno da Moses Robert e Martin Williams nelle Indie Occidentali danesi.

Mugghiare in conchiglie di strombo
e strida di campane a raccolta,
per guidare 8000 schiavi
che infiammano l'intero
Forte Frederick,
un'affusolata torre di tizzoni.

(Le negre portavano foglie secche
di canna per alimentare le torce).

In quel folle crepuscolo,
dall'altra parte dell'Atlantico,
fu tutto un trambusto di truppe,
uomini turbolenti che esplodevano colpi,
affocavano polvere nera, ma anche la conquista
del rum scuro e dello scuro caffè,
un basta a chi stermina e affama
i neri,

grazie al raffinato, aristocratico massacro.

Quando alla fine Moses e Martin furono imprigionati
le teste mozzate,
il loro sangue scottante fu luce a se stesso,
un arcobaleno sprofondato fino alle ossa.

III.

Ora, qui, dove i cani austriaci latrano
e ululano le cagne austriache,
e rosicchiano la carcassa di Venezia,

io grido: «Viva San Marco!»

Voglio un'aria scorticata da vulcani —
come nelle Antille danesi.

La *Libertà* non è mai prematura.

[**Stretto di Gibilterra / Passio per Formentera,** 6 *dicembre* MMXXII]

The Head Slave Drafts His Valentine

I love her: This *Truth* strikes home
As unabbreviated *Panic.*
So, I'll act closed-hearted, close down
Her two gold eyes that shame the sun.

I imagine my love's futile—
Like August leaves. It's a mirage,
A ju-ju joke. A dark, pint-sized whore—
A blue-smoke slut—that's who I'll "wed."

If she's wrinkly and crinkly as wool—
And shorn—I mean, quickly sold off
Like any creamy, treacly cake, I'll grab
And tap instead a gabby, gap-toothed wench.

Thanks to nervous, sullen *Repulsion,* I want
My white-mare nightmare, her stinging sex,
Plus grapes pressed to flood. Lesser slaves
Gotta chow down on monotonous, fishy tarts.

If Lady hates me, I'll spring a tornado,
Spraying spunk. She merits my animal
Services, frankly, and I want to mount
Her coral sex to research a dirty canto.

I do plot to insinuate, in her milky schism,
A sinuous insemination. I have a bad hand
And wicked eye. So what if she shows iced
Pallor and molten tears? We two must mate:

Like Frankenstein's Monster and his Juliet.
I'm sure her navel proves a vortex of sweat.
I seem to amble innocently—
Like a pious ape, dreaming of us becoming

Two divine hunchbacks. Yes, yes,
I do feel "my race": It's an edgy sheen,
An amusing tint, and as hard as iron,
Where I'm darkest, and, most devoutly, *hers*.

[**Pordenone (Italy)** 22 *septembre* **mmxii**]

To Brother Tuppam

Queen's Bush
Mount Pleasant
Canada West

October 22, 1849

Sister Mary Teal asks I write you,
as a member of "The Standing Committee
on Canada Missions,"

re: Bro. Theo Washington—

that primitive Methodist minister;

for I am now in Canada
to learn facts respecting
the Colored people here.

The Negro man Washington—
an alien—
is incapable of transacting business,

and so Mary Teal should execute
Power of Attorney,

lest the Washington Chapel and School
be lost.

(That top-hatted cleric hath no head for numbers.)

We must act before excitements and gossips prevail,
and we go from saving souls
to losing cash donations.

For the sake of securing God's House,
quite solemn is our need

to dethrone Washington,
to defang him.

The Good Lord knows that I've no desire
for this world nor mundane *Substance*,
apart from life's necessities.

My concern is to advertise the *Gospel*
and circulate Bibles—hand-over-fist.

This wretched business with Washington—
the severe, non-stop *Struggle*—
no grateful *Aid* forthcoming—
almost suggests cathedral spires conspire gainst *Joy*.

Oh, how our prospects for a *Miracle*
so dark ahead are!

May the Law mold me *Holy*.

The schoolhouse should be
a House of Salvation,

not a debtor's prison—
for those whose purpose is *Charity*.

Grimly, the practicable effect of *Abolition*
was to unchain livestock,

and the lurking *Mischief*
of the necessary Good Deed,

is that unschooled mouths—
uninitiated eyes,
untutored ears,

heed impish, spittled words.

We've unleashed divines—
wild-winded pastors
among black sheep—

like Washington,
who can't reckon,

and now our accounts go bankrupt!*

You must publish nothing of this!
I prefer my position unknown
and seemingly unknowing.

Difficult now it is to affirm
the progress of our *Charity*.

The necessity of educating the Colored people—
"Canadians"—
requires much measure of *Aid*
from friends in the States:

We can't persist in our work
without means of *Subsistence*.

But the prospect now is that our school
will be broken up.

The Colored brethren—
such as Washington—
are sometimes not ex-slaves,
but fleeing miscreants,
tigerish remnants—
offal of the most awfully criminal....

---

* Cf. Page 298 of the Bankruptcy ruling of the Milanese court.

Our worthy labors in establishing
the colony of Colored folk
in Canada West
were premature perhaps:

Our prospects are blasted.

Unless some worthy element
like Teal—
displace Washington's execrable jowls
with a character imperial,
sovereign letters,

to dissolve his "governance"
through the same charcoal
or ink

in which you receive this urgent
missive.

—*H.A. Luzer*

[**Flesherton (Ontario)** 2 *août* **mmxiv**]

Transit to Spring

Spring is comin,

so slow —

after the ponderous *Winter*,

oppressin;

and *Freedom* is closer —

though still a ways off;

so we anxious pray

a chance to vamoose —

when, where, there is *Warmth*,

the sun, exploding, cheering,

welcoming

our belated homecoming,

icy shackles, melting....

[**New Brunswick (New Jersey) 12 *mars* mmxiv**]

বসন্ত আসছে ■ জর্জ এলিয়ট ক্লার্ক

দীর্ঘ শীতের পর
এক নির্যাতন পেরিয়ে
বসন্ত আসছে ধীরে ধীরে।
যেন স্বাধীনতা খুব কাছাকাছি।
যদিও এখন পর্যন্ত আসেনি
সেই জন্যে বসন্ত পাথরনায় আমরা
অপেক্ষা শুধু বিজয়ের।
কখন
কিভাবে
যেখানে উষ্ণতা
সূর্য
বিদীর্ণ করা উচ্চ স্বর
চিৎকার
দেরী করে ঘরে ফেরো
বরফ গলা
সব কিছুকেই স্বাগতম।
বসন্ত আসছে ধীরে ধীরে।

অনুবাদ : পারভেজ চৌধুরী

Transit to Spring[*]

---

[*] Trans. Parvez Chowdhury.

The Confession of Celia: A Missouri Slave, 1850*

Evening brought black cess and white cloud—
tar-trapped light—
until a cock's dazzling caw,
then dawn's discoloured brilliance;
but, first, *Harm* befell a blushing whiteness:
gore runnin as repetitious
as April floods.

★★

Siegneur's unpent *Lust*—
nay, his unrepentant *Lust*—
unpenned
my pent-up *Rage*.

No penance of light....

Now he is petrified bone bits;
a wash of ash.

(This ink is also wet cement.
Once it sets,
my noose tightens.)

★★

When I was a chit of 12, he was 52,
an earth-caked widower,
come a-courtin to The Slave Mart,
and swung a lamp to swing off shadows.

---

* Cf. McClintock.

(The light was pale as a wasps' nest;
the light stung just like wasps.)

His whistling trader paid off,
Farmer McGregor pleased to feast off me:
Once coin sweated palms,
Vice lurched imminent.

He broached me in the coach
trundling to his farm.

My pain was not decorative.

Despite his trove of pearl-tint grandkids,
he fancied a fresh, golden lineage of flesh.

(He'd don a billygoat guise
in his dotage.)

He cobbled me a brick cabin,
cozy, flaunting a fireplace,
and oversized, feather bed,
wherein he stumped his trumpeting stalk,
privately,
to diddle me into mama-hood, multiply.

Such was my job on his farm:
to be his unacknowledged concubine
and conjure new niggers.

He was unconscionably self-serving.
He was happy.
We were a disgruntled pair.

His glutinous loins knew me as female;
my heart knew me as *free.*

★★★

A "buck" chose me for his Eve:
His *Courage* encouraged my *amour*.
Our lovemaking was always double-or-nothing.
We'd both grunt, "Goody, goody!"
He liked my liquid core.
I liked giving it to a man I love.

I cuckolded Mr. "George"; I scolded his daughters:
"Farmer bother me again,
I peel off his face."
I had that deadly *Inclination*.

But that abrasive prick wouldn't quit.

On his last night, he cometh again
to commit his nocturnal *Inquisition*.

Clipped im with a poker.
Moaning.
Struck im again. (Had to.)
He looked surprised, but he quit moanin.

(When the metal bit down on his skull,
he felt the crunch of my *Anxiety*.)

****

While rain splintered night
and pelted earth,
I donned galoshes,
took up axe and razor,
and carved the stubby cadaver
to gristle, guts, grit,
and fed these pernicious stuffings
to a soft inferno.

Come morn, I swung a bucket of ash,
chipped and charred bones,
a truculent belt buckle,
one recalcitrant eyeball
(I stirred it into the *Termination*).

The mix looked like peppery salt,
but parts were a greasy mash,
a hash of blotchy grey tones.

★★★

When Massa's coral-cheeked grandson showed,
whistlin
at the cusp of sunlight,
I give im the pail to strew the burnt mess,
dump all into the river,
pumpin now a smelly gutter....

But the child was lackadaisical,
and let the ashen eyeball
wash up on rock,
and the belt buckle rest luculent in grass.

Y'all found these proofs,
and come charge me with *Atrocity*.

Naw: *Baas* was atrocious, was the *Atrocity*.

★★★

To get sumpin outta Shakespeare,
ya gotta get thee to a plantation —
where *all* are products of *Damnation*.

Although nothing's as catchy as *Conspiracy*,
I did kill alone.
I prosecuted solo; I executed singularly.
I let out that old man's venerable juice.
My hands were the "diseased tools" of the *Deed*.

My sable man, my stable love,
who's dodged your dragnets and patty-rollers,
is long gone
(likely up Canada),
and I pledge he be innocent.

****

My ink cracks the paper.
I do not scribble and defraud.

My "victim" was only — and truly —
a silver-pated, gold-plated rapist —

a bogus Christian,
a ceromatic* seraglio-boss.

Farmer McGregor now raises weeds.

He was a thorn.

I was his scythe.

[**Windsor (Ontario)** *27 octobre* **mmxii**]

---

* Latin: Mud-caked.

Escape to th'Escarpment!*

River jumps pell-mell, pewter;
singular but spiritual,
we collide into rapids.
Smell of *Newness* refreshing air.

Sunburned water looks a dreamy treat.
We yank our arms through liquid
in a cranky swim,
to discard blood-crust darkness.

Slavery be as smothering as drowning:
So, we surge forward
through priceless ointment,
veer north to bereave brutal species —

massas. *Free!* Clouds look uncommon —
beautifully anarchic, snazzy —
and Niagara rapids come sticky
whitewash, a nigger baptism, frankly,

skimming o'er pulsing depths,
hear nubile chirping,
the ascendant song
bridging marsh, river, rocks:

Liberty's a step-by-step recipe —
flight as naked as a leaf.
Set down a scent
that's aromas of snow,

* "The circle with the lettered bar across it symbolizes the Underground Railroad...." — T.H. White, *The Book of Beasts*.

as we—fleet—flee
whip and lash of *Inquisition*,
to tumble into surf,
draft a gasping epic.

We surge into chill,
plunge into cold,
every joint singing.
Ah, the wrack of nerves!

(Our graves be gashes in grass—
if pattyrollers' throaty guns
get wind of our wending,
through snickering, whickering wind.)

There's *Turbulence* of slogs,
mud-up-to-hips, bogs,
snagging of thorns,
tugging of branches.

Tense fires last night.
(Sparks bellied up
till dawn's moist grease—dew.)
We envisioned this verge—

falling into Upper Canada,
out the virgin ocean, Erie,
lime-fresh swells at the start,
the high-tide pummeling,

as we cross scissoring torrents,
our gravel-pricked skin—
grittily grave,
till we come up, resurrected,

shivering in flaring, flagrant night,
under a John Bull North-Star,
a thousand threads of starlight,
amid rumours—murmurs—of *War*.

Home to a domain of black maple
and wine, cut out of shadows,
all of Niagara hollering due east,
a tide, thundering, overwhelming.

Emerge into a Platonic sun,
an ex-cave-dweller's dawn,
.light brighter than fire,
enemy of shades.

We're two glistening beings
where stars shed ecumenical light,
afar from a too-economical dictator—
iron-hearted,* snow-headed monster!

Labour yields to *Liberty.*
We rise from sable ripples,
negotiate barbs, fences;
calm choppy heartbeats.

At this frontier, surf and sand
conduct tender dialogue—
gold overlapping gold—
as in a Huck-Finn Finland.

(You ford skittering glitter,
crinkled silver;
you enter Ontario;
you bring the light with you.)

[**Kingston (Ontario) 12** & **13** *février* **mmxiii**]

---

* Cf. Sade's hero, Coeur de Fer.

Voice of the Fugitive (1851)

By Henry Bibb

An absconded, inveterate traveller,
I hold a dossier that glosses *Dross*,
To stymie each Dixie bounty-hunter;
Slam doors *pace* each damn border I cross.

The idiotic spiel of the Congress,
The bullet-pocked cadavers the Supreme
Court okays (them ofays be fraud artists),
Drafts Canada as delectable *Dream*.

An unalloyed outcast, I dash through bush
To appear—impromptu as *Deity*—
Where excess soil can be salvaged from brush,
So corn stops harvests of *Starving*. Only

Reputable ex-slaves are welcome here;
Yet, to gain *Freedom*, I was murderous:
My master's one corporeal cinder....
I chased the clip-clop of clomping horses.

I'd send embassies of poppies southward,
Where his body blazed, if now the fire's out.
(Who could wean his flesh from those flames that poured,
After my knife gargled his gurgling throat?)

Thus, I've desired this far-flung *Solitude*,
Crossing curving water's braided fathoms,
And set myself where I now sit and brood
On dread *Necessities* that breed *Freedoms*,

That make ex-slaves, black, uprooted diamonds,
And no longer subdued puppets, but prime
"Traitors" to *Fakes* and *Hypocrites'* hymens —
Slavery's backers — crackerjacks of *Crime* —

Much worse than beasts, that lot: A fiasco
Of *Theology's* their *Apocalypse* —
A Republic of clotting blow upon blow,
A Democracy of unknotted whips....

Free now, I seek a woodland nymph (*Whim* and
Omen produce *Women*), to help witch wine from dirt,
Stimulating limb and posture, to stand
As one, hale and hearty, whole against *Hurt*.

A wife to lumber about in timber,
To tear down pine, pile hay, and hang vineyards,
Who labours fierce, and at *Love* is limber,
I yearn, to league with me, brave gainst graveyards.

A black woman in snow-white woods, a bride,
Succulent (after abducted horses
And an unbelievable *Homicide*),
I woo, intense, to anchor my chorus.

[Gatineau-Hull (Québec) 28 & 29 *mai* mmxv]

Harriet Tubman Proceeds

As mum as a mime—
    as mute as a mime—
I steel my face, deadpan,
    as I "steal away"—

stealthy, husbanding
    even breath, to get away—
trace that North Star
    as magnetic as hearth fire.

I never whimper like some bitch.
    I maneouvre like a tomcat.
"No man's a-gonna hinder me":
    My darling gat doth spit *Defiance!*

My travels to escape,
    unravel—delicate as shadows,
but just as indelible:
    I stick close to hurrying

darkness, skip the moon's
    magnifying silver,
and know—uncannily,
    where footing and handholds

are most secure.
    I move reticent, unspeaking,
skedaddle my troupe northward,
    wade through gore (if necessary),

to edge, or sidle into Canada—
    ivory snow and black pines.
Check how I arrive—
    bold face as a glacier.

[Edmonton (Alberta) 28 *Nisan* / *avril* mmxiii]

Marathon

To run the marathon of the wind—
crash through bush and brush—
as hungry as moonlight is for night—
and live off velvet, rabbit meat—

to crack and suck bones as hollow as thirst—
or swallow bite-size dirt as I hide,
wallowing in grit, bathing in it—
to disallow my flight,

my *Freedom* dream, which maps field
and forest as medicinal green, oh but I must!
Caught, my wings will be chopped off,
my body fenced in afresh,

allowed no ration of *Inspiration*,
Freedom once more utopic, a fancy,
my nights locked in barracoon brooding,
my days wracked by sockdolager sobs,

my flesh taking *Barbarian* disgusts—
uninterrupted injuries—
the whip, the lash, the brand,
the fists, the hound-dog bites....

Preachers' barking lungs,
slaves' scathing songs,
congressmen puking sanctions,
the quibbling mechanisms

of lynchers' pulleys
(ropes draped over tree branches),
drive me to hunt the horizon,
to seek the oily abyss of woods:

Or smother in whirlpools,
or skulk in gutter dirt, hoof-broken turf.
Location is Yankee *Affliction*,
but *Healing*, if it's Canada....

[Barrie (Ontario) 12 *mars* mmxv]

Letter from Mary Ann Shadd (1853) *

C anada West's fields compose a frosty chequerboard—
half glazed-mud, half Canadian Shield.
in that rimy air, our tongues feel thwarted.

The crops show blighted outcomes:
Sunflowers falter, coolly enmisted.
The weather's iron, tough as meteor strikes.

Clotting snow stymies us.
Disease comes in and out of *Winter.*
Uncle Tom falters: He's a sick, Coloured man,

abandoned by his own people.
So many difficulties in Canada!
It's an error here if preachers

don't carry weapons.
The disadvantages of a new country:
Starving farmer and panting fugitive

must seek miserly *Relief,*
and can't proffer *Help.*
Canada's a wayfarer State,

really. Negroes are as mobile as *Thought,*
and can't be calmed by canting politicians.
Scribbled words scare em—

---

* Shadd (1823–93) edited the anti-slavery newspaper, *The Provincial Freeman,* near
Windsor, Canada West/Ontario, in 1853, thus becoming the first woman newspaper
publisher in "Canada."

as if Devil wit.
They're used to scavenging—
and stop at stoops

(or stoop at stops)
in search of free grub
and a free burgh.

The Fugitives trust no white, no black.
(Don't Christians license *Torture*
as a "test" of *Love*? Ask Christ....)

They deem the snow appalling,
shrouding,
and dread the wind's malignant hiss.

But America's leaden—jailhouse—
Constitution
renders us as fickle as a kaleidoscope.

To scatter like milkweed,
flock like loose leaves,
fluxing in tether to a tempest.

[**Helsinki (Finland)** *6 juillet* **mmxiv**]

Salutations to "General Moses"

No shotgun stares her down.

In stratospheric darkness, lisping light,

she, bundling us all like some virtuoso violinist,
scaling through notes,

she directs, leads us, with unstilting *Bravado*,

to bring us out the wilderness—
slave farms,
ungovernable pastures—
to *Liberty*.

We run, lured by the North Star,
but armed with a single pistol
(hers),
as she filters us, ghostly,
through millions of pines,
phantasmal as a swamp's will-o-wisp.

Reputedly good-fisted and handy with guns,
she's neither punch-drunk nor trigger-happy,
but will inflict *Violence, impersonally*—if need be.

The gal's a slick arrowhead slicing through night
No: This gal's an unbound wound,
smarting, seeking *Freedom*'s balm.

[Banff (Alberta) 7 *avril* / *Nisan* mmxiv]

George Boyer Vashon Drafts "Vincent Ogé" *

L ight is never overworked.

Through the night, I unpent pages,
regurgitate Ogé's tale
(a compound of brine and wine —
more or less like Byron's),
to dispel, cancel —
the brawling claptrap of slavesters.

(Their *Integrity* is like ice:
it drains away
soon's they get heated up!)

I don't aim to top
the top poet
for *Liberty* (*et aussi* libertinage):
Byron.

No: I'm an unascribable poet,
taking grog and ale for my muse.

This night-day-night,
my words vent in a black blizzard —
a gale that should —
like fixed bayonets —
drill — or skewer — all eyes.

---

* On August 31, 1853, in Syracuse, NY, Vashon (1824–78), a pioneering African-
American lawyer, wrote a fragmentary ballad in praise of Ogé, a *Métis* hero of the
Haitian Revolution, immolated by the enemy French at Cap-Français in March 1791.
Cf. Sherman.

Y'all might damn me as a political poet,
a heretical poet.
Fine:
I want to grumble drums and trumpets —
and be heard, clarion in *Combat*.

My ballad must blow bitchy.

Singin of Vincent Ogé,
my ink's gonna singe;

wet fire's gonna smite my pages.

To know *Courage via Language* —
to conjure a bronze foot, an iron brow,
a lily wrist snapping a leather whip,
while trees start to shake down escalating leaves
as September homes in,
and there's little upraised laughter
outta the White House or the Black Belt —

I resolve to dissolve
my substance into ink —

silent water,

silently roaring.

[Madrid (Spain) 8 *octobre* mmxii]

The New York Times *Uncovers Arson*

"Slaves packed that burning house.
It was—I tell you—the worst weekend.

"Under a flame-scorched moon,
so many howling, weeping souls had *Hell* right here,
and came to char and ash and smoke.
It was pitiful, pitiful.

"Not even our most anxious guitars
get close to the precise noise
an infant makes
as fire eats through the flesh,
turning the body
into a coffin—
no—just an urn for ash.

"The flaming, perishing 'niggers'
looked like they were renouncing flesh
to become *Perfume*.

"Torrid immolation was their church.

"These 'runaways' had sheltered in the decrepit homestead
near Charleston,
but were betrayed,
and once betrayed, trapped,
and once trapped,
eligible to be destroyed.

"(The intact bodies looked like blackened fish—
fat, juicy, charred.)

"The night was ash, roars, crackles, crying,
moon, timbers, flames, embers, tar....

"Under the ragged moon,
Reality turned jagged;
Living beings got snagged:
A shimmering mishmash—
a night of flame and ash—
heart-strings sagged out-of-tune.

"The fire erected a barrier of light.

"Against the darkness, a pure pitch-colour,
the blazing house resembled a bird cage,
suspended, set afloat, close to earth,
as beams snapped, floors caved in,
and ex-slaves quit hollering
in their *de facto* prison,
and settled down to *Incineration*.

"To be Romantic, when some jumped,
flaming from windows,
becoming chimeras of light,
you could say
they were foolish, carnal saints,
electing *Martyrdom* over *Servitude*.

"Or you could say they were bogus migrants,
fake refugees,
seditionists against The Republic,
and fraud artists in their claims of ill-treatment.

"(Many do skedaddle to *Gam Sham**
in spidery caravans,
lurking, hiding, scurrying,
infiltrating nooks, crannies of woods,
as discreetly as poisons
slip into soups.)

"You could number them as 'subhuman devils.'

---

* Cantonese: Gold Mountain (i.e. Canada).

"Yet, my nightmare privilege was to hear—
mid hectic roaring—
each crackling diminuendo of the darkies.

"The moon was more bronze than ivory.
Then showered down indifferent starlight.

"Anyhow, when the sun come up,
only dust rose too,
and I saw a taciturn piece of roof—
Futility in all that quiet.

"Raking the embers, I felt sick to find
a prune-shaped man who'd burst open,
his guts frying like all the pork
he likely loved to eat.
I found also a body singed hairless—
resembling a black jujube candy
or a twist of licorice.

"One mother had a tarpaper spine;
her face was a charred shoe.

"I even stepped on—and squashed—a heart.
It had been burnt, but not the blood still within.
It squirted out as my foot pressed down
on the slippery, dirty flesh.

"I had to navigate fluid meat.

"The house had largely broken down.
The dead were largely invisible under my bootsteps.
They were scraps—silent scraps—of *Nothing*.

"Unexpected feces did crop up—
here and there—
a kind of dark, cherry mash.

"I stumbled over a hybrid body,
a mulatto weeping caramel:
His cadaver was a brownish, patchwork quilt.

"I noticed a babe already a lantern
of lustrous flies,
incommensurably putrid.

"Then, the sun was iron;
the house was a shadowy clearing;
or a bitter orchard.

"The burnt-over area resembles gravestone shale
or a tar oasis.

"I did not infringe upon any house of light:
Only a carnal loss.

"I couldn't linger in the hot wreckage —
lest I put my clothes to flame.

"There was a dissipated breeze —
a lot of charred nudity —
and lacerating sunlight.

"How could my remorse
be any more passionate than Morse Code?

"In this South Carolina forest —
swamp, lilacs, and mosquitoes —
these people have made a pitiful finish.

"None of this report takes sides
in the disputation over *Slavery*.

"Yes, the environ was horrid,
the event, horrid.

"But we all die:
Green maple leaves turn gold maple leaves.

"Even doves go into the furnace—
the cold ash pit that is the grave.

"Sooner or later, our letters are smoke,
and our dark dreams
are illumed by worms.

"No crows will fuss over this burnt meat."

[Tessera (Italy) 24 *septembre* mmxii]

New York Times *deconspiră o incendiere**

„Sclavi împânzeau acea casă arzând.
A fost—credeți-mă—un sfârșit de săptămână îngrozitor.

„Sub o lună pârjolită de flă cări,
urlând, hohotind, atâtea suflete erau în iad chiar aici,
și se preschimbau în cărbune și cenușă și fum.
Era jalnic, jalnic.

„Nici măcar ghitarele cele mai stridente
nu pot reproduce exact zgomotul
pe care-l face un nou-născut
în timp ce focul îi devorează carnea
transformându-i trupul
într-un sicriu—
nu—doar într-o urnă pentru cenușă.

„«Negroteii» înfierbântați, muribunzi
păreau să renunțe la carne
ca să devină parfum.

„Jertfire toridă le era biserica.

„Acești «fugari» s-au adăpostit în gospodăria decrepită
de lângă Charleston,
dar au fost trădați,
și odată trădați, prinși în capcană,
și odată prinși în capcană,
numai buni să fie distruși.

„(Trupurile intacte arătau ca pești pe grătar—
grași, zemoși, înnegriți.)

---

* Traducere de Diana Manole.

„Noaptea era cenuşă, strigăte, trosnete, plâns,
lumină de lună, aşchii, flăcări, tăciuni, smoală....

„În lumina unei luni zdrenţuite,
Realitatea se destrăma;
Toată suflarea se hărtănea:
O amestecatură sclipitoare —
o noapte de cenuşă şi dogoare —
corzile inimii se lăbărţau dezacordate.

„Focul înălţase o barieră de lumină.

„Pe fundalul întunecat, o culoare pură, profundă,
casa în flăcări semăna cu o colivie de păsări,
suspendată, plutind, aproape de sol,
în timp ce bârne plesneau, podele se surpau,
iar foştii sclavi renunţau să strige
în închisoarea lor de facto,
şi acceptau să fie incineraţi.

„În spirit Romantic, când unii săreau,
în flăcări, de la ferestre,
devenind himere de lumină,
ai putea spune
că erau sfinţi naivi, reîncarnaţi,
alegând martirajul în locul servituţii.

„Sau ai putea spune ca erau asa-zişi imigranţi,
falşi refugiaţi,
secesionişti opunându-se Republicii
sau şarlatani care pretindeau c-au fost prost trataţi.

„(Mulţi o iau din loc spre *Gam Sham**
în caravane ca o plasă de păianjen,
pe ascuns, pe furiş, târâş-grăpiş,
infiltrând pădurea, câtă frunză, câtă iarbă,
la fel de discret precum o otravă
care se strecoară în supă.)

---

* În cantoneză: Muntele de aur (Canada).

„I-ai putea socoti «diavoli subumani».

„Şi totuşi, privilegiul meu insuportabil a fost să aud—
în mijlocul vuietului trepidant—
fiecare scrâşnet din amuţirea treptată a celor tuciurii.

„Luna era mai mult de bronz decât de fildeş.
Apoi a început să arunce o lumină indiferentă.

„În orice caz, când soarele s-a înălţat,
se mai ridica doar praful
şi am văzut o bucată taciturnă de acoperiş—
Zădărnicie în toată acea linişte.

„Greblând prin jăratic, mi s-a făcut rău când am găsit
un bărbat cu burta deschisă ca o prună răscoaptă,
intestinele sfârâiau precum carnea de porc
pe care precis îi plăcuse s-o mănânce.
Am dat şi peste un cadavru cu tot părul pârlit—

semăna cu o curmală uscată
sau o spirală de lemn dulce.

„Una din mame avea spinarea de hârtie smolită;
faţa îi era un pantof carbonizat.

„Am călcat chiar şi pe o inimă—şi-am storcit-o.
Era arsă, dar încă mustea de sânge.
M-a împroşcat când am pus piciorul
pe ciozvârta alunecoasă, murdară.

„A trebuit să navighez prin carne lichidă.

„Casa se prăbuşise aproape toată.
Morţii erau aproape invizibili sub tălpile bocancilor.
Erau rămăşiţe— rămăşiţe tăcute—din Nimic.

„Excremente răsăreau pe neaşteptate—
pe-aici, pe-acolo—
un fel de pastă întunecată, vişinie.

„M-am împiedicat de corpul unui mulatru,
o caramea corcită plângăreaţă:
Cadavrul lui era un preş cafeniu din petice.

„Am observat un bebeluş era deja un felinar
din muşte lucitoare,
degradat într-un mod indescriptibil.

„Apoi, soarele a devenit metalic;
casa era un luminiş umbros;
sau o livadă amară.

„Pământul ars seamănă cu piatra de mormânt
sau cu o oază de gudron.

„Nu m-am furişat în vreo casă a luminii:
Doar într-un carnagiu.

„N-am mai putut zăbovi între ruinele fierbinţi —
fără să risc să mi se aprindă hainele.

„Briza era dezmaţată —
grămezi de nuduri carbonizate —
şi soarele tăios.

„Cum poate remuşcarea mea
să fie mai muşcătoare decât codul Morse?

„În această pădure din Carolina de Sud —
smârcuri, flori de liliac şi ţânţari —
aceşti oameni şi-au găsit un sfârşit jalnic.

„Acest reportaj nu înclină de nicio parte
în disputa pe tema Sclaviei.

„Da, priveliştea era înfiorătoare,
evenimentul — înfiorător.

„Dar toţi murim:
Frunzele verzi de arţar devin frunze aurii de arţar.

„Până şi porumbeii ajung în furnal—
tava rece pentru cenuşă le e mormânt.

„Mai devreme sau mai târziu, scrierile noastre sunt fum
iar visele noastre întunecate
sunt luminate de viermi.

„Nici ciorile n-ar râvni la această carne arsă."

[Tessera (Italia), 24 *viniceriu* mmxii]

Harriet Tubman & Harriet Beecher Stowe: A Debate

Stowe: *Liberty*'s bards finagle verses that lilt of *Struggle*.

Tubman: Poets clad poop with blossoms.

Stowe: Harriet, *this* Harriet —
who's no Judas Iscariot —

assures you I'm strategic:
To letter visions.

Tubman: Didn't Moses muck up fat bodies with sharp blades,
dilapidate a palace with disgusting murders —

and bade God bombard Memphis with stone and fire,
clog roads with horses, chariots, Hebrew Refugees;

so the high-dudgeon "Gypsies," pursuing,
in heavy gallop,
floundered in nostril-stuffing water,
so dead horses piled up in sky-high sludge?

Thus was the oldest *Grief* —
Slavery —
indecorously extirpated.

Stowe: Miss Tubman, or "General Moses,"
I caution:

One who swings wildly a sword
may soon prove herself its sheath.

Tubman: Miss Stowe, or "Grandma Moses,"
I bade thee remark God's Moses:

The Divine Ten Orders—
that rustic *Calligraphy*—
scribed scrupulously into stone—
brooked no profligate diction,
no forgiving asterisks.
The words were harsh:
Obey, repent, or perish!

Stowe: Tis best to blast ink cross paper,
than tinkle inklings of swords.

Tubman: I lead ex-slaves through angry rain,
and traverse from starving bower
to hungry glade,
where winds lour
and frost numbs tongues with chill.
Exhaustion lames us,
but we limp and skulk,
shadow-low,
sheltering behind magnolia,
or hiding where pines hang down green boughs,
while a lamp gives light, not heat,
or a small fire crumbles snow into water.
A cutting feeling—and frigid—is
our crouching, cringing,
like hunted beasts....
Yet, thus we suffer until we slip
into Queen Victoria's America,
abandoning households of whippings and gruel
and *Molestation*....

Stowe: Hew to the Christian example of Uncle Tom.

Tubman: Hew to the Christian example of Uncle Sam.

[**Cambridge (Massachusetts)** 26 *février* **mmxiv**]

Chain / Reaction*

His heart ain't whole.
His heart be a hole;
he taketh brandy for a bandage.

His clan is gone cold;
got sold off, old time go.
So him massacre massa —

axe zigzagged throat to heart —
and locketh himself in the liquor cellar,
plan on bein soused,

when he get dragged out,
hanged, lynched:
Same difference.

Bet the harsh drink goeth down
sweet;
if gore-salty.

[**New Brunswick — Newark** (**New Jersey**) **12** *mars* **mmxiv**]

---

* *In memoriam*: Amiri Baraka (1934–2014).

Spirituals 1: 1–7

God never say no mumblin word:
Cryin for Christ, crossed, His tears thundered.

Our Good God be a Man of *War*—
He perch in Heaven and judge all prayer.

I hate the Cross, that accursèd tree
Made our Lamb's blood drip like honey.

But ogle Jesus now, scribin *Poesy*—
Bright sparkles sear the furthest sky.

Wily as Homer, that reverend Bard
Gleans soulful sweets from His lyric orchard.

Ol Adam and Eve, like us, be black:
They fall down to Hell, but Christ haul em back.

Take out your pencil; pick up the Book—
These measures save us once-damned folk.

[**New York City (New York) 23** *janvier* **mmxi**]

A *Prologue to* Uncle Tom's Cabin

By Josiah Henson

K entucky boyhood:

Adultery was a white boy's hobby,
taking hooch on the "House,"
plus a wench with nothin on—
legs jerked wide to *Pollution*.

Body snatchers
bared ground-down molars—
and fang-like incisors—
to cannibalize kisses.

To drive a "white fork into peppered pork":
Twas *Desire*.

Such were our rulers:
Ungovernable dirt.

One of that number clutched at mama
to crack her open,
bang her into a coma
(really),
treat her to peremptory, acrid *Dampness*—
while she wept,
her tears oilin his "spigot"....

Pops proved adamant bout preventing
Mama from neighing, snorting,
under a man who takes poop for soap.

Pops stabbed his boots into Le Dracu Franju,
tattooed crimson the man's bristled face,
so our tyrant assumed the Gothic blush
of shoe polish.

But pops didn't stomp the cockroach.
He backed off;
that dishevelled slave had to run.

Doc Franju hustled up a posse —
accomplished fast in that contemptible Republic
of vicious bumpkins;
snatched pops out the lyncher-infested woods:

100 lashings his broad, black back notched.

Blacksmith dinned down the blistering leather.
His fat-muscled arm was buttressed
by a huge jug of plonk.
He'd take a swig, then swish down the lash,
as he flogged up a ruby sweat,
to distress my daddy beyond *Redress*.

Mama whimpered to witness this *Violence*,
but her soul was mutilated when Doc Franju
tore wide her bodice, slapped her breasts,

while the blacksmith heaved my fainted pappy
up against the humiliatin whippin post,
pressed his sable head gainst the maple wood,
and nailed his right ear to that erection.

Pops got to howling, and now our owner
left off pawing mama's breasts,
and approached father and pulled out a *pukko*,*
and, with atrocious, cussing *Malice*,
hacked off the left ear
and tossed it to leaping, yapping dogs,

---

* Finnish: Knife.

while a coven of Caucasian churchgoers —
in ape-like postures —
brayed,
praying.

Pops' jaws looked a bawling cavern
as he staggered free the nail,
his right ear, half-lopped and haggard,
and Franju hissed —
mimicking the lofty softness of a pope —

"That's the payback, Caesar,
for striking a white man...."

Dander still up, massa grabbed mama
and jabbed "home" his dick right there.

[Haikko (Finland) 10 *octobre* mmxv]

The Ecstasy of Linda Brent (a.k.a. Harriet Jacobs)

I do testify: *Love* cannot be quashed.
Together, our bodies mashed and squashed,
Wrecking every idea of *Chastity*—
Until the fact was gone. *Adieu, Virginity.*

In no way was I promiscuous—
Or "loose" or wanton or irreligious.
But a slave has no chance or choice over
Who "studs" her—rapist, husband, or lover.

Were my sex only mine to mine,
Righteousness would prove feminine,
And no division and no divorce,
And no woman taken and broken perforce.

I don't booze up; I don't play "Whore
Of the Fields" or "Queen Sheba the Moor."
Still, I am black, but as beautiful as
Th'Ethiope face of the raised-up Jesus.

Africa's in my step and in my sway,
My singing lips, my bronzen flesh display.
I fear no white girl; I dread no white man:
Good looks do good; I catch as catch can.

White ladies yell, "Christ!" I preach, "Lord,
Have mercy, swishing Thy scythe and Thy sword
Against sinning master and serving slave:
Damn all those who don't give-a-damn! Save

Fire and brimstone for those who raped
Wives and girls. Gift bread and wine to th'escaped."
I'm no saint, cos I claimed *Freedom*
To not be a virgin sprawled out as victim....

Marriage is divine, yes, though men are not.
I obey my heart when blood flushes hot.
Am I immodest? I feel I'm honest —
I sip honey thiefed from a viper's chest.

I don't believe I stray, nor e'er pervert
Thy *Word*. To join flesh isn't to coin dirt.
The slave woman's virtuous who loves
Vowed swain of her choice, as Thy *Gospel* proves.

(*Liberty* isn't crude *Libertinage*.
To think *Freedom* is *Fooping*,* is mirage.
Rude is the oppressor, lewd the oppressed,
To interpret being *blessé* as being blessed.)

[**Guelph (Ontario) 23** *octobre* **mmxi**]

---

* Cf. A.C. Clarke.

To Critique Edward Mitchell Bannister*

You scrutinize your routes, your rivers—
St Andrews by-the-Sea, New Brunswick—
but Yankify—yodel—your Canuck voice.

You remember the red-crushed-rock beach;
sketch this *Truth*;
although schoolbooks' wrinklings of ink
omit your Atlantic waves.

America is home—
a wide-open prison:
Negroes put down roots,
incarcerated.

But you are not as insolent as The Great Republic—
all the unbelievable havoc of its speeches.

You are a phantom pariah;
your paintings hang in the shadows of museums,

oblivious to your solid-gold future
as a Victorian pastoralist,
a painter whose brushstrokes drip tears,
or curve the dark naps of the sea—

and whose canvasses may be termed
"high" bastardy,
a "Creole confection" in oils.

---

* Born in Saint Andrews by-the-Sea, New Brunswick, Bannister (1828–1901) was the
first significant, African-Canadian artist, but had his career in the United States.

Art is glinting *Splendour;*
Oppression is the manufacture of *Murk.*

Thou art an anonymous nigger in the U.S.
But *Ugliness* is blind to *Beauty.*

[Saint Andrews by-the-Sea (New Brunswick) *Noël* mmxi
& Niagara Falls (New York) 1 *janvier* mmxii]

Glimpse

As she was scooping it,
the iced, maroon-tint melon,
falling from her hand,
mirrored her Sicilian skin.

Where has the African *not* been
to imperil imperious *Whiteness*?

The Maltese warn children,
"Jekk ma toqghodx kwiet issir iswed":
"If you do not stay quiet,
you'll become black."

The ice-serving girl, she of
the melon melanin,
need only know
that colour is sweet.

[Sliema (Malta) 23 *août* mmxi]

Thomas Chandler Haliburton
Regards Liverpool, 1855

Mr. John William Graham—
manager of Tate & Lyle Sugar Company—
Oxford-colleged, a classicist,

thrills to see the humongous ships,
brimming with snowy sweetness,
steam towards refinery, distillery,

while black soot infiltrates nostrils,
tangles into hair,
sets lungs belching black phlegm....

Such is the toil of *Pleasure*,
to ratchet up profits
as implacable as the Crucification:

The steamer exhaust hurts lungs,
soils clothes, faces,
so chalky children look suddenly,

"wonderfully" (they imagine) vile
and filthy, like heroic waifs,
or cantankerously ugly

as printers' devils,
their fingerprints bluntly black
(no ornaments of other tints),

and whose vividly scrawny frames
will likely crumble under bobbies' batons
in just a decade

or half decade—
in this brickyard dump of Empire.
Anyway, unfortunately too,

the sugar mill specializes
in multiplication of ogres—
spectacular amputees—

stumping for coins before churches,
stuttering baroquely,
but only themselves to blame,

for such bumbled job performance
as to mishandle or tumble
into fine-tooled, well-oiled machinery,

and become fodder for the pen
of Mr. Dickens, who takes *Ire* for ink,
so as to besmirch *Capital* reputations....

But Mr. Graham will be Sir Graham,
if he achieves greater heights
of sugar output and wherewithall,

pouring mountains into ships' bellies,
thus bloating the ledgers' pounds,
even as he distracts himself

from the cries of self-mangled minions
via romancing fanatically skeletal,
sugar-pale tarts,

so gleefully anemic—
subsisting on whores' wages
(absinthe equals drink and opium equals meat).

However, outlawing *Negro Slavery*
mandates using nurseries,
Kindergartens, as labour

fulfilment centres,
to top up quotas required
at mills, factories, brothels,

disgusting, but enriching;
thus, the innocent dormitory
now upstages stink,

and model *Youth*—
pale Adonis, fair Venus—
waste to melancholic, graceless *Ruin*.

These beings mature, cancer-rife,
or fall prey to geniuses of *Vice*—
passionate as leeches—

who love nothing less
than to eviscerate every anus
with a syphilitic organ.

Mr. Graham thinks himself no bad boss,
to talk up workers' sickliness as "noble,"
or to pooh-pooh juveniles broken

down to oozing bones,
suing *Salvation* in alcohol
or starry-eyed sermons,

their inebriated jaws slobberng on bottles,
or urine-tasty male organs,
obstinately pallid,

like sugar at sight, but sour in scent;
or the kids get sold—
a seven-year-old

to a seventy-year-old,
whose joy is to finger a *Virginity*
until she screeches, bleeding.

Such is the sovereign *Tyranny*
of factorists like Mr. Graham,
that *Vice* is enabled

to enact intolerable freaks
upon urchins,
to so injure "white niggers,"

their young brains and fledgling genitals
turn diseased and degenerate.
The fungibility of black slaves

for white girls and boys
means moneybags gorge now
on unskilled muscle,

on forever-illiterate cradles,
and once they've exacted all *Wealth*
and *Productivity*,

discard these *de facto* Morlocks —
to starve or steal,
be harlots

or hang by hangmen.
Thus, Englishry turns Negrory,
insensate souls,

no better than rats,
who must nurse on liquor
and fatten on sugar.

This antisocialism attitude
explains Mr. Graham's mimicry
of swine —

his round-gut, piggish aspect,
puffing Greek and grunting Latin,
as he manhandles a wench,

reaming dirtily a thinness
fed by clouds.
He decants fishy smells,

sweats out a fever of movement
in a pretty rut,
soon flooded with a sugary meringue.

[**Liverpool (England)** 12 *octobre* **mmxiv**]

Pamphlet to the Electors of Canada West (1856)

(By Judge T.C. Haliburton)

The ex-States ex-slaves
are only as "fugitive" as was "Boney,"
ebbing from Moscow,
indelibly a war criminal....

The blackamoors barging into Canada West
(Upper Canada), hankering for *Liberty*,
are now anchored
on 600 acres
of prime, Essex County turf,

where, "free at last," as they so chortle,
they are dusky busybodies,
buzzing and huzzaing
pulpit palpitations,
as opposed to pouring down sweat behind oxen.

Their farcical "escapes" justify,
so thinks this minstrel rabble,
unchecked *Insolence*,
so that they may waive *Circumspection*....

And may compose a café class,
and so make pubs their parliaments,
and cough at *Caucasian* Christianity
and scoff at Judeo-Christian mores
and Greco-Roman laws,
and parade themselves scandalously as our peers—
as if they were unblanching Britons!

I wager their swaggering *Nonsense*
puts this harlequin throng
at risk of pacifying dungeons,
and/or the pointy end of daggers.

Make the Guineas as governable as graveyards.

The Colony's rulers must pare down
the specious vermin,
wrest back acreage from these crooks and crones....

(The *Law* should be such a smothering sheet in cover,
the sable race finds no quarter to inhale and increase.)

However, those who remain in Canada West
must show digits gone frigid—stumped—
from digging, with bare-hands,
into ice-locked earth.

Useless it is to entertain impetuous *Charity!*
Why slap together schools granting whole loaves of *Education*,
when niggers well make do with crumbs?

Why encourage blackies to lisp and spiel
Liberty and *Liberalism?*
Better that they eye a trek,
an odyssey back,
to Dixie,
utilizing the power of their own boots,
their legs like muscled coal,
and abandoning their coffined progenitors
(let them unfurl potato roots),
to seek servile employ
in their former States.

The border is an underestimated *Threshold*.
We must fence and *defence* it,
sternly recycling southward
every black nose or toe
that broaches the *Boundary*.

Southwest Canada West
can be a peninsular *Paradise*—

if the Negro serfs never become
as half indigenous as the cursèd *Métis*.

Better that they—bewilderedly—moulder
in some hollow, frozen edifice—
a tomb, a sepulchre, a sarcophagus,
with drapery of leaves, peelings, vines, moss.

Or let em be tied so much by *Lynch Law*,
they strangle—
as they stampede.

[**Vancouver (British Columbia)** 26 *octobre* **mmxv**]

Letter from Rev. King

I.

I write to vouch you thanks for the box of clothes,
plus the 3 barrels of clothing
the Ladies Auxiliary Sewing Circle sent

from Amherstburg, Massachusetts,
to Amherstburg, Canada West.

It is a fitting measure.
New clothes may fashion once slaves
into natural-born Canadians.

Indeed, the penniless, lash-bent Africans,
comin to Queen's Bush
after journeys as fearsome as *The Odyssey*,
seek *Charity*
to stay the Poor House
and stay out the Penitentiary, eh?

II.

Nevertheless, I gotta confess —
Abolitionists in the Canadas
face above-average *Unkindness*,
a supercilious *Disparagement*,
for our *Cause* —
bruited about in Boston —
is viewed as "sinister" and "Republican"
here, in Empress Victoria's frigid domains.

Praise God for your unexpected letter of *Relief!*

With your coins at hand, I feel
much assuaged to my *Situation*,
which is difficult—

practically a crisis—

for the Negro man, once-refused *Fellowship*,
refuses my pulpit,
though these are days
of *Devilry* and *Degeneracy*.

I strive to keep em—at least—
10 miles from *Drunkenness*—
and encourage em to plot more houses
round Queen's Bush.

Too many in the Township
be destitute
of the beseechin of the *Gospel*.

God bless. I end.

Truly,

Rev. King.

P.S. Maybe *Abolition* requires swords:
        To melt slaveholders' hearts in their own gore?

P.P.S. (Nevertheless, the niggers be 100% *Trouble*,
        and 90% are best off as slaves—
        a gaggle of scraggly crows.
        Damn!)

[**Nouvelle-Orléans (Louisiane) 21** *juin* **mmxiv**]

The Love Song of Charles Baudelaire (1857)

Volcanic breasts, Arctic with pent-up milk,
Yet, sun-singed, gold-tinged, as if smouldering,
I accost, would grasp, tenderly, Jeanne, Jeanne,
But you slip away, so *Ecstasy*'s ephemeral.

I versify, *Mulâtresse*, your adverse flesh,
Such gold-leaf, lemon-melanin meringue:
Africa shades you, overshadows you;
But Europe poisons--corrosive — your core!

Do I love your sex, your tribe, or your hue,
That blend of *eau-de-vie* and darkest rum,
That hot lightning bolt and black muck merger?
Mercurial Moor, did Satan mint you?

I'm stupefied, even damned, Jeanne Duval!
I thought I was conquering a jungle
In loving you, but, no, I'm lost at sea,
In your body, my bed, and our basting.

We propagate quaking waves, savage tides,
Shaking movements, as we surge, flesh merging.
Nothing of you is ornament; all is
Organic: I'm rooted and uprooted

And re-routed by our rhythms, fluxing,
Conjoining *Calvados* and *poire* liqueur:
Thus, your coaldust kiss defiles the Louvre,
And your golden waist wrecks all *Classicism*.

[Cambridge (Massachusetts) **30** *janvier* **mmxiv**]

À Jeanne Duval

By Charles Baudelaire

Madonna of black-bum bastards,
Madonna of tears soft like turds,

Madonna of tar nipples taut,
Madonna of noose and slip-knot,

Madonna of the bullwhipped ass,
Madonna pale enough to "pass,"

Madonna adroit as *Coitus*,
Madonna salty as mucus,

Madonna, spectral, coffee-hued,
Madonna, delectably nude,

Madonna, so above *Reproach*,
To you, I'm loathsome, a cockroach,

Scuttlebutt, and so you regret—
Drained anisette, stubbed cigarette—

And pray I die, or live as dead,
But pay thee gold and give thee head.

Madonna of *Depravity*—
Antichrist, anti-gravity,

Ante up dog things, all sick shit—
Antiphonal to thy *Poet*—

Thou, haunting *salope*, slut, or
Noted, quotable paramour,

Thine is *Empire*, all I want —
Thy emancipatory cunt....

Unspeakable harlot, I speak
Morals to you that you think Greek —

Or dumbfounding or folderol,
For "preachers — leeches — bleed the *Soul*,"

And I'm "hybrid fungus" because
I set thee in verses, succubus —

My *Corridos Prohibidos*,*
Where your strong *Wrongs* sing out self-righteous....

[**Niagara Falls (Ontario)** & **Batavia (New York) 31** *janvier* **mmxv**]

---

* Mexican Spanish: Forbidden folk songs.

Jeanne Duval's Riposte

I.

Chucky's *Grief* melts like frost
as his *Lust* steams up.

An unloved, disagreeable jerk, drab with *Loneliness*,
bwana wanna take me, have me, as his Carib Venus.

His craving? To contract dandy *Fooping*.
But that absinthe-lush be as harmless as Christ.

Meek, weak, is *every* bone in his physique,
as he displaces his face upon his "slave's" facetious pillow.

He's a dreadful man to desire
such a disdainful woman—*moi*.

Convictedly, I step on his heart;
I fuck out his brains.

II.

He dreams I'm licking lavishly his "pipe"
as he moans lines, epically groaning.

Ink trembles, splatters, a page,
as his sketches disjoint my *Anatomy*.

Arias of womanish, *femme noire* femininity—
our glories—high notes—his tongue and lips hum.

The Makar mustn't publish, but sing *Blasphemy*:
Bastard verses, unapologetically, energetically evil.

[Ottawa (Ontario) 15 *janvier* mmxvii]

From Amherstburg, 1857

Don't we work to back up *Mercy?*

We love —
as Coloured people cannot —
intelligently, steadily —
opposing excitements.

Yet, due to past abuses,
they are distrustful
(naturally)
of our disposition

(our sometimes blackguard *Whiteness:*

Each "jolly" breach of melancholy skirt,
a girl's haunches set sprawling wide).

So, I admit I've felt sinking —

felt like sinking —

save for the steadying grasp of a *Friend* —
her balanced eye

(but unsustainable, sadly,
given the exigencies of *Distance,*
plus the fact she is — *Mrs.* — Moodie).

I confess: My *Soul's* distressed
by the dour incubus of *Colour Prejudice* —
mine own
& *theirs*
& theirs against *ours* —

resolving into *Jealousy* and *Suspicion.*

I plead the Coloured Brethren,
come into my house,
so we can pray out our *Rancour*,

but they refuse to darken my doorway
(no pun intended).

So I can't recommend
extending missionaries
to descend upon Canada West
to enlighten the Fugitive Coloureds.

(*Money* makes more people useful.
Send *Savings* to salvage souls.)

Surely, no missions now will obtain in Canada
anything like *Comfort*.

We are stuck betwixt the *Coloured Ignorant*
and camps of Mohawk Indians —
even more intransigent,
being Catholic....

We should dispose our faces towards
the heavenly Canaan,
but our feet stick fast in feces and muck:

We mimic damnable Dante's *Damned*.

We kneel in a convulsed state
and sob impulsively,
eager still to light a golden lamp
in the paradise of God.

To be free of *Colourphobia* at last!

(Lest our very souls strut into a slaughterhouse.)

Let's furnish Bibles and Sunday School booklets
to the Refugees—
the trodden-down spawn of Africa—

the ordainedly ineradicable "Calibans"—
the probably inexpungeable "Savages"—

to sanctify *our* souls.

Charity is negotiation.

Besides, their "God bless ya" is so hearty
and adamant.

Yet, they disembark here as destitute wretches.

See Sister Fidelia, aged about 45,
mother of 14 brats,
who begs merely a hut
for herself and two toddler boys,

plus a Bible,

and the latter will be presented shortly.

Respectfully yours,

—*Brother Whipple*

P.S. Mrs. Moodie's an Abolitionette.
Thus, our cheek-by-jowl, face-to-face *"tête-à-têtes,"*
must not be revealed to common knowledge,
lest they be misconstrued as "carnal knowledge."
I expect your *Discretion vis-à-vis* this point:
Or I'll skewer your belly on my sword-point....

{Omitted Admission:

Sperm should spray and smear a wench—
make *café liégeois* of her asshole—
so a gamahucher feels fresh urge
to launch raunch
upon her haunches and paunch—

specially if she's an old bitch—
a matron—
or better—
a widow!

As is *practically* Mrs. Moodie.}

[**Liverpool (England)** 12 *octobre* **mmxiv**]

William Hall Halts the Rebellion at Lucknow, India (1857)

Hot stink of mud
Clogs nose tight. Guck,
Spit, slime, and crud
forge gasping muck.

I slip on shit
and gut-shot gore.
Bullets won't quit:
Pell-mell punch more!

Scarlet butcher,
surgeon-dirty:
My self. Smutcher
of *Life*, flirty

with *Death*, fiercely
scrapping iron shot,
I ain't scarcely
scared. Watch God wrought

"Injun" demise;
cannons shed blood—
red *Enterprise*:
Men rot in mud.

God kills, but can't
Himself know *Death*:
Each man's a haunt
with dust for breath.

Sunlight betrays
the Sepoy mosque:
Not one shell strays—
all dawn to dusk.

Calamities —
then *Calm*. I smashed
and smote Indies:
Blood sprayed and splashed.

Gumption and nerve
had I: My chance!
I slew, with verve —
brown khaki'd clans.

My heart's callous,
but my chest shines:
Victoria's
medal reminds

all of *Valour* —
this Negro's *Claim*:
Thus, my colour
bears *Honour*'s name.

Though I laid low
brown men for white,
This hour's hero
marks Empire's height —

a minaret
bowing palm trees....
I backed *belle* Brit;
bowed the Indies.

[**Pordenone** (**Italy**) **22** *septembre* **mmxii**]

Chronicle of the Triumph of William Hall, V.C., at The Relief of Lucknow, India

By Sir Richard Burton

Cannon-splintered, the air caved in
as his being—one muscle—
careered behind cannon,
careened the machine,
so that the tense, tawny Scotian,
now a slick automaton,
all nerves dedicated to Sepoy *Rout*,
ripped em—rousted em—from ramparts.

Born was *Hullabaloo*—banshee and barking;
the lead balls howling
as they hurtled down
and smacked into rebels,
splashing *Carnage* about.

The balls struck, thundering, inundating.
Each "palpable hit"*
rendered a Sepoy trench a ruddy grave.

As Hall ramped up each ball,
tamped in morsels of powder
to the belly of the cannon,
and kept yammering, hammering, at the mosque—
like breakers bashing, thrashing rock,
then splintering into sprinkles—
he appeared masoned in bronze,
greasing the *grisaille* sky with fire,
shrinking it with booms of mushrooming smoke.

---

* Cf. Hamlet.

Thanks to his single-handed
loading, firing,
Hall conceived a shrieking breach,
and British troops swarmed finally
into the gore-dashed, black-scorched rubble —
that grim shattering of stone,
and now wrangled over the turf,
rampaging o'er avalanching bits of wall,
into the tense depths,
where khaki nobodies looked pretzels,
a berserk tangle,
with stone-stabbed eyes popped out, dangled;

or men who'd been quintuply lopped
counting as torsos, morsels;

or foes lolling,
heads jutting from their shoulders,
broke off from their necks,
enormous wounds sprawling their brains....

The dusty, dastardly bastion —
disintegrated into shambled timbers and stone,
ejected scurrying, unthrottled cries,

thanks to Hall's buckets packed with gunpowder,
the scattered flashes of his strategic aim.

Thus, the Injuns wept as they bled
and dripped down gore —
or the buggers were trampled under —

for our militants did not slink
through the blazing ruin of the mosque,
but grabbed the grisly crown of *Triumph*,
glistening in the *Slaughter* —

thanks to Able Seaman Hall.

Hall, heroic, was fierce-eyed in the skirmish,
uncaring for *Safety*,
save for his Queen and The Empire.

[**Stratford (Ontario) 4** *août* **mmxv**]

"Darwin's 'Natural Selection' Applied to Slaver Entertainment" (1859)

By Mandingo Appolonius

(as told to Ambrose Dubose
exclusive to *The Miami Star*)

I.

"Somewhere off Cuba,
Maestro and me cloved to as the ship cleavered spray;

"still, the rank tars egged us on,
betting rum and sluts, hog guts and gold,
on who'd vanquish, who'd perish.

"Maestro's hands clattered furious my ribs.
His chipping jabs bruised me nicely.

"Surprisingly, the vessel pitched;
the sudden keeling
set his dark face level and available
to my black fists.

"Then, the ship plunged, and I lunged,
my fingers jabbed deep both his eye holes,
so that em jellies sprung out,
his scarlet screams flung out,

"and I reeled back with the boat's recoil,
and Maestro collapsed, a corpse,
undone by his done-in eyes,
red crap dribblin from the sockets—

II.

"Now, the tars, some delirious with my *Triumph*,
others soured and disgusted,

"turned to usher fresh buggers onto the deck—
drive dark gladiators to gouge each other;

"but the irritated tars, upset by my laurels—
Maestro's eyeballs—

"grabbed me bodily,

"carted him now a carcass,
hefted us both—

"me, pitlessly—

"overboard.

III.

"*Certes*, I had braved Maestro's macabre clouts—
that dismal, salt-spray night—
and had luckily plastered his face pliable as liquid,

"so when we got dropped—likely—to sharks—
monsters glimmering round like slicks of ice—

"Maestro played the purged pig,
and the ravenous sea-wolves skipped me
to worry and havoc his cadaver—

"even the pink innards of his black tush,
down to the black pebble of his heart,
so sundry chunks surged in the detergent flood—

"while I slapped and sledded
a sea like mercury,

"to be cast up here, outcast,

"as despised as any traveller
who spurns kings and captains,
to sojourn where he pleases,
keeping his own compass and map,

"to go as straight as one wants

"as clear as black.

IV.

"A sea-cake, my brine-blistered flesh
all weeds and shells—

"I seemed a sea-borne Caliban—
a clutch of sable pebbles
held together by stringy weeds
and glued on shells.

"So I can't blame the fishwives that caught me
for calling up the constables:

"Either my relic bones were holy
or they were obscene:
Surely, they were distressing.

V.

"Clinched by ooze,
then winched out it,

"I seem a squirt of ink—
a black squid freak in your credulous gazettes,

"so do Miami yokels chortle and chit-chat.

"Is my tale just cockamamie flim-flam?

"Well, there's no way to test bullshit,
save gettin cock-eyed
and sniffin up close.

"Did I clad myself in seaweed and periwinkles
when my shiverin rambles ended?

"If I'm a 'first-rate liar,'
go find the vessel, *The Merry Celestial*,
flagged out of Cadiz,

"and then check your stubborn doubts
gainst the slaver's gambling logs

bout who won that boxing contest...."

[Tallinn (Estonia) **29** *mai* **mmxiv**]

William Hall: Citation for Valour

By Sir Richard Burton

Charging, aiming, discharging,
thudding cannonballs at the Mosque —
while risking the Sepoy *Wrath*,
blistering bullets, grumbling shots —

creating, mid our impromptu hospital
a *Waste Land* of fire,
never ever flinched William Hall.
As I drowsed in the dust, felled,

having brayed into battle.
but now mutely bleeding,
Hall alone kept up the cannonade
that carolled sweetly

like a dove's song in a lion's den.
Then glided up, down, a glissade
of his whistling cannonballs
that cracked th'infernal, Indo fortress,

into which poured our stranded friends,
who mangled the Muslims
into cadavers and rags,
so grass made green of *Gore*.

Like all peregrinating sailors
longing for grape vines and lemon trees,
or the tits of a Haligonian tart,
her tinkling skirts,

Hall's shipped to his Nova Scotian orchard,
home among his people.
We owe him that,
for we owe him India.

Think not that I exaggerate!
A lie breaks us,
but *Truth* makes us:
You hold India because Hall *held*.

[**Eden Mills (Ontario)** 16 *septembre* **mmxii**]

Victoria Summons Hall (October 1859)

Command this hour's hero —
Mr. Hall, to catch the sea,
wave by wave, and surf, unservile,
each majestic swell,

then half-collapsed foam.
Once he fords the spray rampart,
ramping our shore,
he must enjoy every opportunity

for *Caprice*.
Bring me Mr. Hall,
the pitch-faced sailor
who blew apart the Sepoys

and made their Mosque their graves.
Let him sing, sassy as a kazoo,
and encourage our spasms of humming,
while night takes custody of dreams.

[**Frankfurt (Germany) 18** *septembre* **mmxii**]

William Hall, V.C., Remembers

I.

I swept the fort — the Mosque — with bursts,
volleys, the cannon spat.

First —
out of respect for his sacrifice —
I had to scrape the raw brains·
of Lt. Cape
from the weapon's side.

I did next all I could —
to copy Nietzsche's superhuman Negro —

to maim the Mosque,
to tumble the temple into wreckage.

II.

Plasma — dust — a kind of smegma
smeared the battery, streaking it.

My firing was slings of shot.

As Her Majesty's emissary,
I meant to dent or cripple faces —
bronze and copper —
like so much tin.

III.

Sweat flopped—slopped—from all my pores
as I did my level utmost
to crack and crater skull bones;
to scalp scoundrels and pulp em;
to tussle over the yellow dust of Lucknow—
all those cow patties
showing an overlay of gold.

Vultures clustered thick as crows, squabbling,
bolting clots of crimson'd flesh.

IV.

Eventually indomitable,
our Marines surged into the breach
I'd broke open.

They scuffled, veered, booted through dust,
teaching the rabid Injuns
their reward is only manure—

just more and more crap in their mouths—

that we like to slaughter our opponents:

All those who'd mob Whitehall,
besiege Buckingham Palace,
overturn the House of Commons,
threaten the Empress,
and make London a conclave of cannibals
and next brown scholars studying wan, cringing slaves....

But such *Victory—Anarchy*—the rabble'd win,
if we'd let the Mosque remain stuck
in Indo-satanic claws.

Any true Briton must rifle-butt-smack-down tyrants—
deliver em beautiful, mirthless *Extinction*.

V.

Dusty and dustier, dirty and dirtier, bloody and bloodier,
was my solo *Action*,

downcasting—destroying—dozens of upstart, umber faces,

and so,

snagged I this black-shade, star-crossed trophy.

[**Smiths Cove (Nova Scotia) 20** *août* **mmxv**]

Statement on William Hall by the Rebel, Raja Jai Lal Singh, Writ in Prison Before His 1857 Execution (But Lost Until 1860)

Bill Hall likely dreaded the *ferdwite*,*
or he forgot he's *cholos*,**
not *blanco* (white); his bone-garment's ebony.

The cobra-tint panther—
stocky as a chop-winged griffin—
half-Egyptian, half-Anglo-Saxon,
his jaw a shark's,
acted clumsily, clownishly,
this prime minstrel to that *memsahib* bitch Victoria....

(The devil's an ass when not a snake—
and goatish when not swinish:
Such is Hall—
a hash of body parts.)

Scalp his naps and lop his dick? Sure.
Migrated he from childhood Christendom
to adult Sodom.

Definitely, he was out-of-place in India—
being from an out-of-the-way place,
where he was and is unwelcome
(Nova Scotia), that ember of pumice,
that dunduckity,*** cocksucking, persnickety,
white-boy wanna-be,
mouthing anti-Islam *Malice*,

---

* The fine for shirking a military expedition.
** Peruvian Spanish: Coloured.
*** Mud-coloured.

the white-kissing, black-hating nigger,
also hissing anti-Hindu hoodoo,
his lungs pried open

to wonky gurgling,
that "sho-nuff, good-eatin'"* fool,
granting Brit *buckaroos* his baffled *Utility*,

precipitating a cannon's dewy rain —
the tears of Africans,
humiliated by a "br'er" who backs the chalk Caucasians,

and attacks the original — purely dark — Caucasians,
to frustrate our *Putsch* for *Freedom*!
Idiot, idiot, idiot,

the preternatural dolt, Hall,
that human garbage,
must like lickin Victoria's old cunt —
her tea-and-lemon-juice-puckered cunt —

his bulbous nose depthen** in her fulvous vulva —
the grisly Judas,
the undoubtable Sambo,
tottering toward *Slaughter*,
the mutilation of Lucknow,

slaving ridiculously for the whites,
thus proving as disposable and as witless
as an empty chocolate bar wrapper.

Clearly, Hall's secret confidence is, he's white —
a strange, inaccessible white,
an Untouchable, thus touchy, white,

---

* Cf. Fanon.
** To deepen.

an honorary, albescent chap,
sub-blackish,
a *mischling*,*

dispensing *Whiteness* into the air—
electrical scratches from his crackerjack cannon—
to strike down black and brown—actual—men,
liking—but lacking—*Liberty*!

[**Ottawa (Ontario) 8 & 9** *janvier* **mmxvii**]

----

* German: Half-breed.

Upon Commencing to Draft "Moses: A Story of the Nile" (1860)

By Frances Ellen Watkins Harper

Sherry-leaking Pharaoh schemes
    to pyramid his slave gal's gash;
to arrow into her trembling furrow,
    and lodge his seminal *Evil*;
to fasces-axe each virgin temple
    into ragged, hymeneal ruins.

White trotters derive *Pleasure*,
    driving twixt slight thighs,
and/or tonguing their prey
    to sable raw and pink quick.

Once satisfied—
    but only for an hour—
"cream" crusts
    on their mouths and groins.

These identical perverts worry about
    una mujer blanca
*y un musculoso negro,**
    that *esclavitud*
encourages "miscegenation" —
    or *zoofilia.***

---

* Spanish: White lady and a muscular Negro.
** Spanish: Bestiality.

Each Big-House stages jolly *Melodrama*—
 *bestialemente**—
the *Bedlam* bedroom venting
 oily howls, sliding moans,
a lot of muckying oaths,
 while monsieur screws *mulata* daughter,
or her pale half-brother diddles
 the black mammy who gave him suck.

The South markets pasteboard Eden:
 Just a host of milk-face clergy shitting
on chocolate-wash, feces-munching chimps.
 They ought to chuck out their Bibles
and their Plato
 before every chapel's sunk in excrement.

The South is squabbling boozers,
 Frankenstein-crafted Don Juans,
counties of gutless masochists and countless rapists,
 those uneasy gluttons breakin bottles
and hymens,
 and crackin open hymnals with crackpot shouts.

I don't invent the salty conduct that I condemn.
 Many swashbuckling preachers—
despite erratic zigzags—
 to dodge the stink and oink of *Evil*—
will acknowledge that free-for-all *Adultery*
 is the South's honoured *Constitution*.

(They have defenders—
 of course:
Perfumers
 accompanying butchers.)

---

* Italian: Sodomy or assassination.

Even you might argue that *Sin* and *Crime*
    are mere potholes troubling horseback emperors,
or coachmen ferrying concubines;
    that *Rape* itself mirrors
Old Testament *joie-de-vivre*;
    that fair, white gentry don't mind
to double-stuff half-black daughters
    in quadruped poses.

I'd expect Christians to rue
    the dark, primordial, pungent look of dung
and the slithering wounds that open
    wherever churches prove as flimsy as smoke.

Wherever *Law* is illegitimate,
    sons bugger their mothers.

Abolitionists long for *Clarity*:

    Would only the cold spill of black ink
conduct burning, scorching flame,
    truly exposing, *via* righteous *Illumination*,
the "honey-boned harlot"
    wifing every plantation,
her ochre breasts bobbing or throbbing in space,
    as she is seized by the rear,
to ingest the serpentine skewer
    of some glib begetter of bastards.

To straighten thought —
    I am plain:
Fresh Huns are rutting our chaste maids
    in chapels best classed as stables.*

---

* Cf. *Beatrice Chancy* (1801, 1999).

Slavery's context is
    continuously ominous.
Or sinuously ominous.
    (But I din no doggerel.)
I'm glum, not gay:
    A Dixie despot has a whore in bed
even when his avowed wife is begetting—
    in homespun hospital.

This unnatural, but certified *Dirtiness*
    will inspire a brawl of daggers—
cram streams with *Disease*-ejaculating dead—
    prod sable men to godawful *Revenge*,
to grind dainty white ladies
    til they snort and fart,
and next their sullied wombs squeeze out
    babes no better than turds.

A poet says less than a preacher.
    I don't shout or drone.
Nor am I a toothless, yapping scold
    or inveterate *fretchard*.*
I only warn you that—
    as soon as they can—
chain-gang, chalk-ankled slaves
    will tangle blades in slavesters' guts.

Heed: The "Negro Cargo"
    is caustic as cornered rats:
They got a mania for machetes,
    and will hasten to waste
every ivory massa and missy and chillun
    down to a strawberry-and-cream paste.

---

* A fretful or peevish person.

The bureaucrats of *Slavery*?
    Aristocrats of claws and fangs.

I tell you, you are conquerors facing eclipse:
    Your day is already defecated.

[Roissy-en-France (France) 3 *février* mmxiii]

Negro Inventory

(*pace* Léon-Gontran Damas)

Negro is bamboo, coffee, sugar cane.
Negro is a bamboozled coffle of cigar-shade, Cayenne slaves.
Negro is a hurricane.
A hurried caning is also *Negro*.
Or *Negro* is canine, can-do *Cannibalism*.
(*Cannibalism* is the *Negro* definition of *Capitalism*.)
Negro is always candid.
Negro serves as candy.
Licorice, liquor, rice: Commodities weight the *Negro*.
Avarice is *Negro*. So is spice.
Negro is orange or an orangutang's tangy guts.
Negro is naturally chocolate.
Negro is naturally chock-a-block late.
Every organ groan is *Negro*.
Negro is the Athens of bones and the Rome of skulls.
Negro is a priest riving a child's rectum....
Negro is septic:
An anti-septic is anti-*Negro*.
Impudent rotgut—virtuoso plonk—that's *Negro*.
Abrasive at the White House, facing down fallacious applause, that's a
Negro.
Seduction is *Negro*—as is every price reduction.
A violent *Negro* masks an ingenious *Negro*.
Pathological polysyllables get voiced by every anthropological *Negro*.
Negro gotta be as thrifty as is *Breath* itself.
Or *Death* (itself being *Negro*).
Negro is shark mouths, piranha mouths, barracuda mouths,
That bite down as they talk fishy *Negro* talk:
Their words cut pieces off everybody—just like *Negro*
Radicals, who act like any ghetto, razor-blade *Negro*.
Negro breeds broods and brats—

Squalls of girls and storms of boys, unanimously *Negro*.
A *Negro*, to put down roots, erects headstones, not huts.
Negro is homeless. *Negro* is rootless; his groves are ruts.
Negro is the core collapse, the chief crisis, of *Christianity*:
Each honest *Negro* doth say, "God save you—and fuck me!"

[**Enfield (Nova Scotia) 21** *septembre* **mmxiv**]

Inventario Negro[*]

(*pace* Léon-Gontran Damas)

Negro el bambú, el café, la caña de azúcar.
Negro la engatusada hilera de sombra de cigarro, los esclavos Pimienta.
Negro es un huracán.
Un castigo con prisa también es *Negro*.
O Negro es canino, puede ser *Canibalismo*.
(*Canibalismo* es la definición Negra de *Capitalismo*.)
Negro es siempre cándido.
Negro sirve dulce.
Regaliz. Licor. Arroz. Comodidades pesan al *Negro*.
Avaricia es *Negro*. También las especias.
Negro es naranja o las entrañas picantes de un orangután.
Negro es naturalmente chocolate.
Negro es naturalmente choca-un-bloque tarde.
Cada gruñido de órgano es *Negro*.
Negro es el Atenas de huesos y el Roma de cráneos.
Negro es el cura montando el recto de un niño....
Negro es séptico:
Y anti-séptico es anti-*Negro*.
Impúdica matarratas—golpe virtuoso—eso es *Negro*.
Abrasivo en la Casa Blanca, encarando el aplauso falaz, eso es un *Negro*.
Seducción es *Negro*, como lo es cada reducción de precios.
Un *Negro* violento equivale a un *Negro* ingenioso.
Polisílabas patológicas son dichas por cada *Negro* antropológico.
Negro tiene que ser tan ahorrativo como el mismo *Aliento*.
O la *Muerte* (que es *Negra*.)
Negra es la boca del tiburón, la boca de la piraña, la boca de la barracuda,
Que muerde mientras habla cosas sospechosas de *Negro*:
Sus palabras cortan pedazos de todos—tal como los *Negros*
Radicales, que actúan como cualquier gueto, *Negro* navaja.

---

[*] Trans. Andrea Martinez.

Negro reproduce prole y mocosos —
Chillidos de niñas y tormentas de niños, unánimemente *Negros*.
Un *Negro*, para echar raíces, erige lápidas, no chozas.
Negro es indigente. Negro no tiene raíces, sus arboledas son surcos.
Negro es el colapso del centro, la crisis principal de la *Cristianismo:*
Cada *Negro* honesto de hecho dice, "Dios te salve — y cógeme!"

[Enfield (Nova Scotia) 21 *septembre* mmxiv]

Longfellow's "Black Snake Blues"

Let Hiawatha molest a guitar;
worry strings as if stirring mud:
His mumbo jumbo's nothin but gumbo'd muck
cause his heart's a distress of blood—
a pitter-patter, splattered amount—
for a blankety-blank Godiva dubs him "no-count."

Troubles be vultures gnawin on his bones.

Evangeline be a two-buck,
buck-tooth whore.
outta Acadie, y'all
(outpost of *accidie*).

Mmm, mmm, mmm.

Hiawatha remember, he remember,
back when they got down in one bed,
crashed together like Iliad strivers,
burnin like Troy,
his Trojan horse
rompin past her gates,
til the blanking flood *banketh*.

But no (ex) slave can know true *Constancy*.
Love among the free be prone to decay.
Chained-down, Evangeline always pray to get away.

So, now she's liberated,
denominates herself as liberal,
uninterested in a debated
bed, and uncoupled from the ideal
of the couple, and feeling
that *Feeling*'s more vital than vows,
her heart enjoys sumptuous reeling:

No more must she bed down a spouse.
(Hurt too much like scratchin a louse.)
She gonna love someone else, someone else.
She gonna love someone else!

[Vicenza (Italy) 17 *avril* / *Nisan* mmxii]

Ante-Bellum, Autumn 1860

By Abraham Lincoln

I.

These United States are not a potential *Tyranny*,
nor are they a doubtful *Tyranny*.
They are half a *Tyranny*—
a type of the tyrannical.

In half these states, maybe the better half,
Freedom can't exist
outside a necessary *Conspiracy*
to shackle and wrack th'Africans.

Many Ivy League whiz kids cogitate
to ensure stable boys ain't whipped,
but outfitted in white chiffon.
Others weigh crops of chains,

or count barrels of manacles.
Tea is polite;
whiskey is *Politesse*.
A paper peace is kept

though *Grief* thrives like grass.
Civil *Loathing* is the Congress—
realm of oratorical detritus.
Banshee politicos shriek in razor'd darkness.

Consensus is bullish,
dissent is mulish.
Committees stampede, trample, run amok.
Black bulls cover each black mule.

Between salty protests —
divided ministers divvying up the Gospels
(odd believers who cup ale and pray) —
a tender paralysis

holds governors, dreamers, and slaves.
Storm clouds bust into tears
or applause.
The antique aroma of rain refreshes.

South of this White House —
precincts clogged with slaves —
Compromise is tarred and feathered.
Desolate bridges purge this redoubt of poets

and peacemakers. United Statesian
warmongers rowdy up on rum;
their horses snort, whinny,
imperious, imperial,

as all chatter of *Secession*.
If only our forefathers had had
a less self-serving *Revolution*
and hadn't dethroned monarchs

to set up slavemasters,
whose silk-and-velvet decrees loose
unconstitutional, black codes and black, unclean corpses.
Friends, I'm no fan of the Negro!

But our *Freedom* is faulty,
thanks to faultless ruins
of *Logic*, or *Greed*.
(*Misanthropy* is *Theology* spiffed up as social science.)

II.

I mint fresh shadows.
The future is a score whose melody
is obscure
and whose composer is yet anonymous.

Greatness is *Anguish.*
Power delivers *Pain* and begets *Sorrow.*
But patriotic are my shivers and my howls.
See my First Lady — my boudoir honey,

her face is faded silk.
"Breath is insipid,
that's not inspired
by love or verse,"

speaketh Walt Whitman,
Citizen Bard camping on the Potomac.
(He sleeps with *Poetry,*
he sleeps off his liquor.)

Strange how proverbs unlock poems!
Look up: A starling floats like a fish.
Soon, stars will bar — contradict — binary stars.
Thus, I conceive uneasy eons of *War....*

Late summer is us,
breathing,
still not dead.

A startling speech erases —
or engraves —
my epitaph.

If *War* there is,
the first shot kills me last.

[**Virginia Beach (Virginia) 11** *novembre* **mmxi**]

Douglass Anticipates Civil War

A hot-lead umbrella will overcast Richmond:
Meteors—metal—striking buttery-gold
will fringe its sides,
singe the tyrant Davis, and shred his flag

(but that rag will sag nicely natty
if it doubles as his ratty shroud).

Bade the Confederates rush at us as grey *Hostility*,
but drop fast before our Union blues,
our engaged, warring statues,
who kill-slay-kill with strident *Agility*.

The battlefield must sprawl steel-riven,
exploded men
and crumpled steeds,
broken down to horse hair and hooves.

War will win a South
worthy of the North!

The Rebs' farcical, peevish "Prez"—
Davis—
why, his face will be our foothold.

(Cap'ain's brash moustache, beard,
will dangle crooked as blacks razor his mouth,
scrape his lips, jaw—a crimson, cut-rate shave.)

Epic—our need.
Epic= the *Dead* dug up.

Once we commence, sir,
rats will pour down every Rebel chimney
like big, black, pelting rain drops,
sincerely.

The slavesters'll brave rain as alive as fire—
their own vital fluids,
welling from gulches of wounds,
until they drown, face-down,
in the brackish tide—
their own corporeal sludge.

The very sun will smart.
Bullets'll zing and unzip air;

Men will copy mangled flowers.
Ravens will feast on shot-out brains.

Octopus every magnolia with Southern traitors,
hanging.

Every sweet-mouthed, Latinate lawyer,
once spic-and-span in the *Slave Mart*,
will become marble garbage, offal.

Let these slavesters be as fastidious
as felines finessing turds with dirt;
still, they'll stumble into tedious graves, all quicksand—
in what was once sumptuous grass....

Let our blows come down as intermittent,
but as persistent,
as waves
that cannot be waved away.

I pray the South's grey-clad sons
get cast-down in torrents,
that their skeletons "catch cold"
and shiver in the earth.

Lincoln!

Let dandered-up black men wrangle white devils,
wrestle em into *Arrest*,
their pinions pinned down.

Next, usher em into hitherto uncontaminated *Eternity*.

[Berlin (Germany) 11 *mars* mmxiii]

The Narrative of Lincoln States [Not His Real Name]

Ars atrium omnium conservatrix*
is Memory.

I.

Like any grown child of God,
I can't remember my first steps,
my first words.

But I'm Imbangala
of Angola.

From out the avocado-coloured sea,
rode a "blackbirder" —
come from the *mondo depravados***
like a lash of visceral lightning,
striking south from Madeira,
to enact a drama of *Destruction*
off the coast of West Africa,
some island they'd charted;
no, chartered.

Crawled ashore — I say —
a mob of dingy beasts,
light-hearted brutes,
who, backed by tar-faced, blond-scalped blacks

(snakes who know our grassy hideouts,
vipers who rattle a demonic demotic),

---

* Latin: The art preserving all other arts.
** Spanish: World of the depraved.

showed genius for improvising *Brutality*.
They were rum-insane canines, but canny
with raucous whip, caustic blade, spastic musket.
Astute in *Barbarism*.

Conglomerations of blood,
clammy blood, grimy blood,
peeled from black backsides,
jumped from torsos, faces, spines,
sprung from a mouth, a sex, an eye,
to splash an ascerbic burgundy on the earth....

II.

The Portuguese pirates grabbed us pell-mell,
every sort of *sorte*,*
man, woman, toddler
(I was all of seven years,
approximately),
and herded us on board
their black boat,
then below planks
in seminally filthy air,
crummy light,
screams, screeches, shrieks of shackles,
knifing at ears.

Colomares,**
a rancid ship,
stashed us, spoon-huddled,
on floors of mixed bodily fluids —
in their stock-in-trade, marine stockade....

---

* Danish: Black.
** Latin: Dove of the seas.

A race measured by *Bloodshed*
commenced at once to create
a race of miscegenated stock—
a polluted, sullied, and sullen race....

(A naked, young body—
whipped, branded, chained—
is extremely fuckable
in dreamy ways.

To flog a woman,
to jerk about a man,
to render *Copulation* viscerally grotesque,
excites anti-Semites supremely.)

I remember only vignettes:
red gore, black flesh, green fields,
gangrened flesh, burnt-sienna fields, black ichor.

Diligent devils—ringmasters—flicking whips.

Stinking Alvear's Amontillado
(out of Mantilla, Andalusia),
once tasted in Imperial Rome
and in the Moorish Empire,
now drenches yelling women

as they are tasted.

Slave ship
bullhorned by bullwhip.

An opaque epoch:
An atmosphere of daggers.

Rust brands necks, ankles, wrists;
whips snap buckling spines.

I saw my parents slaughtered
awfully like water buffalo.

III.

Always old ligatures on young limbs,
new ligatures on old limbs,
teach that blackness
is *History*'s truest *Tragedy*.

My first sale: Rio,
imperial Portuguese harbour.

My name's now spelled, "Antonio."

I help cut sugar cane to sweeten
the sour coffee
another slave harvests
and still another slave brews and serves....

The universal *Economics*:
Labour comes cheaper than *Capital*.

Cotton is a soft commodity,
but sugar is as hard as currency.

One takes a pointed pole, a machete,
a plough, a hoe—
or, rather, a spear and a sword—
to slash or cut that tall, tough grass—
cane—
that is sugar.

The sugar lands manufacture
milk-white millionaires overseas
by mangling black millions
in southern seas.

Better still, alchemical sweat
scums off—
Presto!—
into rum.

IV.

Now 18 and well-muscled,
I'm sold again,
to the New Republic—
God's Shining City on the Hill—
America.

(After an aide to Alvar Nunez Cabeza de Vaca,
an otherwise anonymous Moor,
the first known darky on Yankee soil,
who outlived shipwreck nigh Texas,
fell a six-year slave of the Karankawas*—
arch bowmen who hunted, fished,
and kept dogs—
and escaped
by trekking southern deserts
to Mexico City, 1536,

I am the latest Negro landed in America.)

My new, now-"people's republic" port:
New Orleans.

Again, I'm no person,
just a purchase,
a thing retitled "Antony."

The barker harrumphed,
"The best-blooded slaves
in this hemispheric Republic
are tethered on this turf."

---

* Dog lovers.

Up on the auction block,
the bland, unblanching tycoon
disposes of the "productive catalogue" —
mother, lock, father, stock,
straplings, boxes, and babes,
kit, kids, and kaboodle.

Before us,
the white-trash, bluegrass rednecks —
who define the Republic —
bray and huzzah.

Prices get bargained up and down;
white fingers poke or pull black genitals,
tap at teeth and gums,
palm and squeeze muscles....

Sold off,
our lot turns into th'U.S.A.'s sunburned *Diversity.*

V.

Our doyen's smile catches on his teeth,
omnivorously carnivorous.

He strut like his butt dump gold coins.

Frankincense phrases
fart from his Frankenstein mouth.
His Sunday School chat insists,

"Slavery is God's commandment
(your punishment):
All *Being* is held firm —
like ball and socket:
Note the silver chains of the stars."

Here's my reading:
a *dracu* clan—
survey black folks
and tell each other,
"Here is gilded blood to suck."

Thus, even if we do
"a biblically laudable job,"
sweating to fatten others,
our shackles ain't shaken off.

Hard money is silver,
measured out, calculated.
But it matters not:
we get no deep-pocket *Accumulation*.

Rather,
the whip froths black upon my back;
black plasma outs.

Iron manacles hand and hand;
my sweat purchases only gruel—
a gut-ready, gritty swamp.

We eat doled-out, dried up, dusty cake,
suck and slurp dingy, mangy water.

One gets used to a bellyful of crap.

Black mammies weep like paddle wheels;
black babies shriek like windmills.

VI.

Creole is a colour in Rio—
and a calculation in New Orleans.

My liege opens a stable:
He parcels out young girls
to service stallions;
mere boys to stud mares;
all while he ogles.

Or he sprawls gawdy bawds onto oily sheets;
or compels the most pulchritudinous Ethiope
to mother a motherfucker for a plutocrat.

A glimmering *mulata*—
all unimpeachable cream-and-peach—
or the buxom, hassled, pure black "hussy,"
or the gal of translucent shimmer
(the shade of fragile, Pedro Ximinez grapes),
can all be pressured, promised, processed,
so that God-shouting lady
sees purple bruises flower upon her yellow butt;
or some blue-gum bastard gets flogged
to spur on "irresistible" jiggling.

(Should she turn up her nose at such "sports,"
a mother still must turn up her bottom....)

Giggles follow bawling;
howling pursues guffaws.

VII.

My own beloved gal, Clio Patrick—
a hint of whiteness in her ebony,
a scratch—
exhibited, extra, a high-class spirit:

Never always a slave,
but always a black woman,
she never ever was subdued.

Cock-eyed and fish-lipped,
unquestionably grimy,
a sanctified social disease,
our Chief toppled on top of Clio.

He pounds fetuses *into* Afro'd women's wombs.

Pines murmured.
A pine, darkling, fondled velvet dark—
and *not* vice versa.

VIII.

Sobbing, she disclosed his *Crime.*

(I realize careful *Violence* is good:
A Jim Crow, Caucasoid Christ
has gotta die.

Don't be harmless,
or you'll be dead:
I told myself rightly.

Now a death-head stamps my every dream.
Courage plate-metals me.

I have a chastening remedy—
a useful torment—
for "Mr. Jim."

My ten fingers want ten daggers.

Bleeding is usually unpleasant—
save when it is unusually pleasant.

Violence must be exact—
a haiku;
or it is *Carnage*—
an epic.)

The moon is a weak, stark,
sickly white thing.
It mirrors putrefying Caucasians:
A bad sign.
I creepy crawl under firefly light.

I catch the devil at prayer;
he has neither guts nor gumption.
I snarl, "Get fuck off yo knees!"
My once-owner drops hard, on his butt,
whimpering.
I hiss, "Get fuck off yo ass!"
I ram the musket barrel in his gut.

Stars squirm like pale slugs
in blackface night.

The ball bites into his belly.
His bowels explode:
Vomit throngs the vacuum;
gore gasps out;
he pukes up chuckles.

(To burn his bones and poop on the ashes,
to uproot his rat brood and his other brat vermin,
would've made me laugh out loud,
wrest Bedlam outta Dixie.)

Free at last! Free at last!
All it took was a musket blast!

This refrain ran through my brain—
as melodically—oozing—as the Mississippi—
as I hightail it outta Louisiana.

IX.

A murderer or a rebel,
I fled Back-and-Forth America,
that opulent *Disaster,*
land seesawing over *Slavery.*

I raced through a fair bit of rain,
and rain all through Carolina too.

The River Jordan is deep and wide:
Gospelled Africa on th'other side.

But how else to be free?

I could not divest myself of melanin
and slide into depraved white skin.

I did not want to end up done-for meat,
a rope snaked about my neck.

(The simplicity of string and stick
is *Lynch Law.*

Yet, hanging *seems* painless
compared to a hammer
being laid to one's bones,
crunching and crushing them,
til scraped nerves scream.)

I prefer that my grave dirt
be ink.

X.

And what about the brazen *Hypocrisy*
of my pursuers and accusers?
I slew the man who defiled my love:

But how many Negroes have perished,
not due to factual *Crime*,
only *Insinuation* and *Allegation*?

Often gals deflowered —
or gone to seed
(who ply their keisters as supply-on-demand) —
or some perfume-halo'd Jezebel,
a gap-toothed grimace
and a gape-legged stance —
can bid a black boy
become a cadaver,
his parts disassembled....

Yet, painted dainties camp out
near Negro "bucks,"
crave and wink at
"the cargo of bull studs,"
and, when night falls
like a widow's dress,
flour-ivory fingers
grip ebony muscle
as some "eager nigger" —
mining "snow" —
sinks down his shaft.

Come next ruffians and yahoos
grab, stab, winch, lynch, strangle, and mangle
each unlucky "Othello
of the bordello"....

Generazioni di assassini,
bearing the pigmentation of pigs,
scissor off the sable phallus
for use as church tapers.

---

* "Generations of assassins" (Freud).

River Nile, where all our blood flows stark red,
Our last-born are cursed, our first are dead.

But the honest *History* is not
black rods plugging white pigeonholes,
but the negative reverse,
spawning a fleshy gilt.

(Ponder—wonder—how many masters
acted "Mr." to some slave-chit "missy,"
mastering her as if she were his "Mrs."?)

XI.

Britons! Albion's children!
You may wonder what is my scheme,
my purpose, in this prose.
It is multifold:

Ignore all counter-pamphleteering drivel:
The Lesson of *Revelation* is,
Violence must permeate the Cosmos
to impregnate—bring forth—*Justice.*

Thus, I say to bondsmen (and women),
in terror and trembling,
bade your masters pick maggots
from their babes' half-crushed skulls;
let your sighing knives
silence the Horse Latitudes
where statistics and steeds get jettisoned as bilge.
The whites only have what they took:
Blacks must *take back* all we deserve.

Liberation—elation—
bests *Patriotism.*

Honour to Nat Turner!

Follow "General Moses" —
Tubman,
who tramps "runaways" through swamps,
shoots em tombstone-dead if they run back.

Turn on a dime
and give no quarter:
your plug-nickle life
ain't worth one red cent no how.

Study how your compatriots, fellow citizens,
resolve "The Nigger Question":

"Take kindling, even dry twigs,
a jug of kerosene,
several feet of good, strong hemp,
lash the subject bucks
with bullwhip or horsewhip,
and then lash these reject jigaboos,
one by one,
to stout trees,
then build fires at the varmints' feet.
Bathe their tar-baby flesh in kerosene,
then strike and toss a match,
and step back;
watch flames eat their tarpaper flesh,
turn black, black skin
into a pristine element,
pure black carbon,
turn human skin to ash, smoke, and dust.
Then, throw a barbecue.
Doom all niggers to trigger
living fireworks."

Brethren! If you do not wish to campaign
and kill for your *Liberty*,
then at least come North
to the British realms,
to shadowbox with snow flakes,
yes, but live in free winds.

Flee sawdust stars, crowbar-jawed crows.

All us chillen who once got whipped,
now got wings,
ways and means,
here in the True North.

XII.

Whither the *emancipados*?
Anywhere ex-masters
can be held liable for the big bucks.

Just trace our tongues....

Our brown faces mirror white fathers exactly;
Our 'Ebonics' echo pallid, unpalatable preachers.

English is porridge in our mouths.
Language goes salty, gingerly.

(Behind English literature,
spy a suppuratin sepulchre.

Cf. *The Old Testament in the Dialect
of the Black Districts*:
It demonstrates pidgin speech
is as pungent a parley as is Tchaikovsky.)

Europe is not a cathedral;
it is an abbatoir.

Now, my European, Caucasian readers,
I ask you,
Why do white folk do what they do?
You must admit out loud,
you often concoct a scheming *Mafia,*
spurred on by genocidal *Greed.*

Note that your "Great Helmsman,"
Columbus,
instituted *encomienda;*
cargo'd to Spain
loads of chained "Injuns";
pit his trained, wolfhound dogs
against recalcitrant captives,
ripping them to shreds....

XIII.

Soon to die, now aged 70,
interrupting, abruptly ending,
my personal century
(and a century is formidable for lost time),

I have been a killler by necessity.
I remain a liberator by deed.

Do not list my acts as crimes or sins.
I was not free to be virtuous.

1861

[Ottawa (Ontario) 24 & 25 *janvier* mmix
& Nantes (France) 26–30 *janvier* & 2 *février* mmix]

---

* Slavery.

Julia Ward Howe Composes
"The Battle Hymn of the Republic" (1861)

Untrammelled roads admit no unbridled horses:
Violence outpaces prayer.

Apple blossoms vanish violently:
Beauty just gets blown away.

Ideally, we plant trees, not corpses;
prefer *Husbandry*, then *Harvest*.

But, during *War*, even poets shatter
into factions of lines.

The ruddiest *Chaos*, chanted in *The Iliad*,
brandishes patriotic bugles, imperial flutes,

nothing peevish.
Consider blown apart presidents:

Their carcasses torn open, their blood
suddenly enthusiastically everywhere,

no defiance of enemy guns possible;
wives instantly widows beside.

Mothers! Temper all hallucination:
The Army schemes to injure thy sons!

Vengeance directs *Eternity*.
Tools rate less than armaments.

Pogroms enact gory *Indulgence*,
but this vice (of "civil combat") bleeds our *Manners*.

Unfathomable armies —
untethering slaves —

unhinge *The Republic*,
undo the *Constitution*.

[Cambridge (Massachusetts) 29 *mars* mmxiv]

Jefferson Davis Opines

I've sought a career of usage —
to underwrite applause *via* plausible deeds:
To tax the cotton Midas' mansions,
to keep the sewers spic-and-span
(in theory).

Assuredly, I back our grandees' *Georgics*:
The habit of profits for our plantations
puffs belly and proffers *Bellicosity*.

Now, observe Lincoln:
Somnambulist on a tightrope.

Why should not a *Constitution* be as guiltless
as a heroic soldier's rags?

I say our Confederacy should enshrine *ergastula**
and make wine, then make water,
then fertilize the charm-schooled, Tea-Party dames.

I do accuse the Union
of irredeemable *Savagery*.

We must slash the jugular —
answer their troops as if we are dressing meat —
and be butcher-glad gladiators,
and cut to pieces every Union dog —
every sniggerin, nigger-lovin dog —
ignoring their wanton snivelling,
so that they gulp their own bones and fat.

---

* Latin: Underground prisons for holding plantation slaves.

We will adventure—neck-chopping jocular—
put down each sordid, Nordic bastard.

Our swords dice up
the Lincoln *Constitution*—

all that phony bologna.

[**Gibraltar (United Kingdom)** 5 *décembre* **mmxii**]

Upon Re-Reading Othello

By Adah Isaacs Menken*

Desdemona's virgin-snow whiteness:
A dead-end.

Better that her *chatte* had been stretched
by Othello's spitting sword
than her lungs had been stopped up
by the blackamoor's fists.

Not even *Love* can marry
blackest black and whitest white —
with no inkling of grey.

Besides, only a Caucasoid god
could dream up Eve as a nude —
fluorescent albescent —
save for her piss-hole and shit-hole.

Hard for Othello and Desdemona
to amalgamate and checkmate *Sterility*:
No matter *Great Hymns of the Faith*,
they are illegitimate *Royalty*.

Their wedding serves up a *Titus Andronicus* feast
of bile and guts.

How can Othello husband an ivory lady —
while black women groan in chains?

---

* Philomène Croi Théodore (1839–68). A "light-complected," "Black" poet outta
Louisiana, claiming Jewish identity (thanks to marriage), she became a transatlantic
actress and sexpot, a star dramatizer of Byron's verse.

Shakespeare's errant:
Othello is Samson;
Desdemona is Delilah.

[**Kamloops** (**British Columbia**) 7 *Nisan* / *avril* **mmxi**]

Sojourner Truth's War Measures: A Ghazal

I.

I'm torn twixt the smoky Old Testament
and the gore-smeared New Testament.

To be like leopards, swift, hungry to kill:
Defines my politics *vis-à-vis* slave owners.

Viscerally clot the chains;
Garrulously unknot the whips.

Hunters nurse passenger pigeons on whiskey-soaked seed,
then bullet down the addled birds

to stuff pigs and sustain slaves.
Such is *Economy*: *Want* and *Waste*.

Prurient Puritans chowing down on pork and grape
expel a smug smell, rancid, cancered.

II.

How can I hasten to *Chastity*?
I quit clouds that fog up *Thought*.

Ain't I a woman —
as stark as a mother, nude with her newborn?

Mother? Her crotch flowered;
my head came forth, extruding, shouting down this *Hell*.

Hell awoke and spoke its mind:
Devils crooning lies at lecterns, pulpits.

Hell is where the white preachers metaphorize,
"Bang, bugger, every black bitch."

Hell defines a goddamned zoo of a Congress:
Donkeys and elephants, curs and rams.

Human *Evil* forces bipeds — black beasts — to breed.
Graves go missing, but no one ducks *Fucking*.

The virile *Unvirtuous* lurk and skulk
where virgins pass, unclaimed, claiming *Virtue*.

Fish hooks snag on foreskins. Jig.
Fish hooks jerk labia. Jug, jug.

Words growl, swarm ears,
while another sopping pussy gets eaten — slurpingly — out.

III.

My by-name* suits a psephologist:**
It's as stimulating as votes.

Each vote's a boomerang
in ornery, ghoulish Ameri — *KKK* — a.

Pro-slavery or Negrophobic.
Anti-slavery or Communist.

Skin rips apart; blood erupts abruptly.
Bullets cripple bones, bully skulls.

Suddenly, trains carrying rum barrels
and dead people, Confederates, brim over.

---

* Nick-name. Was born Isabella Baumfree.
** A student of voting.

Obviously, the road of *Progress*
is completed with slime.

Maggots blanket
a lead-poisoned army.

Rain, wind, and cold—*Pluviôse*—is all the weather.
Pogroms—orgies—rip apart the Republic.

[Ottawa (Ontario) 14 & 15 *janvier* mmxvii]

Whitman Compiles His Leaves

I.

A Yankee bard is a poet-and-a-half.
His language is struck—
roaring, alive—
from anvils of pulpit and press—
sermons, newspapers—
the forges (and forgers) of citizens.

He must show no little stature.
Each page musters flurries of song.

He mustn't be a reclusive virtuoso,
some clandestine *Genius*.
His theme must *hit* the public—
hard, hard, ever harder.

II.

Anti-slavery is my chosen cross.

Slavery is no *Kindergarten* struggle:

The American poet cannot encompass it
with tent-show slogans or gimcrack rigmarole.
He forbids all newsprint malarkey.

I am that man.
I am that Poet.

Messianic—nope, quixotic,
I, Whitman, tilt at *Slavery*—
because I accept to bear
the *Constitution*'s stigmata.

I have neither a glass eye nor a glass jaw.
I have an earthquake laugh, a volcanic heart.
I do not arrange garlands of ink.

III.

I canvass civic *Destruction* that resembles
the late ruction in France:
each brother now beholds the other
as a rival to sabre through the skull
or cannonade — slaughter — to pieces.

The murdering is *Medieval*:
Men clout and tear each other —
tooth-and-nail, hand-over-fist —
or bow to bullets' nefarious applause.

I know of what I report
(echoing the can[n]on).

I've been a fumbling nurse
among the Union's wounded;
have waded tides of smoke
still swamping battlefields;
have seen the earthy lilies that are young corpses,
their flagrant, disgraced *Nakedness*,
intrusively gleaming....

IV.

To Europe's classical (farcical) bards, I say,
our Yankee vs. Rebel war's an ideal *Tragedy*,
staging the sour odor of shot-down doves,
red-matted cotton,
red-splashed sugar.

It is dynamite blasts of wounds—
each one a ruddy vent.
It is fog-incarcerated stars.
It is unpronounceable amounts of living fluids.
It is "white trash," yellow-bellied—or lily-livered.

But I am undismayed.
Americans are not drunken Philistines.
We are not tarred-and-feathered outlaws.
We are *God's Republic*, trying to free *even you*.

I see sable Apollo, rising, beaming, from snapped chains.

V.

I am the Verbatim Poet.
("*Beauty* is quotation.")
I report the malignant triumphs of battles.
I repeat Baptists' tambourine-bashing hymns.

My ink is my supple harmonica.
(Each poem lilts a *fasola** liturgy.)

I'm jotting down the primitive epics
of slaves—
i.e., our primary-colour blacks.

Yessum, I approve the styles of vulgar minstrels.**

Yep, I be as blasphemous as a saint:

Messieurs, regard my edgy signature:

Wet, it glistens like a guillotine—
blade gobbling tyrants.

[**Niagara Falls (New York)** *La fête du Canada* **mmxii**]

---

* American: Four-part harmony in song.
** Cf. Pound.

*How It Strikes a Soldier**

A shuddering morning—
stink and stutter of cannon;
smoke volleys, solid, then fritters into wisps....

We cringe like rabbits,
digging at roots—
grass clogging mouths,
our breathing lavish with ants;
a shipshape pall sinkin down on us—
the penumbra of the clash
twixt fire and dry wood—
bullets and the panic-stricken—

bullet-stricken—

dyin.

Can't spy the immortal salute of sun to soil—
grass, preening;
but do feel grass downpressed—
velvet as a coffin-lining:

We shack up with cockroaches.

[**Batavia (New York)** 9 *mai* **mmxiv**]

---

* Cf. Browning: The poet, not the gun.

The Siege of Port Hudson, Louisiana, May 27, 1863

By Captain André Cailloux

Surging into the liquid ravine —
no footing in muck
for muddling man or horse —
each step's a slog,
each canter convulsive.

Troop of the 1st & 3rd
Louisiana Native Guard —
ex-slaves plus blacks whelped free,
at first was barred from *Combat*.

But Rebs stymie the Union, smite the whites.
We're what's left.

(I wanna jettison the horses;
jug and chug fresh water;
our ale provision is only good
with salt frosted in.)

Commanded, we charge.
Despite sabre-slashes, bayonet-gorings,
we guffaw in the mouths of guns.

Ragged lines limp in simpering *Slaughter.*

Bellies flood with tears and snot;
an ungrudged fluid —
smudging scarlet —
zigzags out.

Shot and cannon cripple
languid *Greenery*;
or splash swimmers into pond-scum.

Whizzing steel scissors elms,
junks willows,
splinters shadows into tendrils.

The Confed fire's no measly trick:
No prohibitions apply.

We Union blacks beg vulgar rock
to yield some platform,
for bracing.

Otherwise, we lurch about,
slipping, tumbling,
conspicuous as dark clouds,
make child's-play targets,

except Rebs also seesaw and yaw
through air bristling with misfires —
swooping engines that pummel or impale —

so one's as apt
to skewer one's own comrade,
as to spit the "foe."

The long smell of smoke almost smothers
face-mashed boys' weepin for soon-sonless mothers.

And drink messes up some men's aim,
for there's less pain droppin dead while drunk.
Thus, they drub their brains
with drab beer
(unsalted),

and loose a gumbo of lead
as likely to sink
a stately, shimmering pelican aloft
as it is to nix
a grey-clad slaveholder.

The Big Sandy Creek be swamp,
just splinters and red foam,
a groaning sepulchre.
Voices curse as boisterous as whores.

We bring on fresh horses
to trample down bobbing bones,
but some boomerang up and back—
like brilliant, reverse windfalls.
Hooves deliver such splashing blasts,
bones fly up in a sad storm,
some still showing fragments of cloth.
Air looks a chequered quilt of pirate flags.

These wetlands, this jaunty brew,
feeds grinning gators.

The dead are novel soldiery:
They form a pontoon bridge for cavalry.

If I outlive this swamp,
I'll sport in Naw Leens cribs:
Only the grave be more irresistible
than *Coitus*.

Since the heart has four chambers,
shan't a (black) man please four wives?

Ed. Note:
A musket-ball tore off half of Cailloux's head.
His screams split in half too.

[**Peggy's Cove (Nova Scotia)** 4 *juillet* **mmxiv**]

At Gettysburg (July 1–3, 1863)

I.

Nothing so vigilant as bleeding.
Every cannon belch

fashions artisanal apertures
of eyes, assholes, lungs.

The pounding ricochets
torch wheat and corn and cotton.

Cowards scram, stumble over legless feet,
cropping up in orchard and pasture.

Or step upon some mumbling husk,
skedaddling mouths, squelching lungs.

If only frail flesh could blunt bayonets!
No: Bone's as crushable as a rusty tin.

Men turn into meat — rare, medium, and well-done.
Greedy horseflies conduct Coroners' Inquests.

Dying, grown men ain't shy to beg
to see mama one last time.

Each one bays like a butcher.
Luckily, wounds don't hurt long.

A pack of horses, avalanching,
pitches upon the invalids.

Whole regiments become front-line coffins:
Case baby-faces ranked in caskets.

II.

Gettysburg is a green furnace —
an *Inferno* of incinerating grass.

In the cannon-splayed fields,
smoky *al fresco* —
the anguish of metal among milky fire —
I survey Gehenna's frontier —
Hell recovered —
thousands of cadavers congregated
like pale, rotten mushrooms —
fodder for a prudent farmer.

Thanks to all the leaden lightning striking soil,
cemetery worms jump and butt against caskets.

Soon or late, though,
the battlefield's again a field
as silent as Sunday prayers
and as sanitized as a lawyer's crimes,
and all is shiny,
thanks to the cleansing ranting
(what outdins noise)
that is rain.

[Ottawa (Ontario) 14/9/14]

At Gettysburg

A fateful cannonball sent axes
flying,
hurtling into his face;
best buddy got diced.

(The hatchets crab-scuttled sideways
in mid-air, like dynamic cleavers,
then banged hard his face
and bit chunks out his chest:

This *War*'s as necessary
and as nasty as a toilet—
so many good men are flushed away
for bad reasons, bad decisions,

bad strategies, bad politics....)
Though inoffensive was my pal—
in this *Offensive*,
his actual eyeholes now are dung beetles' dug-outs.

Lead came to live in his breast;
he now goes to live with worms.
(Every soldier be a bag of bones;
ready—snappy—dog food.)

[**St. Catharines (Ontario)** 12 *mai* **mmxiv**]

Death of a Union Soldier

By Walt Whitman

Lopsided bleeding:
An uncasketed cadaver,
his lily face scarlet-painted....

Hear my tongue, so inadequate
to describe the outlandish ochre
of the unhurt rest of him.

The heart, really, is bloody meat,
and the proof is,
the soldier's autumnal fall
in his springtime youth.

(Nothing as tautological
as intestines.
Nothing as scatological
as the heart.)

Intolerable newspapers black his name,
so I, too, know who he was,
as he was known to his comrades
and their diaries of calamities.

At burial, a brief violinist
serenades his bier.

When the shot penetrated his heart,
no one saw any pink flinching.

His morals never were overturned.

[Niagara-on-the-Lake (Ontario) 14 *juillet* mmxiii]

Confessions of a Union Spy
(or Ode to the Confederate Dead)

I anchor at New Orleans—
ape a decommissioned mastermind,
a big-money pal
to General Lee himself.

I'm a half-hearted veteran
and full-dress playboy,
a gent of effortless hardness,
given to cavalier derring-do,

to blast virgins' very hollows,
steam open their minds,
purge my seed in their maws,
until vulgar tears burn.

The jaunty call-girls
flock bout like mosquitoes.
(Our desperate *Insouciance*
is what you might deem *Passion*.)

Bed is unusual brevity—
les dames blanches,
these relaxed fiends—
screw in iron angles, unconventional angles.

I climax in each velvet prison.
Listen: I'm destroyed to death.
The night's sheen
glimmers.

Each kiss is as deadly as bad wine.
Smell the miasma!
This stifling waste
reeks sickly of slave trafficking.

I act as dissolute as dawn or dusk—
an "ex-Confederate"
who floated down the sea-green gulf,
down-at-heels, bit by bit,

wanting a consignment of queen bees
to spur on my spurting lust
into inexorable *Desecration*,
positioning New Orleans as

"Super Flumina Babylonis,"*
a secular sepulcher,
home of the nursing poet,
the gravedigger poet,

Poe country—
where ominous spoils
that disfigure *Beauty*
go to purchase disfiguring beauties.

My luck is Midas-positive.
Behind, beneath, under,
multiple, inarticulate moans,
a violated face

shouts out secrets,
or breathes out news,
in grey *Convulsion*,
that soon cuts down a battalion.

---

* Latin: "By the Rivers of Babylon." Cf. Swinburne (1871).

Blossoms blaze a branch.
A saffron blossom scents the eve.
A lady's scattered plumage
welcomes our kinless sin.

J'adore le champagne,
also this sour woman with beautiful tits.
I take oysters and Champagne
et cette cochonne.

Love is pleasant battle—
dancing piano legs—
Coitus staving off *Decomposition.*
The sword she grips is mine.

I'll be happy when
Grant and Sherman
carve up Lee's horse for their dogs
and the true Confederates

face no shortage of graves—
after confronting intricately mutilating firing squads—
Surgery that's *Butchery*—
their corpses pitching into swamping sludge.

Hyvästi!*
Mes vieilles belles!
Each menial mistress
is as unfailing as a jail.

Hyvästi!
Each congenial concubine—
adieu our vulgar tupping—
I exit this execrable sinecure.

---

* Finnish: Farewell.

An ideally filthy Plato,
that is Nietzsche.
Each brothel's a parliament;
each fundament craps booze.

I arrange orgasms of wine,
plus the worm and apple of *Sex.*
(*Style* is painful
before it is beautiful.)

Why brood over bread and wine?
Crucifixion counts less than *Resurrection.*
Our struggle is bodily.
We are invisible cadavers.

[**Virginia Beach** (**Virginia**) **10** *novembre* **mmxi**]

Whitman at the Front

The gunfire, explosive, fumes clouds,
frail as wilting cobwebs.

The *War Economy* recycles metal crap—
bullets, medals, bullets.

The generals, inveterate schemers,
dream blood runs true
as a gunner's aim,
but it splatters,
smearing everyone,
shooter and victim alike;

it slathers everyone, everything,
with the cavalier *Objectivity*
of prostitutes,
squirting.

I inhale glum, morose, atmospheric lava,
hear drizzling sobs,
as I slosh among the wet, newborn corpses
in this undiluted *Hell*,
rigor mortis settling in,
unsettling to see,
as live eyes go blank as statues' orbs.

Guns bicker and bark, blather and botch.

I slog under the translucent muck—
the smog and murk—
with a prerogative of ale—
to doctor workable ailments,
to nurse survivors through *Bereavement*,
to okay even obscene *Grief.*

The *Infernal* is incarnate here,
just because the Negro, our brother,
is deemed ineligible for *Liberty*,
but not insensible for *Servitude*.

The South's a constituency of demagogues—
a species of hostile lungs,
unspeakable lungs—
as bullying as a butcher,
crowing gainst the blacks,
rousing so much *Calumny, Persiflage*.

Now, too many perfect cities are suddenly
swimming in flames, drowning in ash,
their streets showered with cadavers—
a defecatory defilement.

II.

I'm like a single leaf of grass;
my apocalypse is solitary.

But my lyricism is true
because my feelings are true;
and no writer is dead
who's read aloud;

for *Poetry* is the transcendent branch
of *Biology*—
visceral, scatological, sexual, and spiritual:
Never petering out,
even when the body is petrified.

To be raised up from the dead,
to be stood up whole amid men forever horizontal,
sets one apart as electric, extrusive, maverick.

I have insolent loins,
libidinous thighs,
and allow *Libido dominandi*
and disallow *War*,
its packets of smoke and pockets of fire,
the grisly uniforms bandaged in stains,
the young men's limbs put to holocaust,
the black sun's scarlet beams,
the orchards dug up for tombs,
the dutiful bleeding of the prone,
the pouncing blood of the bayonet wound,
the prodigious belligerents come to corroded *Brilliance*,
the young souls now silent and visible as ghosts,
the sandpaper tongues burnt up in screams,
the maggots that are every corpse's harem,
the uproar of lice,
ubiquitously, uniquely iniquitous,
the crusade excruciatingly crepuscular,
the posthumous perfume....

I fall in love with the remains of poets
as the sun tugs the night into view.

I acknowledge the Underworld,
but I'm not consigned to dirges.

A lifespan requires consumption of *Sex*,
production of *Love*:
That's everybody's *Affluence*,
here and now, to lick, suck, fuck, kiss—
to explore every diamond sinew
in greedy sacking—
the voluptuous ransacking—
incessant ploughing of *Beauty*—

the lanky Adonis planked on the bed;

not trusty *Grief,*
not guiltful tears,
hard as mud chunks dried;

not to savour cesspools.

[Krakow (Poland) 11 *mai* **mmxv]**

Frederick Douglass Lauds the War

Bad government is slushy in its core;
gangrenous in its extremities.
To medicate such circumstance,
a scythe serves better than a scalpel....

Thus, Negroes must gusto into battle,
act cocksure, gunpowder saints—
and scythe down Dixie, axing
every spindly, horseback Frankenstein.

I don't cringe to thrust every black son
into *War's* awful crimson,
or the Gospels be ripped up,
the *Constitution* left a rag.

Let iron be blessed,
so cannonballs crush each Rebel chest.
Let lead—that sobre ore—
polka-dot every Reb and puncture still more.

Blizzard down now incinerating shot:
Unfurl corpses where once stood men;
paint stubborn, grey bursts that cloud the sun;
watch ichor throw up from throats and necks

like so many sudden, miniature volcanoes;
spy flying, chopped, lopped bones,
battered, scattered, doubly bloody,
plopping in a cascade of limbs.

Lincoln's *Mancipation Proclamation* is nothing,
unless it's the lumbering of soldiers
longside mumbling guns, cumbersome,
and malignant cannon chucking bombs.

Our Cap'n can't be presidential, adamant,
lest weapons blast, recoil, then blast again.
Plus those slain slaves decomposing at Harper's Ferry
implore our teeth, "Tear the slavesters into carcasses!"

It's time for corpses to pile up
in a black clutter.
Now, the South must feel
a strident smashing—

as when a hand slaps dead a fly.

Lincoln should always sit discontented
in a theatre:
He should perch restless at every recital,
every drama, every droll, minstrel regalia.

Our proscenium stage is *War*!

Let us see front-page tombs for whole armies,
The South's lads' so shot-splintered,

latrines serve for their graves.

[**Berlin (Germany)** 11 *mars* **mmxiii**]

Frederick Douglass Considers General Robert E. Lee

I.

The Confederate Napoleon is a statue
of solid, gregarious excrement.

I hear his dainty prancing,
the style of a dessicated dandy.

I'm told that he's as brainy as a dictionary,
but I hear only his lunatic twaddle.

I witness only the blustering pantomime
of a degenerate general
who likes to mix his brandy swigs
with lashings of blood.

II.

Cannons' grunting shots —
smoking weights of metal —
all miss him,
so far.

So, we miss his grumbling funeral:
To cast cloacal him in a cloak of muck.

III.

I'm glad for the deliberate tumult —
the unequivocal maiming of the South —
that undoes *Tyranny*
and Lee, the strict pervert.

When we triumph,
Lee tumbles,
a burnt-out star,
his soul submitted to a crushing *Darkness*.

[**Moncton** (*Nouveau-Brunswick*) **20** *mars* **mmxii**
& Sydney & Glace Bay (**Nova Scotia**) **20 & 21** *mars* **mmxii**]

Sherman Marches to the Sea

To "make Georgia howl," indelibly,
I bid grass scorched,
then scraped bare —
by milk-complected ladies on all fours —
weeping whitewash tears;
and still I torch their mansions and their barns.

Spare churches? Try to.

But I condemn the Confederacy
to lapidary ashes.

To skewer plump cows and skinny calves —
crush hen's hot eggs
and then behead the hens —
and crumple every chalk-columned mansion,
so that even pastors know *Disquiet*,
That's the inventory of *Victory*.

Dixie must shrivel like a gibbet, only bones remaining.

We must decimate the Rebs ten times over,
plus sack their crops and hack their critters.

I do urge the Union boys to be decent —
not too disdainful —
and gratify no brute urges.

(Undisciplined *Murder* is undeclared *Treason*.)

Our civilian enemies
are problematical scoundrels —
to be handled with handcuffs.

But their goods merit bad treatment.

We locust their palaces,
boot-heel-crush their antiques,
stab their portraits,
bayonet their wedding dresses,
crash their fine china,
melt their silver into bullets that will kill their sons,
and torch all that can't be wrecked:

So voluptuous is the murk and flame,
the very sun seems dilapidated.

We unchain the niggers,
so that *Slave Law* is confounded by *Black-Ink Fact.**

(There's no way to anchor birds.
Once freed, the slaves display
the lightning flash of flight.)

By departing from *Compassion* and *Caritas*,
we will deliver Lincoln
Georgia for Xmas.

Such is our intuitive *Gravitas.*

Understand us as a shrieking tornado
plucking up the Confederacy, root and top,
then chucking all into fire.

(Traitors must be indubitably broken.)

I swear I condone no *Molesting.*
I command all my Othellos—
"Wedge thy weapon in no white womb."
Any United States soldier who flouts this rule
may as well stick his tongue down a shotgun barrel
and tug the trigger,
for my *Chastisement* will be cruel—
to the umpteenth iota.

---

* Not "alternative facts" (cf. the Post-Reconstruction U.S. president).

Once we meet the sea—
victorious
as the ranked waves ceaselessly advancing,
then we can get as drunk as a wet rag,
soak up vitriolic alcohol,
and *then* we can wed willing women—
wild-haired women whose clothes are vines—
one-night only—
and press antinomian boots into springs,
and pound home till each quim brims and spits,
and *then* we will commandeer locomotives,
leaning, inclining North,
chugging smoke, shunting us to *Relief,*
while Atlanta is yet smouldering ash....

Once we've won,
we leave the South's Authorities gasping,
rueing our accomplished ruptures.
Like angels with truncated—or shorn-off—wings,
they'll survey an extinct Eden—
a backdrop of cannonball-stumped-down pines—
a shivering mishmash of grey uniforms—
a throbbing broth of faces, bearded or boyish.

Quintessential Conquistadors,
spectacular Assassins,
we'll re-package Georgia as embers, cadavers.

Johnny Reb will wallow in his own guts,

when we establish our *Pax Americana,*
dawn will bestow an indissoluble gold light.

Men!
I spy that great morning
in the offing:

The grey dead bleach
ass-down in their grassy vaults.

[**Windsor (Ontario) 27** *octobre* **mmxii**]

Lincoln Plans for Peace (Pace *Appomattox*)

A*prilis* cometh—
unanimous melt-water streaming
under the Capitol's bridges
reaming Washington's ravines—

following the horrible, endless January—
those two faces glancing backward and forward
at *Hell*—
the tornado *chiaroscuro* that is *War*—

contention of lead, steel, iron, fire—
and damnation of *Flesh*—
its bleeding ruination.
I so do want to savour

orchards trembling under rain water.
So many good people have perished
due to good aim
and good metal of adversaries.

Battlefields' oozing soils—
churned, baptized, by sanguinary urine, ruddy tears—
host Union bodies,
I'd like cast in gold.

Every corpse has a face like beaten earth
or pressed-down snow.
The *Constitution* is, in truth,
a whites-only song,

the spouts of breath
of our Union boys,
plus the answering Southern shouting.
The road to Appomattox

was a cloud of iron—
flame-beamed, blood-seamed.
Earthworms now dissect the dead—
painlessly—

to detritus.
Lee came at me—
on behalf of Davis—
a lot of frisky galloping

plus black-soil exterminations,
totting up to 500,000;
each Virginia field—
after the crimson binge—

floods wholly violet.
The dead know verminous caresses:
Flies gobbling up the gore.
In *War*, a victor can't be sluggish

at *Slaughter*.
His *Conscience* is his molars.
A martial president couples *Cruelty*
and *Theology*:

A just God desecrates our enemies.
I know these truths....
Damn! Even Gettysburg is now
a battalion of flowers,

after the wine-red bleating
of the bayonet-defeated,
their salutations to mosquitoes;
after the mad-dog *Ferocity*

of contending "cousins"....
Magnolia offers a serene stink.
I look out over cratered fields—
still as sunny as America—

and I spy, finally liberated,
a rustic, imitation Africa—
a flourish of melanin
among unspoiled dew.

I hear the Negroes—
each brazen throat—
the puce cackles that stir us all.
Their "spirituals" sound *romanceros**—

the anthems of a people
poorly suited to *Caution,*
who have *Liberty* insurgent in their veins.
Lead no longer jumps from guns.

I'm the big-shot *blanco*—
no toothless, Head-of-State—
who made the South undertake
an unpalatable inventory of corpses

under a falling roof of crows.
Bronze statues and stalled cannon brood
on this fire-shattered Republic;
yet, I feel Mozart-exuberant.

I ready the tempting thudding of wine
in cork-topped bottles:
Wine is a gratifying brine!
So, I hunker down before ranked bottles!

True: I dreamt recently
I was a lamentable cadaver
in an amenable coffin.
But no *Tragedy* ends decorously.

[**Frankfurt (Germany)** *26 juin* **mmxiii**]

---

* Spanish: Ballads.

*James Madison Bell** in "Canada" (1865)*

Ten years back,
dodgin pattyrollers, bounty hunters—

then veerin into the Canadas,
fordin the yelpin, snarlin rapids
doggin
my leap cross Niagara,
marked a tumultuous gesture—

to slip free Uncle Sam's
ulcerating shackles.

The starry sky shouted—
Great Lake Ontario halloed—
"You're landed;
you're grounded;
here you can be rooted."
Prayer was all I needed.

True: Canada is as untamed and coarse
as a sunbeam in *Hell*.

Yet, at Niagara,
winepress medicine
caroused in and caressed my belly.
Made me piss gales.

---

* Bell (1826–1902), an African-American poet, resided briefly in Canada.

A free man wanna hog a super-size pig
and a dame ultra-soft as a cloud.
Land where trout flickers in wet air
and next blazes on a plate.
He craves black tea bubbling like tar,
black grapes squeezing out green pulp;
a forest that's a treasury of feathers
or a storehouse of furs,
with plumes of chirps and whickers.
His village gotta be a kingdom of grog.

And Canada *ain't* uncivilized.
Trains leap canyons and lope along rivers.

Both Yank and Dixie Yahoos holler,
*"Viva los blancos antropófagos de la tierra!"**
Never can Negroes satisfy such snow-white criterion.
Rather, we gotta cakewalk and second-guess —
grin like Uncle Tom;
cavort like Jim Crow.

The Republic is as shifty as an earthquake.
Slurs and bluster raise cane — and welts.

Too many organ-groaning Transcendentalists,
spirits wheezing diatribes,
Black Sabbath, Sunday-School blasphemies.

No wonder the States convulsed
and split into warring halves,
ending only in attenuated shambles,
the proliferation of the dead,
and Lincoln's demise
after a one-gun salute.

---

* "Long live the white supremacists of the earth." Cf. Philoctète.

My ink—smoking pitch—chars the lily page.
I'm not a well-fondled poet
like Dickinson—
her pages rustling and ruffling like taffeta gowns.

Nor will I ever be as head-bloated and shrivel-hearted
as a senator.

When I have ink,
I like my pen's radiant gliding—

dissident to any plain-white poet,
with a pink mouth and a brass medal,
honey-drippin and toilet-trained,
who, a "Patriot,"
lauds the purging of "Injuns"
and praises belligerent government, preachin,
"The President's turd is the biggest!"

And their hearts are in error.

[Rönnäs & Helsinki (Finland) 3 & 4 *juillet* mmxiii]

Letter of Jourdon Anderson

7 August 1865

Dear Mr. Patrick Henry Anderson:

I've your letter, of July 4 (mine own "Independence Day"), and am glad you've not forgotten a man who bears your surname, whether or not he's your natural heir. I'm gratified that you beg now my aid to repair your civil-ruction-blasted business, for it was my advice that saw it flourishing, *ante-bellum*.

Yet, I'm surprised that you still breathe, sir, for I did expect the Northern soldiery to hang you by the neck from the nearest magnolia, given that you quartered Rebs at your mansion and slew personally a Union soul, who lay helpless—legless—in a hospital bed. (I presume that the victorious Northers were not told of your evil—and feckless—murdering.)

Be that as it may, plus your having fired two would-be-slaying bullets at my fleet shadow, I never meant you harm. I did love the old Plantation—and your wife (Miss Anne) and daughters (Miss Annapolisa, Miss Mary, Miss Martha). If there's a Paradise, I expect to see them there, and I wish you necessary success in your own expectations of the Afterlife, sir.

Now, I'm doubtful that my requested return to your employ and lodgings would be good for me, for your son, Jack, intends to shoot me should I grant him myself as target. In contrast, Canada West is tolerably good. I earn $25 per month, and am supplied clothing, victuals, tools, and books.

Yes, my home is a hut, but is *mine*, as is my wife (who bears the honourable title of *Mrs. Anderson*), as are our children—Miles, Jane, and Georgina, all Canadian pupils. The teacher says that Miles could be a poet, for he is so naturally smart (bless his soul), and the girls are Sunday-School proper. Whenever our neighbours remark, "You were all Dixie slaves," I answer — and I bade all us Coloured Andersons answer, "Our *Slavery* was no disgrace for us, for it was not our choice. However, it is a damning discredit upon the white folks who deemed it honourable." That we keep your surname affirms that I hold *Anderson* as a fine name *in my own right.* In Tennessee, though, due to the losses you sustained in attacking the Union, you have devalued your patrimony to the extent that it is nigh accursed.

Anyway, sir, I'd be inclined to think better about a return to Tennessee, if your wages could exceed or match those I pocket presently. (No need is there for you to fret over having to guarantee my liberty, for Dixie is cannonaded all to dust, and the Lincoln Party, upon making Tennessee a "liberated Department" has issued me my Freedom Papers.)

Nor is Mrs. Anderson disposed favourably to return to your overlordship, at least not without a guarantee of *Good Faith.* For us, your *Sincerity* must be gold backed, or flaunt a cash deposit. Otherwise, we cannot make out your purpose, positively.

To help us let bygones be bygones, we request cordially that you restore us our back wages. For me, that's (conservatively) $25 p.m. for 32 years; for Mandy Anderson, the amount owed is $8 p.m. for 20 years. A cash — or gold — payment to us of these arrears amounts to $11,520.00. Our immediate receipt of our just compensation would allow us to feel better about contemplating employ with you again.

Yet, I must also advise you to revise the above figure upward, given interest rates, though you may deduct the cost of our rags, three doctors' visits of mine, and one dental extraction for Mrs. A. I've no doubt the balance is in our favour, and no bankruptcy will be visited upon your holdings — which descend, you will confess, from your "grabbings."

If your payment to us would represent a hard loss for you, I assure you we Coloured Andersons, will be pleased, upon receipt of the cash money, to take you into our employ, and assure you of due payment and fair treatment in the exercise of your agricultural labour.... (We would also let you stay on the Plantation, dwelling in one of the old slave cabins, which we would outfit better than you had done for us.)

Thus, I urge you to send us the cash owing, by express mail train, and address your envelope to Mr. Ivor Winters, LLB, of Windsor, Canada West, in U.S. denominations (everywhere negotiable in Canada). If the termed amount or its likeness is not in our receipt within the next 8 weeks, I will consider your letter insult, fraud, and deceit, and of no credit to you.

I hope you have everything in writing. Indeed, until we have reconciled our accounts, you are, in fact, indebted to us, your unpaid "slaves" — i.e. workers.

We northern Andersons trust the Good Maker has opened your eyes to the sins of you and yours, for making us toil for generations, without recompense. Here I draw my wages every Saturday night. On your plantation, however, never did I — or any Negro — ever see a pay-day. *Now* is the *Day of Reckoning* for those who've cheated the labourer of his hire....

In replying, please also state your plans regarding the security of our younger Andersons, especially the girls. I'd not have them yield their *Chastity* save on that day they yield our (your) surname and take those of husbands. I do remind you that your son, Henry, did violate their Aunt Matilda, and her daughter Cassandra, with no answer from you, save grins. I assure you that, if you so much as allow Henry to breathe in the direction of my daughters, or my wife, his life — and yours — are forfeit at my hands. My *Violence* will be earnest....

I should also like to know whether Tennessee has good schools for ex-slaves and their born-free children. *Education* preserves *Virtue*.

I close here: "Howdy" to Jimmy (James Earl) Carter III, who I thank for knocking Henry's pistol aside, as he was aiming at my horse, thus injuring only our swift shadows.

[**Liverpool (England) 12** *octobre* **mmxiv**]

Post-Bellum Negro Inventory

(*pace* Léon-Gontran Damas)

Now cometh the intermittent Negro;
the concomitant, impenitent Negro;
the precipitously iniquitous Negro;
the my-way-or-the-doorway Negro;
the two-faced, dual-citizen, double-talkin Negro;
the cotton-pickin, banjo-pickin, nose-pickin Negro;
the recidivist, throat-cuttin, Republican-Party Negro;
the lavendar-gum, ivory-tooth, indigo-sable Negro;
the tubercular, diabetic, syphilitic Negro;
the wino Negro, the yes-and-no Negro;
the hobo, itinerant, nowhere-to-go Negro;
the alcoholic, Catholic, imbecilic Negro;
the low-class Negro with high-water pants
dumped in a high-water-table grave;
the Negro doctor, the Negro solicitor;
the bamboozling and/or wham-bam Negro;
the purple-lipped Negro slipping off white shoes;
the Negro who sleeps at your table and eats in your bed;
the Negro of magnificent assets (auctioned off);
the denim'd-down, damn-y'all-to-*Hell* Negro;
the Negro who departs at sunset for your house;
the Negro of needless sentences and useless explanations;
the green-eyed Othello Negro with Desdemona-smelly fingers;
the Negro who alarms, the Negro who appals;
the Negro whose sex imposes midnight on a cloudy nymph;
the grinning, easy-going, germ-carrying Negro;
the Negro whose head is stuck inside a lyncher's rope;
the Negro whose teeth are aluminium and diamond;
the silly coot Negro, tomcatting and dogging twat still;
the Uncle Tom Negro, quick with Bible verse and razor blade;
the Negro spewing Machiavelli and chewing macaroni;
the thankfully soft-hearted, crankily hard-headed Negro;
the Negro who never lets your blushing wife rest.

[Ottawa (Ontario) 17 *octobre* mmxiv]

Instructions Upon Emancipation

By Frances Ellen Watkins Harper

*R*acemen, beware *Ostentation*—
and *Artifice*—

or backslide like Sisyphus.

The Race can't tolerate
squishy, guffawing *Negroes*.

We must be as clear as arithmetic:
Style is never imprecise.

II.

Bother to wash:
Off-colour scents get *Labour*'s sweat
blacklisted as *Stench*.

Obligatory *Cleanliness*—
Bible recitation plus soap—
helps us surpass—overcome—
dingy, white brutes.

True *Christianity* permits no *Filth*,
no alcohol.

III.

Undeniably, English must be our *Grammar*,
not so much gaseous rubbish.

Spit out gravelly pidgin,
that rotgut prattle.

Cough up the ordinary lump
of chewed-up vowels,
spittled consonants.

Black ink and/or purple-face speech
must preface grim, utilitarian *Striving*.

No second-rate English,
no third-class conversating,
puts us first.

IV.

End all unblessed *Coitus*!
Quit begetting bastards!

This *Humiliation* trails each *Patronym*
like unremitting soot,

or makes *Genealogy* awful iffy.

Enchained, black men were forced
to play Minotaurs,

to be sullen bulls
and multiply the masters' herds.

Now, *Redemption* demands ex-slaves
push ploughs so hard
sparks fly up from stones and rocks,
and earth seems to spit fire.

Get letters, then crops, *then* children.

V.

Scions of Moses,
be as enterprising as is *Medicine*
versus *Illness*.

No meadow or miscellaneous pasture
that's ours
should be left unfrequented
by shepherd, farmer, or vintner.

How can anyone struggle *sluggishly?*
Shall we let *Hunger* bite our guts?

I'd gladly myself be
a poetess of *Sweat* —

replace Sapphics with Georgics —

to heap up popular *Wealth* —

sun-bright wheat and gilded cakes —

and mint hearts as treasured as gold.

VI.

To be flamboyantly kind, loudly generous,
is to be ostentatiously, congenially ruined.

If beggars, we'll be repellent,
despicable, black-face vultures.

We must project a civil colour,
a civic shade:

To be as *Substantial* to this Republic
as oxygen is to breathing.

[Montréal (Québec) 4 *mai* mmxiv]

On Queen Victoria

By Karl Marx

She is not necessarily ugly —
nor symbolically loathesome, toad-like.
Her throne-sitting is violently placid.
She believes the butchering done in her name
must be decorous.

In every portrait, spy her arms —
annulled wings:
She is a black-decked hen
brooding in a nest of nettles,
given to furtive fooping
of English cocks all crowing,
all clucking to swallow more of Africa,
more of Asia,
more of th'Americas,
the two Indies,
and even more of *Europa*,
more and more and more.

Yet, behind her decorative patter,
there's *Terror*, radiant as the sun
that ruddies her global, oceanic realm,
each bloodbath dawn and each sanguinary dusk.

When I see her, stooled perennially amid chilly darkness,
her skull sloshing with tea and sherry,
I see the odalisque of Tennyson,
the black widow of yellow-sheet bards.
(Hear her um-ing and er-ing
her canon of limericks.)

Is she, perhaps, amiably awful?
I see a blackened, pale carnation;
a lady as cadaverous as a raven.
(Her sex must be an agony of thorns.)

The lady is garbage.
She's rotten, not wholesome.
Yet, she's a succubus less interesting
than the mature fly
that she resembles —
a maggot come into its own.

She is, really, worse than grotesque:
She is obsolete.

She credits she has a right to sourness,
to be transcendentally — and hungrily — carnivorous,
to model a genealogy of hemophiliac progeny,
to read telegrams whose dotted ellipses
trace out snippets of corpses,
that leak sighs and moans
(the orgy of a *séance*).

Doesn't she know,
vis-à-vis Albert,
that the dead stay dead,
if never quiet?

I spy her obsidian *Chastity*.
(Her dead husband is a unique eunuch.)
Her face admits a vampire's surliness.

Her empire is cannons barking scripture
in Gothic lettering,
trumpeting petty-bourgeois *Götterdämmerung*,
the slippage of mansions into sewers.

[Antigonish (Nova Scotia) 22 *mars* mmxii]

Adah Isaacs Menken's Compromises

When naive (because a "called" gal starts young),
I acted a sweet wife's tart substitute.
Upon her husband's taut truncheon I swung:
His supposed *Love* posed me as prostitute.

The shock of organs—twinned—in collision,
Chiming to primal pinnacle (frolics),
Addicted *moi* to each male emission—
That whitewash wine of swine alcoholics.

My school-slate chalk accompanied white-thighed
Seductions, the carnal hydraulics of
Teachers and preachers who took me, cross-eyed,
Had me, so *Evil* violated *Love.*

Soon, hubbies dubbed me, "pale-face *negrita*—
A cat-gut-skinny Stradivarius,
Tropic trophy, a white man's chalk cheetah,
Still *belle* when his wife ages carious...."

Thus, I'm "escort," the slut-associate,
The lounge "lush," and the circus poetess,
To each man crude as a dug-up toilet,
Craving to tup a "Half-Breed" or "Jewess":

I'm one by birth, the other by marriage,
And can be "Caucasian" or "Other than,"
Or "Oriental" (my supple carriage
Backs my spiteful masquerade as "Indian").

Read my gleaming letters, their glazed, dark ink.
Decipher henna, if you'll see me plain.
A "quadroon"—queerer, clearer—than you think:
Each beige page, *Rape*-ripened, I reap in *Pain.*

[Boston (Massachusetts) 15 *mai* mmxiii & Liverpool (Nova Scotia) 29 *mai* mmxiii]

Darwin's Editorial on East African Slavery

I.

Each slaver's a caterwauling *Concubinage*,
never a hushed-and-holy *Cathedral*,

and resembles more a *Hindu* pyre on the Ganges
than it ever can *Noah's Ark*.

The *Shame* of it never seems shameful,
but defiant.

II.

In the minute opacity of the hold,
where Arabs hold

th'Africans,
whose very tongue is plaintive *Memoir*

(spooky, crude, heart-rending),
an ominous fragrance bakes.

The Muslims generate ubiquitous *Chaos*—
as I've witnessed in Zanzibar—

when they creep into the floating cells
to rinse daggers in gore.

III.

I look overboard at the memory:
Water reflects my objective face,
but tears summon *Reflection*.

I remember a coffle of blatchy* beings,
plopping, one by one,

into murk, dark as night-steeped mud,
while vessel boards squeaked wretchedly,

as each African took his, her, bitter step,
down into unfathomable, liquid *Hades*.

Disappeared they
like a torrent of shadows.

The manhandled "livestock"
took together their plunging,

each one drowning, chained,
in succession,

their legs and feet attempting gallops,
except they had no purchase on this surface,

or, rather, *Immersion*:
It was a submarine,

seafloor platform,
they could only reach as bones.

IV.

Yes, the recollection is awful.
Each African—*blatched***—by God

or Devil
looked *cytenish****

---

* Black, dirty.
** Blackened.
*** Sickly.

as each emerged from the hold
where the Arab tars

waded through a mass latrine
of searing stench,

to pluck up the sickly,
chain em,

then walk em overboard.
I do not maunder.*

I wish wine could answer
noxious questions.

But daemons refuse burial.
They must be cast out.

V.

I agree:
The blacks lack even cattle smarts,

and they oughtn't be confused
with being our equals,

unless we are ourselves,
"injurious characters,"

impossible to rehabilitate,
who never advanced from the jungle state.

[Cambridge (Massachusetts) 25 *février* mmxiv]

---

* Grumble and/or ramble in thought.

Paradise

By Harriet Tubman (1869)

I.

May God dispatch the shrewdest demon to *Hell*—
Every bullwhip villain and every lily-dainty belle.

Take Dixiecrat and autocrat, that miserable *Mass*—
Make em suffer insufferable *Hostilities*.

Lavish on em taxonomies of pains:
No economical hurts. Nay! Splash out their brains!

II.

The ex-slaves who nipped North were impatient
Travellers, wanting to breathe freely and clear vacant

Lands, to snatch at light, refute Arctic cold,
And busy themselves, weaving wheat into gold,

Where nectar-fond bees sip flowers in ballet,
And seas debouche sweet drink, quenching each valley.

III.

Let freemen roam about—in place—like branches
Or roots, til autumn crops cascade in avalanches.

Our vulgar *Apocalypse* must be our *Harvest:*
Gilt-laden vines, plated ham for breakfast,

Copper-green buds upon delicious fields—
The pine cathedrals that *Baptism* yields,

Amorous eats amid glamorous beds,
Dark wine flooding—thudding—from huge hogs' heads,

Fat poultry, fresh-killed, yielding chunks and sharp,
Suckable bones, plus handfuls of small-fry carp,

And unexpected *Treasure* of creamy desserts,
The pleasure of sugar that sweetens all hurts,

And uncompromising whitewash that is milk,
What soothes the belly like swallowed silk.

IV.

Now we meet a chilly phase, facing subtle
Foes, who seek our *Liberty* to scuttle,

And chafing for our re-enslavement or decease—
These Ku Klux Kleptocrats, such red-handed *Sleaze*,

The Bible Belt terrorists, the Gothic Klan,
Who drag black saints to white-hood *Execution*.

Dixie's shoddy elites reconstruct *Corruption*
As statesmen-like *Bloodshed*, the mob's disruption

Of *Law*. But if our *Happiness* should multiply,
We nullify their *Crimes*, annihilate their *Ecstasy*.

[Tallinn (Estonia) **28** *mai* **mmxiv**]

Le Bateau en état d'ébriété (1870)

(*Après* Arthur Rimbaud; *pace* John Thompson)

Sluicing *louche*, cannibal-corral'd channels,
The pilot just gave up: Threw up his hands....
Cos howling Red-Skins arrowed barbs—scalpels
That nailed sailors—Christ!—to masts: Scalped ampersands....

I couldn't care less for the quartered crew—
Those whores portering English cotton and
Flemish grain. Cut-throat ructions are their due....
I slam through waves, untrammeled, now unmanned.

In the turmoiled, roiled tides—stormy, strident,
Weird as babes' dreams, surge I through winter-white
Surf, while peninsulas soggy, verdant,
Unmapped, host riots—black ghosts' screams hacking *Quiet*.

A sea is tempests, awakenings! I—
Tempered, crafted—bob, deft in the wash—
The endless combers of *Eternity*—
Where dead darkies' eyes beam—dark lamps of ash.

Sweet as acid is to an assassin,
Black waves inundate—grate—my sinews-seams;
The charred seep, pitchblende vomit, a wet ton,
Tore off my anchor, scattered drowned men's frames.

My only refuge? This sea-worthy *Poem*—
Star-soaked, tar-rippled milk: *Verse*'s reverse—
Blackness blushing inky, but floating "chrome":
Spy a philosopher's corpse—sharks at nurse,

Dyeing the blue straits, now ruddy with *Dawn*,
But deliriously, as if ablaze,
Straying, spreading wine-red stains as crimson
As the pooled blood of *Love*'s treasonous lays....

I know lightning-veined skies, volcanic spouts,
Whirlpools, twisting eddies; I know the *Night*,
And *Dawn* that surprises doves—mourning droughts—
And I've seen what men muse is outside *Sight*.

I eye the sun, lowering, hint at *Hell*'s
Purple blotches, orange sewers, ruddy figments—
The trembling death throes of *Tragedy*'s belles—
Quellings like floods that shatter Parliaments.

I view blue-green, Northern-Lights-pastel'd snows,
Or *Dusk*'s gleam stroking rouge the sea's eyelids;
Or black, crab-like clouds suppurating crows;
Or gold-and-blue rays veiling white-bride beds.

For months, I've chased somersaulting tides (much
Like cattle—stampeded), trampling down reefs,
Forgetting that Saint Mary's sun-bright touch
Allays—soothes—the Atlantic's panting griefs.

I moor at strange, phantasmal Floridas,
Where human panthers' eyes mate white flora
And rainbows reach, wide as two Canadas,
To bridle, at sea's end, glaucous fauna.

I see engulfing marshes, in ferment,
Net in reeds some Leviathan, rotting!
Spy water thrash and crash coral cement,
Plus horizons cataracts wash, clotting—

Plus icebergs, tin suns, gilded skies, pearl floods,
Splintered wrecks spiking umber-sand bottoms;
Swollen serpents, lice-pestered, crept from muds,
Writhing through sunk rigging like black, squid fumes.

I witness barnacled slaves, dorados,
In blue currents, and grey sharks, murmuring.
Foam-flowers laurel my timbers. Tornadoes,
Ineffable, whip my sails all a-wing.

(At times, the martyr *Sea*, scored by crossings,
Vaunts me easy upon her sobbing bust,
Where shadows flaunt blood—poppies, tossing—
And there I bide—like a nun lost in *Lust*.)

Near isles, I cruise, while at my gunnels, squawk
Raucous quarrels—dashed-down *merde* of white-eyed birds,
As I drift slowly, let frayed knots unlock,
While drowned slaves, backward flock, adrift, in herds.

(But I, vessel caught in a cove's tresses—
Tempest-tossed, under skies where no birds sang—
Could not be dredged if gnashed to carcass;—
Save for bits where hands—Hanseatic—gang.)

Heaving, spiting encumbering mauve streams,
I block the blushed sky like a Trojan Horse,
Lichened with white mists and green-azure beams—
Those dream garnishes great poets endorse.

I run, harassed by electric, frantic
Tides shocking my maidenhead, while the glut
In my guts is slaves the North Atlantic
Weighs as black-gold, each an august ingot.

Waves' blows tremble me—as if *Behemoth*
Is bucking me—a moth, while maelstroms groan—
Fathoms and knots distant. I cut a swath
Through blue graveyards while white cathedrals moan.

I skirt ship-scuttling archipelagos—
Isles whose flame-shot, cloud-churned skies seduce
Sailors: "Is it on such nights, when *Time* flows
Endless, one sleeps, exiled—*Time*'s own refuse—

The *Future*'s ghost — dead amid mocking birds?"*
True! I weep much! Dawns knife my heart! All moons
Slay dreams; the sun eats eyes. Sick with *Love*'s drugging words,
My keel feels torpor; each sail swafts or swoons.

Europe's sea's are all piracies, unless
I sail a cold, black pond where *Dusk* embalms
Realms with perfume, and some boy impress
My craft where *Crises* pass into *Calms*,

And embark me now, wallowing, o waves,
In memory of slave-ships' cotton wakes,
Displacing, with boyish glee, slaves' toy graves —
Slit-eyed wrecks — those lees belching fat sea snakes.

[**Funchal (Madeira) 18 & 19** *décembre* **mmxv**]

---

* Parrots taught a single word: *Motherfucker!*

Anatomy of La IIIe République (1870)

By Alexandre Dumas, fils*

I.

Seat yo black backside; face facetious lecturers—
feces-eaters,
chalk-pale guff-speakers:
Lap up *Lechery*—

Can-Can of cant
(can't):
no can-do—

of *liberté, égalité, fraternité*—

and no pretense either.

(Even th'Emperor—
Louis-Napoléon—
was frank crap,
caca granted a crown.)

And the dark-pigment pimps of Pigalle
dicker, thusly,
"Milk-face *hombres* quail,
fearin sable snakes."

Meanwhile, thugs mug as bankers;
rapists doll up as pastors.

---

* Cf. Fanon, always Fanon.

Paris be Pigalle, not the Louvre.

La Sorbonne apes Le Moulin Rouge.

II. *Prélude* (*circa* 1867)

See? Baudelaire pipes drooling poetry—
gamey verses—
cause he wanna bed down Jeanne Duval,
Queen Creole siren
(whose *négligé* displays nappy, silken *Négritude*).

He wanna screw that puffy-nippled, voodoo chile—
that foxy, tropic minx—
inimical to *Morality*;

he lusts to litter
white blossoms on her pubic velvet

(though he laments his shrimp-size prick
& testicles—small as a sugar-lump).

He pants to lap out her pussy-hole.

He talk up her beauty,
he brag of her beauty;
he lists the ornaments
of this elemental *Beauty*;
and he is tender, ardent,
as his anatomizing eyes
graze upon her every atom;
while she puffs opium
in an opaline light,
and he wants to gallop, equestrian—
no question, yessirree—
her gynaecological *Beauté*—
her biological *Bounty*.

Instead, he jabbers—
rank blabbing of an alexandrine
slid from *vers blanc* to ink-black blues.

But it's a true-blue, blue-gummed gent—
some pigeon-toed, pidgin-tongue darky—

who snags Duval's chocolate-sweet ass
by slingin elegant, snaggle-tooth *Sass*.

III.

Paris—*Métropole*—cries to its colonies,
"Mo' cocoa, coffee, cocaine *encore*";
chides,
"Y'all think a piano
a coffin for a pony";
and damns dismal ports
as "vortices of *Crime*."

Frère, Br'er,
go from Martinique to France—
come from Egypt to France—
ya enter a maelstrom of broken mirrors,
becoming now a congenital criminal
et un bo'n *idiot*—
even if your soul
is as complicated as Macedonia's
incestuous, but variegated tribes.

Afric dude, freak
in the Caucasian college
and/or citadel,

yo *Existence* sours like palm wine....

IV.

Negro intellectual,
ya confront
a blunt, contrapuntal *Race*,
even as ye sip icy wine in infernal August
and count the vermillion, vermin-ridden corpses
of Franco-conquistadors,
now ended up speared in Tahiti —
or Tunisia or Vietnam.

Écoutez!

The crux of French history;
the matrix of French history:

Black Eiffel Tower
penetrating pale Arc de Triomphe.

White muse, black penis.

[**Halifax (Nova Scotia)** **25** *septembre* **mmxi**]

Discourse on The Negro

By Charles Darwin*

The blacks originate across a blistered, puckered sea.

Our hearts pump liquor and/or acid,
so the Negroes can't decide whether we favour
Good or *Ill*.

They consider us akin to gods—
or Apollonian demons—
or cold *Glory*—
or obliterating storms—
and we don't disappoint.

(What is Europe—
but insurgent sunlight—
doves flashing amid grapevines?)

We deem their societies more earth
than sky,
more dirt than *Metaphysics*,
more sperm than tears,

and so their alleged "humanity"
seems spurious.

---

* "He is no Dante, no sadist." —T.H. White, *The Book of Beasts*.

In southern Africa, one excavates
knocked-down cities,
untenanted temples slid to rubbish,
smoking ruins unhousing gutted swine,
no-head chickens,
javelins juicy with gore,
and things sliced to bones and meat—
even human things:

Don't blackies tear out guts,
use em for epaulets?

And Negroes be goat-footed centaurs:
Scent a *Coitus* tang—a mustang—smell.

Spy em goin at it—
Minotaur tupping Sphinx
(from the rear)!

So unlike us (if unlikeable) Europeans,
for whom *Sex* is vinegar
and *Death* is ambrosia.

We ferry em to *Salvation*,
Civilization,
but for our pains,
we hear fathoms of weeping:

We cruise a salt sea of tears.

[**Capri** (**Italy**) 21 *février* **mmxii**
& **Pompei** (**Italy**) 23 *février* **mmxii**]

Ntshingwayo kaMahole*
Fits Guards to Battle Britain (1879)

I.

The Anglos parley *"Peace"* and promise
a hands-off government,

but their ivory fists grip iron guns,

and their vessels shudder, clanking with shackles
they label "fretful *Necessities...."*

Next, their horses' reddened hooves
crumple down—shred—Zulu bodies.

(Her Poets Laureate exhale dreams
The Queen's economists dispute.)

Their cannons spit, *"Law!"*

Our drums spiel, *"Liberty!"*

Our *Strategy*? To inflict gory *Damage*;
to expunge Victoria's fungi-pallid forces—

à la manière
that Crazy Horse** dismayed Custer's Yanks.

II.

Universal is a corpse—
the message it howls.

---

* (1809–1883).
** Tašúŋke Witkó (1840–1877).

Thus, deliver each Briton wounds
vast as Zululand,
so each pinked face resembles
the anus of an animal.

Be heroically despicable:
Perpetrate *Hell*.

I summon no stingy phalanx,
but soldiers irrevocably monstrous —
at the very fulcrum of *Fury* —
whose *Murdering* is no sham,
no cringing, *et* nothing retrograde,

so Anglos expire, flailing, impaled,
and plump up piles —

like raw shrimp shish kebab.

Unrepentantly repellent, unleash
a torrent of *assegai*,
a downpour of spears,

to clog white throats,
infiltrate white lungs.

(A spark imposes fire!)

Britannia broaches our kingdom
to clasp our chrome and diamonds,

and wasp-sting our daughters

and grasp and vineyard our fields....

Zulus, squash these unnatural slugs!
Squish em into supernaturally putrid slime!

[Uppsala (Sweden) 11 *octobre* mmxiii
& Stockholm (Sweden) 12 *octobre* mmxiii]

Ntshingwayo kaMahole Outlines Strategy (1879)

*S*ubtlety is diabolical *Courtesy.*

Urbane first, next hectic,
we'll toilet the British:
Watch bluebloods, expiring,
royally fecundate our fields.

Hurl spears through backside or down mouth!
Treat scruples with playful *Contempt.*

Free Azania demands a crimson deluge —
bodies shed like red leaves;
white troops harbouring flooding wounds.

Each collapsed steed, steel
shrivelling its guts,
splays a general:

Personally, I'll tug out his eyeballs and tongue,
while his smelly belly toggles my blade,
and his comrades sprawl bout in pieces —
like wolf-torn cows.

Hear the Anglos croak Shakespeare,
as we shake spears —
and they croak
(exasperating croaks).

Men, churn our grasslands into an ocean of skeletons:
Let impudent dogs —
punctured by our dreaded barbs —
drown,

while their white throats hurtle out ink;
blurt polluted puddles.

Our chore: To engineer
i.e., agreeable *Corruption*.

To hear each white corpse groan
like creatures unenlightened.

I want each foe to feel the agony
a man feels,
when a bamboo thrust in his prat
pitches up through his flesh
and then screws through his brain,
while the spitted jackass blares,
terrified by his undeniable dying.

Thus, render our foes abominable meat—
carcasses sprouting disgusting perforations,
ruddy, then pink-black.

(Each cadaver is as public—
and private—
as a garbage can.)

The slain whites'll bloom bouquets of feces.
Vultures will guttle the gentry at will.

I'd trade any Browning poem
for a Browning gun:

To see the Brits scattered like snooker balls—
red and white—
scurrying bout a green baize field.*

I am a dead-aim economist!

Thus, the enemy wavers like the sea's
wobbly surface:

---

* Cf. Fanon, *ancora* Fanon!

Our grievous lances
gyre through aristocrats.

Each one's an unearthed Caligula,
as open-mouthed jocular as an ape —

double-crossed Christ's spit-mirror image —
now wheezing, squelched, in ruddy dust.

[**Stockholm (Sweden)** 13 *octobre* **mmxiii**]

Isandlwana (1879)

The dead—those iron-pierced dolls, akimbo,
    unwound posh, cunt-like wounds,
fly-plastered, fly-pitched.
    We living stumbled scarlet-washed ruts—
no medication possible—
    in that catastrophic midden.

Afflicted by brain-rictus (*Vanity*),
    we jounced to bayonet the blackies,
The Zulus, but trotted too cocky:
    Our lungs sprung satisfied giggles.
Euphoria thrilled our whole corps:
    "Apocalyptic" describes this misjudgement.

In that valley, Isandlwana, we reconnoitered
    a sinkhole abbatoir.
We plunged into it, screams chasing us.
    Howls gnawed off our ears.

Zulu blades smacked us off our horses.
    Our Empire shivered, trembled,
on its foundation of green (grass, or sea).
    Spears jigged—frigged—holes;
geysers crimsoned backs, chests, even faces.
    I thought I was in Troy.

The Zulus surged at us as a horde—
    sable *Huns*, a coal-fisted blizzard:
Each of us felt a tin statue—
    so easily dented.
Africans slew us with grumpy *Indifference*.
    The wind harboured barbed hurts.

The killing cloud of the blacks —
    that hurricane pestilential —
spilled a black blot on our *History* —
    our hitherto illuminated scrolls —
but such is dark-darker-darkest Africa —
    continent bleeding incontinent Europe.

[**Ottawa (Ontario)** **27** *octobre* **mmxiii**]

Encountering Ntshingwayo kaMahole (1879)

"Into the valley of Death
    Rode" our hundreds,
proving Tennyson useless.

Our cries throttled appallingly the wind,
as we lurched to sodden —
surprise —
Slaughter:
kaMahole's pitch-skin tribe pitched us down,
and their fist-gripped *iklwa* —
a thrusting spear —
gusted through each thudding heart.

Percussive exclamations smacked our ears.
Screams caked, moans drizzled,
wherever Zulu *assegai* —
that long, throwing-spear —
homered,
in itinerant downpours.

There was *Damage.* There was dirt.

Our troop shattered like the altercations
of breakers versus boulders,
so that each tiding line
assumed a turbulent edge —
the choreography of crabs —
as we whites leapt, scurried, scuttled,
or stopped short,
our guts pouring out....

No unbroken dust on the *veldt.*
Green turned wet, voluptuous lavender.

Our bright, British corpses,
now plastic muck,
yield shreds of hide to vultures' beaks.

[**Stockholm (Sweden)** **13** *octobre* **mmxiii**]

Darwin's Marginalia in More's Utopia

I.

We imperialist pillagers sabre-slash our rivals open,
forehead to foreskin —

like how gorillas claw open
orangutangs —

acutely uncute, but prosecutorial.
Immaculate. Immoral. Immemorial.

II.

We must strangle France, Spain, Portugal —
the triumvirate —
in a triangle,
prove these Europeans to be third-rate Caucasoids,
whose monarchs head up rusting crowns.

If we but go for the jugular,
our rivals let go their sphincter muscles.

III.

Ain't no nicey-nice blueprint for founding *Utopia!*

The venture requires foes's *Extinction....*

Only afterward can we sight
the golden dawning of our limitless *Expanse.*

[La Línea de la Concepción (Spain) 8 *décembre* mmxii]

Rimbaud, Deposing (1884)

No blue-gum blacks got blue eyes.
But some got green or grey—
or gangrene in gristle sockets.
Salt-frank, pepper-pungent,
the mottled Negro *métis* be.

The tan women indulge
a *Nymphomania* of the pulse—
a craze for it
(my rod),
churning their flesh,
each sylph sashaying like a toilet-watered pig.

I suffer a sugar curse—
to screw down a devil bitch—
whose blackness renders chocolate
the charcoal of *Hell*;
so I take cigars, *cognac*, and cunt
as unconscionable as *unconsummated Desire*;
and pour chalk and then cream
into a figure, *une femme*,
whose wriggling respects no moral,
while my shoulder muscles bunch
like evil lilies in a funereal bouquet.

Saint Venereal, *c'est moi*. I—
Death and *Night* and *Blackness*
(as in Baudelaire)— .
stable my harem.
(*Il-mara sewda r-ragel taghmlu ghuida.**)

---

* Maltese: The soot-skinned wife wears down her husband stick-thin.

To screw carelessly, formidably,
maketh me a goatish god,
as carnal as that killer, Caravaggio,
exemplifying bad-ass *badinage*.

Not for me the aromatic locales
of fake virgins as rank as old fish,
harlots decorated like Christmas trees.

Rather, I want the "spaghetti rod"
splitting the "coffee bean"
(*e quel remir**),
the pinnacles of glitter
amid smoking froth
in a woman's sultry, volcanic vent.

It's to Africa — and *Hell* —
I'm doomed to go.

I've deregulated the laws of *Poetry*;
I've tampered with *Humanity*.

(I've shimmied and shaken myself
between black ankles and shackles.
I've callaloo'd mauve wine, brimstone ichor,
vinegear myrrh, tar sweat, scarlet sugar,
cholera rum, thistle tobacco,
thorny cotton, lightning tears, jigging bullets,
and thundering worms. Cargoes!
Negroes! I've mixed em all up!)

Torture has to be somewhat baroque,
for it is always superfluous:
it is the rococo flourish of *Power!*

---

* Provençal: "And what lustre." Cf. Pound.

Nowadays, I hear inky singers
entertaining crowned heads,
with "authentic" hollers and moans
of field niggers.
You see, there is *Beauty* in *Evil*.

My only caution:
Excess
undoes
Success.

[Valletta (Malta) 23 *août* mmxi]

Whitman* Pens "The Rape of Florida" (1884)

I.

An epic poet's epical** poetic is to conjure
a hero as impossible as any gilding *The Kalevala.*

II.

His oars ply water into sheets, then droplets.
He outmuscles th'Atlantic as he glides to a stop —

a beach, uncaring of alligators or vipers.
Name him Atlassa*** — boldly worldly.

An overseer attempts manhandling,
but Atlassa's Mandingo-blunt fists —

priceless fists,
healthy fists —

squash the white man's cheek, smucking,
so blood squeaks out the weakling's mouth.

Atlassa's blows clatter the overseer's jaw;
the bugger's teeth clang gainst each other;

dude feels awful as Atlassa batters and batters.
Punch brings on punch:

---

* Albery Allson Whitman (1851–1901).
** Cf. Walcott, *Omeros.*
*** Cf. Saunders, *Imaro.*

I imagine two men battling like bulls
hassling o'er a heifer.

(True: The men tut-tut o'er a sweet-eyed,
Virginia virgin, Palmecho.)

Climax: My hero's fist smacks the white man's ear,
so skull bones splinter,

stabbing into the ruffian's brain:
The ear-boxed pugilist flops, foxed—

as when a black bull broaches an arena
and swords thwack instantly his hide.

III.

Atlassa?
A rock unbudged by ocean.

His paddles waketh water;
he glides o'er steep and broadside-seeping swells,

scudding atop snow-edged waves,
to beach—and next go wallop tyrants.

I draft him as resonant copper,
unimpeded iron:

Tempestuous, he stomps on waves
and I hear water snap back.

Impetuous, he deals adversaries
unwholesome *Dereliction*,

wherever the defeated bleed or smart;
well, it hurts like *Sodomy*.

IV.

I dream a hero —

an African —

inside a Negro —

within a Black man!

[Niagara Falls (Ontario) 12 *mai* mmxiv]

Overheard at The Berlin Conference (1884–85)

Great Britain (GB): *Free Trade* will scour Africa golden —
plus whitewash the golliwogs.

Kingdom of Portugal (KP): To capture blackamoors
and their picaninnies in nets —
as if fish —

or chain em down —
as if dogs —

ends here, if not already.

United States (US): Borders cancel battles; treaties nix tussles.

French Republic (FR): Granted snow-pure *Christianity*,
Caucasian *Reason*,
and European *Civilization*,
Africa will be less savage and Africans less black.

German Federation (GF): *Cannibalism* ceases where *Capitalism* succeeds.

GB: Either we deliver *Justice*,
or Africans will judge us plagues.

US: So our *Revolution* schooled George III.

FR: So our *Revolution* taught Louis XVI.

GB: But the *Haitian* revolt tutors all that *Ruction*
breeds *Destruction*.

GF: A frail *Power* winks at *Fraud*
and whips the *Poor*.

Kingdom of Belgium (KB): In recompense for our *Governance,*
we bade Congolese toil at maximum *Efficiency.*

FR: *Profit* bids railroads bushwhack through jungle
and statues stare down lions.

GF: Europe must brake the brazen *Plunder*
that imprisons Africans in a vast penal colony.

KB: *Progress* means tapping* Congo copper, diamonds, and rubber,
while depraved, dark souls hosanna our paleface deity.

GB: Does not Belgium "sadism" the Congolese?

KB: Great Britain cannot lecture any *Power* at this table
on correct conduct in colonies.
Just ask America!

US: *Enmity* can be *Amity*:
Let's set a dollar value for Africa.

GB: Quite! During blackest *Slavery,*
you were masters at weighing the value
of sluts, studs, and suckers.

US: Well, John Bull educated Uncle Sam well.
We Yanks had excellent mentors in *Slavery,*
from you who once played our masters.

KP: And tormentors.

FR: Negroes must toss out Xango
and idolize Descartes.

GF: Apply too liberal the whip,
and hollering blacks will learn
it's scholarly to lie.

---

* Raping.

KB: We want what Germany wants:
Picturesque primitives paying dividends in *Treasure*!

GB: Good governors seek neither undue *Profit*
nor undeserved *Reward*.

US: Fiddlesticks! Your empire requires
the plucky cheating of unlucky peoples.

GB: We privilege good manners and good *Grammar*.

KP: Does that compensate coloured Natives
for loss of *Land*, *Labour*, and *Liberty*,
the swindling of *Profit* and *Progeny*?

FR: Overcome bad policies with better.

GB: We civilize half-naked shakers of spears:
We dress em up with cloth-bound Shakespeare.

KP: Africans relish games and comedies;
laughing, they sweat; laughably, they starve.

KB: Why can't we wing our blue-sky flag o'er Africa,
which is elsewise British, blood-red, as maps testify?

US: If Europe ain't gracious in Berlin,
this already way-too-long 19th Century
will truncate the impingin 20th,
usherin on butcheries.

GB: Crikey! That's just what's ongoing on your Great Plains —
graveyarding the Redskins of the Great Republic!

US: *Destiny* is manifestly ours.

FR: Beware! *Destiny* is fickle.

GB: *Imperialism* is deathless,
a matter of centuries,
not puny human life spans.

KB: Yet, your *History* is studded with wars.

KP: The atlas is a blueprint for ledgers of black ink.

GF: Etch this pale parchment in black ink,
and Venus conquers Mars.

US: Colour our section of Africa —
Liberia —
a bright yellow,
blazing *Caution*.

GB: Pshaw! Liberia is ex-Yank blacks bludgeoning
African blackamoors!

GF: To enrich — finally — blank-faced bankers' coffers.

KB: We bear the Great White Burden purely —
in the Congo — that Pit of Darkness.

KP: But Britain looks a hyena, stripping flesh.

GF: Let no nation here skim others' territories!

GB: We have dynamite, an arsenal,
enough to guarantee any treaty.

US: So, John Bull pledges *War*
if his boats don't hog all our waves!

GB: Why do you indulge such crazy, ghastly *Hate* —
those mass murders done by ghost-masked lynchers?

KP: Great Powers mustn't sound vexatious,
nor meddlesome, nor insolent.

GF: Ambassadors, welcome *Agreement!*

US: All you Old World states crowd
the globe with coloured cadavers.

GB: Dig up your own corpse-ridden history.

FR: First, police the debauching *Butchery*
that daily blights the Congo!

KB: Well, hot damn! France plays the plundering pirate
in Barbary Arabia.

US: We have no designs on Africa.
We seek no "lion's share" of booty:
It's Britain who flashes fang and claw.

GB: Uncle Sam grins as kindly as Uncle Tom,
but his jaws drool and spit white lies.

US: Your grubby chronicles brighten beheadings.

KB: The Congo conjures *Opportunity*!
Count on Belgium to capitalize on the Congo....

GB: Self-appointed saints, you play blameless martyrs.

GF: Is this Europe?
A clutch of unflattering demagogues?
Where are the statesmen?

KP: The former *Imperialism* was unmitigated *Horror*.
The priest Las Casas has scribed the satanic proof.

GB: One failure is the incomplete gobbling
of Liberia.

FR: True: Your short-cut, Sierra Leone land grab
cut short Alfie Russell's presidency.

US: Thus, our gunboats float, off Monrovia —
to keep both "Frog" and "Bulldog" out.

KB: Africa rots, so why not just cart away gold?

GF: A treaty makes for congenial *Imperialism*.
We must come unto Africa
with our *Elegance* unencumbered —

and also bring a lantern glare,

so th'Africans squint at *Splendour*.

We'll not be repugnant parasites —
degenerate, ghoulish —

but show appropriate *Virtue*,

doling out Christ and crucifixions,
classrooms and cuffs

(a measure of *Discipline*
to erase *Lethargy*).

Nothing else is mandatory.
Anything else is lackadaisical.

Ambassadors, all shake hands now.

[Helsinki (Finland) 30 *mai* mmxiv]

Partial Transcript of
The Berlin Conference (1884–85)

Kingdom of Belgium (KB): Empress Victoria needn't swallow
every morsel of the Congo,
but leave a slice for our Emperor Leopold.

French Republic (FR): He metaphysics rubber as "black gold";
so, he works Congolese into coffins.

KB: Unquestionably! *Slavery* fathers sins.

Kingdom of Portugal (KP): Europeans
should be Christians, not merely Caucasians.

Great Britain (GB): Well-born whites!

United States (US): Well-*qualified* whites!

GB: Oxbridge bluebloods must helm Africa.
We're unconquerable.

KB: Save for at Isandlwana....

GB: That Zulu "Victory" was a miracle
wrought by *Hubris*—an error, tactical.

US: In any event, there was a slaughter.

GB: I hear no matter warranting laughter.
Recall: We torched your White House to smithereens.

US: And we whupped your buttocks at New Orleans....

KP: We sniff the noxious stench of *History*.

KB: What does Belgium want? No mystery:
Nothing too swollen; nothing we can't digest.

GB: One piece of wedding cake? Next: The rest?

German Federation (GF): The dogs of *War* are nervous!
Shakespeare's bulldogs bark at every mouse.

GB: Her Majesty has no pogrom tendencies.

GF: If *Peace* is not agreed, we seed *Disease*,
and the English Channel turns a decayed sea.

US: Divvy up copper, diamonds, the rubber tree.
Stash the gunboats and barbed wire.

FR: A real peace treaty must require
dissipation of *Irregularities*:
No more poaching each other's colonies—
like dogs scrapping over bones.

US: The answer is more and more *Free-Trade* zones,
thus ending land-thefts, piracy, pillages,
zigzagging borders, ethnic-cleansed villages....

GB: What *Hypocrisy*! Admit that you make all
South America, outside Brazil (late of Portugal)
your *de facto* colonies. Uncle Sam's a cancer!

GF: Colonies provide illicit *Capital* transfer
to empires; *Plunder* makes Europe "triumphant."

FR: This *Hurt* requires disinfectant!

GF: But a treaty can't be journalistic flimflam.

KP: Respect *Ek Chuah*, the "God of Trade."

GB: You parrot the mantra of Uncle Sam.

US: Properly coloured maps must now be made.

KB: We'll steamship home rum, rubber, diamonds,
ornaments, copper pots, sugar....

FR: And bust female savages' hymens
and hang high each nagging nigger....

US: The problem with John Bull is
the troublesome rotundity of his
belly, a bloating that never sags.

KB: And the spider's branching legs,
straddling the globe.

GF: Is Europe Michelangelo, or a microbe?

US: Britain threatens all with bulging crevices
of graves, an atlas of abyss after abyss.

GB: You know that well, America!
Cadavers piled up—blue and grey ca-ca;
the fallen, heaped uniforms, ungainly.

GF: Nothing's as unbudging as a cemetery.

FR: Colonialism is a glorified *Infection*.

KB: Diamonds render Congo dirt candy—a confection.

GF: Forego this unforeseen *Anatomy*
before it enacts an *Autopsy*.

Split Africa smartly, and no party needs arms,
but only hands to tool factories and farms....

[Peterborough (Ontario) 27 *novembre* mmxv]

Repressed Transcript of
The Berlin Conference (1884–85)

French Republic (FR): Just now, Poe's raven threw itself blackly
gainst the window.
Its wings curdled the grey, noon light.

Kingdom of Portugal (KP): A grim sign!
Psychopaths love their slaughters
as much as actors love death scenes.

FR: That's *War*:
Endlessly contagious, expansive.

German Federation (GF): A Treaty will prevent our navies
pinking the ramshackle sea;
forestall soldiers and emperors
suffering that choking-on-dust sensation that's *Dying*.

Great Britain (GB): Uttered like a plutonic Plato —
or a Platonist Pluto.

Kingdom of Italy (IT): Our Embassy furnishes today's luncheon —
limoncello and lemon-flavoured salmon —
plus pewter creamers from Naples
and a Capri of silver spoons
for the coffee service later....

Kingdom of Spain (KS): And we supply mescal from Mexico.

GB: The worm at the bottle's bottom
mirrors an engorged maggot.

IT: Italy commends Berlin's imperious architecture —
a comfy cocktail
of Baroque and Georgian and Gothic....

United States (US): While we tipple this tongue-dazzling limoncello,
we mustn't ignore the simultaneous business
of preventing the flowers of Africa
from becoming broken petals,
due to the instinctive *Mischief* of empires.

GB: But you Yanks bring a shotgun perspective,
a gunboat vision,
to every single *Policy.*
Consequently, we note the irreparable disappearance
of Red Indian tribes from your Great Plains.

US: Spattered gore must yet blur—
befog—your lenses,
if you don't recall your keen destruction of brown Indians
at Lucknow.

IT: Now arrives the situation of coffee
plus plum-coloured Amaro,
to help your parley attain the dove-cooing heaven of *Peace.*

GF: What do we stymie here?
Deadly rats biting little black girls;
upside-down burials of African chiefs;
the suitcase materialization
of Caucasian carpetbaggers,
delivering Africans slumping cadavers,
or squads of thugs forcing toddlers
to choke on their own kicked in teeth.

KP: How awful that Spanish priests
torched the Mayans' papyrus scriptures!

KS: There's always *Hypocrisy*
in Portuguese *Poesy:*
Consider Camões....

Kingdom of Belgium (KB): Sun-incinerated Portugal
likes green wine, Camões' leaves—
his leaves like peeled off, fresh-used toilet tissue.

KP: Belgium should speak *sotto voce*
for your *Poetry* is paper currency,
what Belgium rips out of Brazil,
where *Slavery* remains *Law.*

KB: Better that than nickel-and-dime *Finance,*
the ghastly customs of (Portuguese) *Poverty.*
You sell your daughters like you sell fish.

KP: Yes, we don't have a colony like The Congo,
where every child sports a necklace of leeches,
and maggots snuggle in assholes and eyeholes....

KB: Follow our Africa missionaries' footprints—
those men as fearless of becoming crocodile material
as moths are of diving *kamikaze* into candles.

Japanese Empire (JE): As observers, we observe,
from our Asian purview,
that Europe acts exactly like vultures,
raining flesh from open beaks.

US: The sinister litters of Europe
practice honed *Dishonesty.*

IT: Dante is our guide here.
Europe's Afric colonies to date conjure
hellish stewing in sulphur and flame,
rivulets of fire, torrential blazes.

FR: On the sea bottoms, black bodies writhe—
all soggy flesh and splattered bones,
a macabre porridge.

JE: (Aside): Is *Whiteness* itself a dishonest *Complexion,*
a perfidious *Complex?*

GB: I shouldn't understand American *Charity,*
for it always shields cynical slaughters.

IT: This is the era of Satan.
All our maps pinpoint colonies that double as cemeteries.

KP: Poisonous winds propel the Belgian vessels.

US: Consumptive scrambling for scraps of Africa—
all this ominous chewing—
has an aspect of *Vanity,* an aura of *Lust.*

GF: Abandon such *Poetry!*
Prohibit it!
Europe mustn't be a cathedral belching fly larvae.

GB: The Yank rhetoric is, really,
"Bunkum, hokum, gobbledygook"!

KB: Must Britain be morbidly, globally bellicose?

GF: We seek a midway between all-out (*Total*) *War*
and nothing-doing *Peace.*

[Guelph (Ontario) 29 *novembre* mmxv
& Detroit (Michigan) 29 & 30 *novembre* mmxv]

Confession of a Jesuit Priest in Brazil, 1887

I.

In Deep South Brazil, October reprises April,
but December rips apart June:
Come frigid cold of fracturing frost,
every crucifix feels chill,
and Christ is affixed, shivering,
cast in half-nude *Disrepute*.

Congregants gang into mass, parley
in clogging doggerel,
while church bells hang together—
like Christ twisted twixt the Two Crooks.

(X was not just of Nazareth,
but also of Nassau—
and Nigeria—
and Niger—
everywhere slave skin foams burgundy.)

One credits that the *Crucifixion* marked simple, judicial *Error*,
for X got damned for disrupting the *ta'afish*—
the golden black-market in stolen bullion.

Thus, my cathedral puffs out jasmine like opium—
a gold mine's worth,
fogging up the scriptures,
but prompting Believers to drowse and dream....

Now a retiree, I'm retro—a pimp,
letting complacent *bourgeoises* seesaw atop me,
flatteringly, while nattering,
"Cripes! Cripes!"

I tell you:
The Crucifix don't need my words
to set it upright.
It is spry, fresh, green wood.

Nor do I let *Prejudice* poison *Coitus*.

Lookit—*merde!*—take a black gal,
delude her til she's as denuded
as a desert,
and you find a greasy spring—
a twat so chafing it chokes a cock.

(That's what I'm talkin bout!
I can't reason in a patristic mode,
or enunciate matheme upon matheme:
Theology be blues, *transubstantiated*.)

II.

Unnatural, the Portuguese Empire bleeds pus—
exported / imported
to Brazil:

Slavery issues one-sided, sordid stories—
tubercular debacles....

III.

But sweet *Recompense* is my slave girl:
The likeness of her black hair is night.

Our bed's fragrance is smoke; our table is figs:
She opens her spice-box; I unfurl my vine.
Milk emits shimmering mercury.

I down her in delicious dew or dusk,
and tender her tender wine —
as pale and as treacherous as a swamping wave.

Our hearts start a-thuddin:
Though she's shy — like Tennyson's gal of Shalott,
Lola burns harlot-hot.

IV.

Being a priest, I should dub females foul;
their perfumes should smell like offal.

Yet, unhurried and unhygienic *Fucking*
enacts no unhappy *Pathology*:
I like it like guillotines like necks.

When I arrow sluts' feathery thighs,
launch a piercing voyage
into the black eye of *Femininity*,
the sex's venomous vortex,
I fancy myself kin to Rimbaud,
who dicked drowsy, brown gals in Bermuda
and dickered with wide-awake, sable wenches in Benin.

In my private church,
Venus parleys with Jesus;
they both wink; they both guffaw.

It's the prude, not the bawd,
who nails X to the Cross —

to punish *Love*.

V.

Ideal it is, brethren, to spread my bird-hipped Negress,
to arc her legs wide as table legs.

Love is daily, sensual labouring:
So I'm the dawn plunderer,
the South's subtle thief,
the treasurer of female toffee.

VI.

There's talk that the plantations are finished,
that sugar is less vital than steam,
that *Slavery* perishes inside a year.

Bah!

Well, until then,
count on it:
virgins' days —
eves —
be numbered....

[Florianopolis (Brazil) 20 *juillet* mmxii
& Puumala (Finland) 4 & 5 *août* mmxii]

Ports Négriers Européens

Liverpool (4894 voyages)

Londres (2704 voyages= fount of Shakespeare's lingo)

Bristol (2064 voyages)

Nantes (1714 voyages)

Zéland (688 voyages)

Bordeaux (480 voyages)

Le Havre (451 voyages)

La Rochelle (448 voyages = launch pad for Québec)

Saint-Malo (218 voyages; & the spider-hole of Cartier,
           that pirate who "bagged" Canada for France)

Amsterdam (210 voyages)

Honfleur (134 voyages)

Lisbonne (92 voyages)

Marseille (88 voyages)

Etc.

Cadix (39 voyages)

[Liverpool (England) 12 *octobre* mmxiv]

Józef Korzeniowski* @
Freetown, Sierra Leone (1890)

*E*n *route* to the Congo, we watch horses thrash
    in piranha pools, kick up red-streaked splashes,
here at Freetown, the anti-Shangri-La:
    Immeasurably rickety, the city
shivers, all slapped together, slap-dab, slapped down,
    even squashed seeming—
like mashed remains of hand-swatted mosquitoes.
    Can't breathe freely here—
insects scurry through air, blurring eyes;
    they pause to snap at eyelids,
sting nostrils, bite lips, gnaw all agape skin,
    then hurry on, but not before
doubling, tripling, quadrupling *Pain.*
    Blight is their diseasing *Delivery....*

Indoors allows no *Salvation,* either.
    Try sleeping with feet nesting on the floor:
Ants virtually eat em up, toe to heel.
    I could almost adore, in contrast,
the Congo, for Freetown has no nympho
    wantons, only bleached-out trolls,
all bedded down with suave "Afro-Saxons,"
    whose fine-fingered diamond thefts
win em such fine-ass *pieds noirs.*
    Still, Freetown is a Valhalla of *cum*—
as bedroom-clammy in reek
    as a brothel, save that we Europeans
are adrift between earthquakes (or Sambo attacks),
    bereft of holy-water alcohol,

---

* Alias Joseph Conrad (1857–1924).

and snake-oil morphine.
    Only swill enough of the booze; then,
Freetown natives seem "veddy" British—
    Fleet-Street, Saville-Row, flimflam artists—
if skilled at snatching busted crud
    and repurposing it as "furniture,"
or remodeling kitchens as lean-to latrines.
    My predecessor here, Dr. Clarke,
left notes that look like my own handwriting,
    though he has his own shorthand—
a spaghetti of ink—
    that gave himself the permission
to punch "the living eye-whites" outta any black,
    and to declare all those little bodies

tacked to matchstick cruciforms as "false,"
    given "This despicable, bashed-together ghetto
in which the niggers teem,
    where their dames are stripped and ravished,
their brats all kicked to pieces."
    So, Doc Clarke commands himself,
"Trash the small-time, Christ statuettes!
    Negroes sport Caucasian fetters;
Africa is under Europe's irons:
    We 'blackies' die in English noose
or under French guillotine:
    Whitehall and Belgium are packed
with buttoned-down psychopaths."
    I've been warned that Clarke is now known

as "Dr. Fuck Up Bald Head,"
    that he, brain-sick, sodomized publicly
his "yellow maid," corkscrewed her fanny
    "until feces dribbled out,"
next splashed her face with gold water,
    then tongued sherry and bade other servants
bugger "the execrable bitch" while he watched.
    He pronounced her a "yellow-skinned-*ed* black supremacist,"
and then went into his paper-stuffed office
    and shot himself in the head,
so fluids were running right out his nose.
    What bothers me especially is,
I wear the exact same shoe as asinine Clarke,
    and now I worry about Kurtz....

Freetown is fine for a lip-smacking, mackerel lunch,
    a celebrity-toasted ale or sherry;
otherwise, my days here are rubble
    and my nights are slime.
No healthy, true-white lady to buck;
    no escape from the evil, whining, blood-sucking
bugs, the fangs with wings, the termites
    and vampiric roaches, the humanoid
vipers, the slick killers with stiff-white-lip
    Grammar, English not sleazy, *per se*,
but utterly void of *Good Will*.
    Time to set sail, to fire up the steam,
to heap up fresh tin boxes, pill bottles,
    clear booze, black boots, and grey revolvers;

to take command of the steamboat and ply
    through gold fever and *Dysentery*,
scarlet *Ebola* and green-eyed *Jaundice*,
    and Yellow Fever and gangrene
that purples black skin and blackens white;
    to—admittedly—vandalize The Congo
as authorized, and indoctrinate
    and damn the natives to prostrate themselves
under the hammer of Great British *Commerce*.
    We will act as liberal *Huns*,
and aweigh from Sierra Leone—
    diamond jungle—
to weigh in at The Congo—
    the jungle of diamonds.

I'm anxious to *flee* Freetown,
    this flimsy citadel, bristling with fires,
to navigate whatever tempests
    caterwauling breakers—
rumbling breaker upon breaker,
    the salt-white, salt-pale tides,
hunched waves, the spattering torrents—
    and speed breakneck from the cringing town,
with globe-bellied sails,
    open to ripping, grisly gusts,
to anchor, eventually, in wine-dark sea,
    and come out to skull-tint shores,
the mother lode of *Bloodshed*,
    symbolized by smouldering Towers of the Dead.*

---

* Where vultures roost on *plein-air* cadavers and tear the flesh clean from the bones.

The ocean is an incurable wound,
    stretching to The Congo;
waves seethe with overthrown slaves,
    black maggots, floundering.
(Slaves build—and never destroy:
    Unless they cease to be slaves.)
Stars burn like Hindu widows undergoing suttee;
    we progress through the white surf
as a black ship,
    as night circles and circles round,
and we tipple through the foam,
    under swarms of clouds,
surging on swells. We do mean *Harm*:
    A surf-supported army is a *Navy*.

The aqua-blue sky, aquamarine-fluorescent,
    matches the sky-broad plains of sea,
where waves flash like shields.
    I'll ferry us to The Congo,
so smoke-black dogs will grovel and lap dust,
    taste the charred cinders of their huts,
while my conquistadors muster the bedraggled
    survivors to cram this "galleon,"
in illegal, but infernally lucrative,
    furtive slave trafficking,
where bayonets wrangle ox-heads,
    or swords hack away at each Afro *Genealogy*,
showing incorrigible *Brutality*,
    slopping buckets with intestines....

We'll pass devolved freaks, nameless tribes,
　　raging tides bearing us beyond
the reach of arrows launched like tears.
　　We'll endure all this *merde*
to glean newborn copper, diamonds,
　　from coffled, bronze droves,
their slaving bones,
　　dragooned by gargantuan shackles.
We'll invade filthy villages, more dirt
　　than architecture, and already greasy
with charring lamb and burning goats,
　　and lay waste to everything human,
feasting on *Carnage*,
　　so we leave male trunks, dark,

studding anthills and snake holes;
　　we'll carve the tribesmen as if they're pork.
We'll be ruthless as pale salt
　　packed in a pink, dull-pus-percolating wound.
Kings, chiefs, witch doctors, poets —
　　will be pared down to penis and testicles,
garbed in rags — if they're lucky.
　　Our steel-faced battalions will stare down
arrows winging like ravens,
　　so we'll desire only to destroy
the blacks, lest their spears rip
　　into our champions, tipping out their brains.
The Congolese are infamous for springing
　　sumptuous salvos of barbs,

plus hurling axes that splash through flesh,
    turning Europeans into ungodly carcass
and unwashed carrion,
    white throats cut short by black iron.
We must leave gruesome trappings
    to mark our passage:
Disgraceful impaling, bowels twirled out of bodies,
    foreheads burst open, sprouting holes,
vultures crowding to dip beaks in flesh.
    We must discharge blasts—cannonades—
of *Slaughter*, glut our white teeth
    on mahogany throats,
crumple even vineyards with flame,
    if we are to cow lions,

to make stiff-back warriors kowtow,
    and go docile into *Slavery*....
I'd prefer that we not be ruthless boulders
    crushing black men into jam and pulp.
I'd rather have deathless wine,
    restless in endless cups,
than trigger unmixed, unadulterated *Grief*,
    all the arrogant bleeding,
all the swaggering breath,
    that is Europe's plot,
to grab allotment and deposit
    of gold, copper, diamonds—
to loot the lot—
    and leave all Africa *History*'s own cemetery.

[New York (New York) 24 & 25 *juin* mmxv]

In the Congo

By William G. Stairs[*]

I.

And we inhaled miasma, mustard taste of VD,
rust stench of TB,

(neither disease worthy of a VC),

got trench mouth at the fore,
diarrhea aft,

and got pestered,
daggered, by mosquitoes,

swarms in brigades —

Angels of *Malaria* —

staggering we doughy whites
all the spook-blacked night.

II.

Here, even *Cogitation* fails:

lungs lava mucus,

---

[*] William G. Stairs teamed with Stanley on his second Congo expedition. On this Tempest-like misadventure, the Nova Scotian *cum* British imperialist likely raped African women, but definitely slew African men. See *African Exploits: The Diaries of William Stairs, 1887–1892* (1997). Stairs Street, in Halifax, NS, is named for the villainous pillager.

heart spits brine,

Torpor sops *Reason*,

the brain clicks — ticks — off....

Too weak to trick —

or torque —

torture — niggers to steady feed
our lucrative machines.

Greed requires *Murder*.
(Our Empire's policy is,
Terror mines *Treasure*.)

We console ourselves:
"The Negro is naturally perishable

like vegetables torn out of soil
or fish yanked into the air."

III.

And we muscled down tusslin quim,
and were unabashedly brutal,

mauling every Negress
with abundant, apt *Delight*.

(One raunchy black *pute* loved suckin
my pudgy white hose, even while
I dribbled bilge and/or spunk.

Pathetic panting did she —
sordid *conne*:
So morbidly *morbidezza*.

I can still see her scissor mouth,
her razor eyes.)

Air assumed a burnt-spice odor—
remains of battering-ram-splattered hymens.

IV.

Jailed us some cargo,
tossed em scraps.

(Their ginger smell bristled our nostrils
with nigger *Intensity*.)

We weren't inhuman(e).

I did note,
now and then,
the odd, sloppy tear
dumpin
outta slumpin eyes.

Make no mistake:

We came at em
with unmistakable knives
and/or gunpowder—
our *lingua franca*.

V.

Next we confronted mandatory *Misery*—
blood-blurred sunlight;
delicate, skeletal, whiny squirming
in louse-infested sheets;
excremental howls;
scathing, scorching siroccos;
bathetic wallows in whisky;

we hunted signs of any cantering gull,
to bring us to cold foam,
urgent *Reconciliation* with a Euro port,

where we'd sidle in,
pour out our sob-story *"Crimes"* —

the Gothic anthologies of *Anthropology*—
grim (Darwinian) *Science.*

Next, we white men annexed—
pounced upon—
women the pallor and feel of jelly,
wives—

to console our inconsolable guts.

[RDU (**North Carolina**) 9 *avril* / *Nisan* **mmxiii**]

Flight from The Congo

By William G. Stairs

After squalling sails —
spittle haze of seaspray

(and we were thankful for that haze,
for sunlight now feels bestial) —

carried thither by tatters of foam,
we swished into Halifax harbour,
blurred by fog.

Happy we are
to bring our brine-burned bones back
to sea-salted coast,
the wash of cold mistrals,

so nicely *North*

of gold fish, gold fevers,
and gold rum
(the gold-gilt Carib sea),

back now to stiff winds,
dangerous *Winter.*

There are no righteous tropics.

We've survived air shrill with arrows —
I mean, streaming, or thorny, with arrows —

the jeering of arrows,
hitting us down,
a jesting gesture —
but successful, as in *Chess.*

We should prefer stringy snow
along the sea strand—
New Darkness
or "Nova Scotia."

Halifax is a hammering clamour of bells—
Sodom-and-Gomorrah churches,
fire-and-brimstone weddings,
bread-and-wine chapels,
milk-and-honey funerals—
Civilization:

We can munch Sicilian bergamot pears,
swallow a garden diet—
not endure guts fed only fodder
or forage.

Here my crew can take a lass—
lips tasting of rain,
hair zesty with April zephyrs,
body as honest as honey—
with skin rose-pink
(conch-shell rose-pink),
her nubile *Utility* proving her *Worth*.

Flounce here some pertinent pillows:

A man can snooze with angels
or booze with gargoyles—

and dream of the bony belles of Ipanema—
or the bonny, big-breast lassies of Bahia.

Over there, down there, south—
where the Negroes camp,
spears puncture us Europeans;
our blood swears against us;
we forego our minds, our ways.

I tire of eyeing crow-dark shadows,
of fearing sudden spears bursting from shadows.

(From flesh, gore unfurled in withering gales.
As spears flew in, souls flew out.)

Our answer had to be cacophonies
of gunpowder. The incessancy!

I want to forget anchorage in a Congo river;

Mr. Joey Conrad (English-parleying Pole)
spitting out plasma-soiled vodka;

nigger huts pregnant with trash and corpses;

too much dust;
dust-laden dew;
too much diarrhea;

the diaphanous darkness,
strangely tangible;
strangling us.

(Chaps:
The Congo is a conglomeration of spikes.
Human skulls brick every castle.)

Fact is—
one *Niger* cunt got wrestled aboard;
her scorched tits
so scorching to see.
Plenty hard alcohol
got her all alcoholic.

We sampled her as a damp, trampled camp follower—
incorrigibly hearty—
deserving heartless, cold *Conjunction*.

We were infallibly greedy:
Liking to stud a stripped-down cutie.

She was unmercifully,
unceremoniously, frigged,
gamahuched, double-stuffed,
so jizz boiled down her butt-crack.

Us unblanching buffoons
made the coal-scuttle chit
a Caucasian cocksucker,
but her breathing *Self* was poison.

Her steel-bright smile was nerve-wracking:
She gave Joey C. a chilling grin,
just as she sucked in his peter,
then bit down unstoppably.

When he fell away, his blood flowering
from his stump of manhood,
those ruddy petals splintered
as they splashed us.

Hers was a trivial *Ruction*,
but I could not bear to see
his unbearable body.

I blared, yelled, *Murder!*

The leering gal,
spitting out Joe's appendage,
got thrilled — drilled — through —
gorged on a sword.

Two bodies tumbled into a swamp.

About-face we went,
to retrace the shadowy passage,
to navigate a stifling river
with a cargo of corpse-usurping flies,
to dodge a *delirium tremens Darkness.*

Halifax is hollow bells, kiting notes,
and soon hallowed blossoms
and hallowed belles
(hollow where it counts), comfy.

I want *Death*-like *Peace*, fresh-water port,
upstart tarts, and volumes of pear wine.
No more skimpy guts.

Somebody, somebody, anybody,
please holler, "Amazing Grace"!

Don't let me drift back into the blue-grey, marine *Hell*,
that wonky *Limbo*,
all that *Heaven*-discouraging voyaging!

Or I shall perish scabrous, albino,
a fraction of a pith-helmet faction,
cut down by darkies as indefatigable as Sitting Bull—
and as indignant as Riel....

Halifax, N.S.
1892

[**Durham** (**North Carolina**) **9** *Nisan* / *avril* **mmxiii**]

Paul Laurence Dunbar Selects a Theme[*]

The great poem should canvass *Confederates*
    plodding tired-out horses,
shatting upon their own dumb, doleful dead,
    across the smoky lines
scarring all Dixie,
    nigh the Appomattox *Apocalypse.*

Being a Negro (or "negativized") poet,
    I combine John Donne and Johnnycake:
That's my untidy *Duty,*
    my tinny, dubious poetics.
No wonder I'll never match, but only echo
    British Library, hardcover bards
(hardy as Hardy:
    Hardy-har-har).

I could enumerate the slaves,
    freed before I ever drew breath.
Yet, they exist for me only as phantom oils,
    or yellowed pictorials,
or newsprint folks, drab and ragged.
    Yet, it would be heroic *Scripture*—
to recover these dark citizens
    left out of famous lyrics,
but written into *Laws* as firm as cages.
    I edge toward a *Direction*....
To recall the slaves' edgy tongues;
    to bless their hollered plaints.

---

[*] Dunbar (1872–1906) was a beloved, bestselling African-American poet, who felt conflicted between producing the Dixie jingles his audiences craved and the "serious" verse that would win him critical acclaim—and a canonical claim.

An epic of hectic *Invective*:
    That's what I should write —
if I'm subjectively objective
    (not abject).

But I'm the (bastard) child of Lincoln
    (shadow of Apollo)
and "Moses" Harriet
    (shade of Artemis) —
the incarnation of *Cacophony*.
    I pluck a *Grief*-stricken banjo,
farcically; I never will pluck a lyre.
    I speak a leafless book.
I slash words into sheets crepuscular.
    My *Poesy* is *Surgery* done wrong.
I know no medicating *Technique*,
    merely a sputtering howl.
You see that I jingle a mediocre,
    broken-tongued *Poetic*,
a jungle *Grammar* nothing papers over.
    I'm the damnable imp of damp ink.

My br'er poets, yes, I'd like to be
    primus inter pares,[*]
my brittle treble
    troubling ink resonantly,
so that you condemn me
    as an irascible, asinine bard,
all cantankerous *Cant* —
    cos I can't descant
à la Shakespeare *et companie* —
    they milk-white lads and dey milkmaid tarts....

---

[*] Latin: First among equals.

Yessum, I trade on my molasses-sweet brogue—
    sumpin southern, wily and whisky-smoky
and pungent as tar, and icy as mint julep,
    a smidgen of ochre moonshine
and pot liquor low-down in the mix.
    That's why my rhythm jitters illicit.

I wish I could author venom-spitting books,
    craft anthems thrumming *Propaganda*,*
or draft tragedies that still bleed, murderous—
    "By Jingo"—i.e., er, janglin *Dialect*.

But I'm a "Yahoo *de* verse," eh?
    Check my "gasping wit" and "gut scream."
It's as hard for me "to carry a tune
    as it is for a nigger to carry an election."
My jottings "strike up a medley of crow
    and harmonica: Mockeries of English!"

Dubbed—as in *Zoology*—a "squeaky monkey,"
    whose lyrics bray echoes (like puke)
or just drool comedies, an upchucking
    "eating up thousands of pounds of paper,"
I merit my critical mangling;
    my *faux pas* mustn't "mislead talented [i.e., obedient]
Negroes"
    (intoneth the Pig Latin-schooled journalists).

Come the *Future*, my words will be so many
    dim smudges,
and scholars will ice-pick apart
    my "plangent, lying guts."

(Roaches and rats rend poems, anyway,
    and parasites pick the poet barren.)

---

* Cf. James Weldon Johnson.

Agreed: My flowers constitute
   a pitiful, worm-blown bouquet.

Consider Mr. Whitman —
   his now-approved,
republican *Fervour*, his *Muse* —
   as egalitarian as manure.

[Berlin (Germany) 8 & 9 *mars* mmxiii]

Paul Laurence Dunbar on his
Lyrics of Lowly Life *(1896)*

Germanic *Accuracy* insists: *Poetry* is *Dichtung*—
or sealed-in condensation;

it cannot be *Poetry*,
if it shows dismissive permissiveness
or cavorting diction—
what spells out abortive, misbegotten inklings.

The "Plantation" School of poets—
the Dixie *jongleurs*—
decant indiscriminate jangles—
the sludge of a "songbook";

they render, really, a sewer's outpouring—
the defecate and urinate of Uncle Sam,
licked up by Uncle Remus.

Their work's result
is *Insult*.

When I eye their rodomontade serenades,
bout "cotton pickers" and "banjo pickers,"
"tar babies" and "dew-pale" damsels,

I spy ruddy toasts readied
for salivating Klansmen.

Profs complain my *Poesy* displays
"imbecility or an ingrate's mentality,"
that my efforts to scale Parnassus
are pitfalls:

Each verse arrives "already damaged
in structure or sense." So they say.

I do regret.

I'd like my measures to encompass candles
and kindling,
to neither be riddles
nor piddling,
but ignite a conflagration,
yielding inextinguishable light.

I'm no elect *Genius*. Sure.
But I strive to tune my tongue
true to each lung:
To ejaculate *vers*
(if not wriggly worms).

My ink's no sweaty *Elixir;*
I flout the watermelon lyrics
of chicken-shit minstrels.

I'm content to be a crow
of *Verse*—
to even crow my verses—
rather than play a tar-and-peacock-feather Uncle Tom.

There's credible song—
even in misspelled, mangled, agrammatical lines.

Thus, I may aspire—
even my small-time brain may aspire—
to invent monuments—
nay, figments—
of *Erudition.*

If it's credible for Duncan Campbell Scott
(the "Canuck" sot)
to rival Sir Walter Scott
(a lot);

perhaps I can echo William Dunbar

(let us say,
in some minor, minor-key way),

the distance twixt us not being far,

if divided by Burns

(or unlettered—vulgar—blues, by turns).

[Enfield (Nova Scotia) 1 *mars* mmxiii]

Papers of Edward Mitchell Bannister, Barbizonian

I.

The troll Aubrey Beardsley drafts pen-and-ink *Terror*—
just true-black, blue-black, real black, pitch-black
blotches of women, twigs of men.

His *Kitsch* bewitches Ruddy Kipling, Dicky Burton—
his faces as cartoonish as an Empire's squiggle cross a map.

Rather ogle Tennyson's rapids of light.

Cast aside Beardsley and his pitcher of smoke!

Tennyson is radiant drink—
gold-leaf mead—
letters that amount to paramount liqueurs.

To approve Beardsley, though,
is to wriggle *à la* Golliwog in a gutter:

The fiend's drawings splay rats in high-heels—
nervous, furtive rodents with dirty tits

(the middle-class owns *Mediocrity,* so boringly unoriginal)—
their *bourgeois* boudoirs plumped on *Plunder.*

His sickly psychopaths—all sycophantic cocksuckers—
and his madonnas show flesh bumpy with boils.

All his subjects invite face transplants.

II.

Ex *Nouveau-Brunswick*—
Saint Andrews by-the-Sea, New Brunswick—
I paint—exult in—bovine pathos—
oxen sauntering as unhurried as sunset.

I stroll amid oiled sunlight,
democratic gold,

and loll in grass
and lounge in moss—

aristocratically republican as Emerson.

Why should I ape the puny excretions
of Beardsley?

I expect to depict agreeably marbled water—
such as the waves of Passamaquoddy Bay—
or reset th'Acropolis,
albeit in a New Albion cornfield.

Being the first African artist in America,
unfulfillable *Excellence*—
never painstakingly pallid nor piebald *Execution*—
is my wont—

should I want
to win

laurels, accolades

(i.e., permitted glissades of morals,
from *Righteousness* to *Sin*).

IV.

Let Beardsley, Toulouse-Lautrec, *et al.*,
spelunk in the abysses of the brothel,
retrieve bodies that are metallic murk.

Rather, there's *Beauty* in a weather-blistered boat,
or in flame-polished eves,
and in pastoral scenes as true as barbed-wire.

Gaze upon the nacreous moon blazing the velvet, sable night!

But open Tennyson and sound silvery music,
golden in the hearing.

His sonnets are stained-glass texts.

But Toulouse-Lautrec, Beardsley, their ilk,
contemplate *Pestilence* that eats through cosmetics —
so Jane Austen's *Emma* is at last unmasked
as model for Gustave Flaubert's *Emma Bovary*.

Their pens surrender bastard scum —
racailles —
gutless lice —
that daylight ought to incinerate.

Just like Baudelaire, these so-called artists
mooch off cum-plastered, *Can-Can* hoochie coos —
those malicious peddlers of tuberculosis.

Discard their rabbit-like anatomies!
Serve em a rinse of wine-like fire —
a stringent cleansing!

Perusing Tennyson,
I'm captive of *Magnificence* —
as unfenced as sunrise.

And I spelunk in the intoxicating honey that's Virgil,
treasure the dreamed-up *Nobility* of *paysans* in Millet,
register the facts of resolutely fat cows
in Massachusetts or in Maine,
their sincere mooing.

Art is arrogant.
My narcissism is requisite.

Give Toulouse-Lautrec his buffoon *Hell*;
grant Beardsley his peep-show *Divinity*.

I will show true as my signature pigment —
chimerical, but indelible — like Africa.

[**Saint Andrews by-the-Sea** (**New Brunswick**) *Noël* **mmxi**
& **Niagara Falls** (**New York**) 1 *janvier* **mmxii**]

Herbert Vivian, M.A., Publishes Tunisia *(1899)*

I.

Just as a paddle withers if withdrawn
too long from liquid,
so does Empire shrivel—atrophy—
if we Britons don't insist on assuming
overlordship of this beach-fringed desert....

Tunis is the fault-line,
the trip-wire,
that will either expand or contract our maps....

II.

The Arab women (says Mrs. Vivian)
are very often yoked to camels.

Yet, it's hard to say which creature merits
more *Sympathy*, or due "animal mercies"....

III.

When camels trample a person,
the feeling is like being pummelled

with boxing gloves: The feet drum soft,
though this buffeting—in effect—drubs hard.

IV.

When a husband tusks into
the virgin's pigeonhole,

he cores her so errantly
that the sex goes from fissure

to crevice.
Goblets emptied of *lagni*,

clink guttural,
as *Lust* brinks unshrinkingly at a man's loins.

Bristled cacti pricks seem her eyelashes
while moonlight rivers the quivering bed—

until the rose-water aromas
finally trend fishy....

V.

Mrs. Vivian got pressed into a harem
via the *Deceit* of a French attaché's wife—

a surprisingly un-French, but chunky Negress;
and she was plied with seductive liqueurs

of licorice and *lagni*,
and was soon splayed in a picnic state

before plates of rancid oil, roast locusts,
fat dates, sun-dried salt beef, plus oranges,

tasteless, mescal-infused cacti from hedges,
gold-and-purple grape vines, and black olives,

and milk, syrups, a camel's hump,
a quartered gazelle, plus half a lamb....

Imagine Manet's *Déjeuner sur l'herbe*,
my wife's fuschia physique

(her blushing, cultivated complexion),
made vulnerable, if fetching,

thanks to white-silk-sheer pants
and gold high-heeled shoes. But

the bed "wasn't fit to even put a horse."
Stink of dirty rags, oily fish, decomposing rats....

Next, a troupe of Negresses crackling
two-stringed harps, emitting roller coaster cackles,

and clapping tambourines, encircled her
and combed their fingers through

her nether hairs (wiry, bristly),
and pinched gaily at her breasts.

VI.

Here, anyone who doesn't sell carpets,
sells quim.

(Tunisians interact on two stops:
Friendship and *Murder.*)

Anyway, a Muslim bride,
divorced often enough,

can be generous with *Virginity*
(offering it again and again,

ad nauseum,
calore galore,

her sugar-coated *Nudity,*
deposits of perspiration,

unmentionable delight of her *Sex*),
to go to bed like grapes to the press.

(A delicate gentleman, I'd faint
upon the prostitutes —

white lace, black stockings —
of Piccadilly's Circus.)

VII.

A white smell in the room:
The fluttering-thighed bitch.

Her plush, uptilted tits
cushioning vanilla seed.

We're as carnal as pigs,
gullible as pigeons,

spooning and drooling,
extraordinary honey:

If my "ugly" piston is churning,
she is sufficiently squealing.

Bovine Venus and porcine Priapus —
declining satyr and reclining sadist —

bareheaded where I'm licking,
bare-assed where she lies —

I'm guzzling at her "wine-skin"
like a dribbling horse.

VIII.

If you believe all Orientals are, at base,
niggers,

appreciate that the most sun-seared Arabs
are hardly as blackish

as the average Sicilian, Basque, or Monégasque.
Naturally, the fabled, sanguinary Moors

pitched dark *jism*, to and fro, in pale *queynte*.
Some locals are Ibero-Numidian;

others be white Berbers combined
with Sudanese darkies;

still others are Troglodytes,
hunched in caves and wolfing dog flesh.

(Mrs. Vivian gnashed several mouthfuls—
half a belly and a quarter of hind—

and determined it has a specific taste,
not unlike what any fellatrix could discuss.)

The Negroes laurel their faces with grins.
Nothing upsets them—

perhaps because they've not endured
the blatant *Evil* of Yank-style "Emancipation."

The blackest of em issue from Sudan,
but the other shady gradations

evince Arab interference.
Surprisingly, even blacks loathe their colour,

and clamour to shower in whitewash,
walloping from a bucket.

Nothing's more disconcerting at night
than to see frosty teeth shining.

Dressed in rabbit-fur rags and ostrich feathers,
much higgledy-piggledy chintz,

Negro "bogey-men" beat booming tom-toms,
and agitate maracas,

to scare off "demons" said to arrive upon
the rust-red flood of the menses....

(Note: The darkies feed their papooses opium
to still their cries.)

IX.

During the day, one will stumble upon
silvery *squelettes*, ivory bones, clay shards

of broken pottery —
as in Omar Khayyam.

(The parchment for books
is culled from shaved sheep.)

What is straightforward in Europe,
in Africa, curves elliptical;
What is metaphysical in Europe,
in Africa, turns mythical.

[**Windsor (Ontario) 23** & **24** *janvier* **mmxvi**
& **Detroit (Michigan) 23** *janvier* **mmxvi**]

Bannister Reflects

To breakfast on pollen, in filtered light,
until night's sooty *Finality,*
along the brash North Atlantic —
the cold, bare, rude boulders —
the shallow vantage point of pebbles —
and to spy Anglo-Saxon moors
reborn in this Moorish New Scotland —
is to suffer hard-edged hallucinations,
stumble among *bric à brac* architecture
of brackish puddles and tumbled pines —
or amble into settler churches —
those squat, toad-like, bastardized cathedrals —
and inhale the giddy smell of molten ice,
all April,
all over mud-flat Fundy....

Against the epic whiteness
of this cold, uncivil, asexual, European America,
we Blackamoors seem foolhardy silhouettes —
despite our strutting, top hat, Creole poses,
and our niggardly muses,
too narrow in thought to loudly blot out
chalked-up Yellow Journalism —
what refuses our Art be hung,
but insists our selves be lynched.

I view Audubon's almost audible *Art* —
the dead-end spectacle,
the obsessive gutting,
the self-satisfied craftsmanship,
of his frigid, morbid aviary,
imprisoned in painting's rigid frames.

The artist is an appropriate usurper
of animate *Nature*—
it suits our adventurous instinct,
to relocate the wild to a parlour—
or a library—
with saintly imperiousness.

My task: To paint Beethoven,
cut with Bojangles,
so that banjo and fiddle
violently displace harp and violin.

To ramble, not rampage,
and commune with spume,
driftwood, snow-foam,
or spill an elixir of silken willows
from paint pots onto canvas,

and to imagine cattle loping through an orchard,
blazed by blossoms.

Or I can try thinking like a horse,
and activate snorts or whinnies
by mottling clear blue
with gaseous white,
the breathy emissions of a chilly pastoral dawn,
a journey in Tonalist chalk.

Tints pinpoint a picnic locale, ripe for *Rape*
(see Manet),
or the iconic, royal black shadows
where assassins lurk as saints are born.

I don't have an odd-job brain.
I paint so I can buy milk
or gasp at wine's insouciance
and lose my balance.

Nor do I exhibit Audubon's casual grisliness—
his hyperbolic slaughters that please
the salacious elites
of America's venomous *Imperium*,
its symbol being an eagle (vulturous)
as inflexible as *rigor mortis*.

Nor am I as smug as a savant—
or purse-proud as Midas.

No, as an "African" outta
Saint Andrews by-the-Sea,
I see my canvasses,
pliant as light,
drafting—crafting—an unmistakeably
Negro Renaissance.

[Baltic Sea: Tallinn (Estonia)—Helsinki (Finland) 29 *mai* mmxiv]

Adrift, in Paris*

"*L*a palette des vins" —
chez Moulin-Rouge —
bleaches black souls.

Each congenial cave where mingle
our shadows,
obliterates savannah and shackles:

Music guffaws, raucous as pimps,
as it cackles —
at our crumblin thatch huts,
or homeland Pygmies
(as tall as uncircumcised hunchbacks) —
or a grandfather's musty penis —
or a mama whose body,
that gold-girdled Afrian bum —
slithers ornaments over silk.

Who here respects the diamond-back crocodile
shimmering in the Congo,
but horrifying the Seine?

The French have drilled all Africa
wells stopped with rat droppings.

To be darkest African at Paris
is to revel in bacteria
(*pissoir et bordel*),
or to be so green-with-*Envy*
or so green-with-*Innocence*,
one lives as prickly as a cactus.

---

* Cf. Damas.

I minstrel myself, "tom,"
play the buck naked rascal
amid the snow of Sacré-Coeur.

At "home," my rat-hole here,
I enter a cockroach factory,
and don't mind the squalor,
for, outside, Gothic police—
canines gobbling breath mints—
hound us, gutter to gutter.

If only we *noirs* would let
our machetes milk blood
all over the Champs-Elysées;

we'd antagonize the blanching *bourgeoisie*,
while our blades would monopolize—
depreciate—
white flesh, the angelic pallor.

The poet *noir*—

après Baudelaire,

après Rimbaud—

proffers a Ph.D.—

après Apollinaire—

in *Assassination*.

[**Paris (France) 19** *août* **mmxiii**]

The Negro: An Anatomy

By Rudyard Kipling

Who can mirror the Negro's terrifying *Beauty*?
The Negro be the breaking point of *Beauty*.

The Negro's insidious, obsidian looks—
like terrorist bombs—
char and/or crumple fragile, paper faces.

The Negro (male) phallus is as ugly
and unbending as a crucifix,
but jabs brats outta bellies.

An alcohol-irrigated desert, that's the Negro.
His is a rum-marinated brain and a brine-pickled heart.

The Negro is as sullen as an itch.
and/or as surly as a migraine.

The Negro warbles spectacular *Grief*.
Listen to his cosmetic sighs.

Immortal twittering suits the Negro.
The Negro is an organ.

The Negro is ubiquitously anonymous.
The Negro holes up in beehives and hornets' nests.

Negroes make do with *"nègreries"** and do forgeries:
Thus, Negroes roam only at night.

The Negro is jumpy sweat and an inky fragrance.
The Negro soul? A lot of stained-glass in jagged shards.

---

* Cf. Damas.

Cajole the Negro! Don't criticize!
They like to be joshed, not judged!

The Negro exercises his teeth on other Negroes.
He be a black, *mouche*-like moocher.

Pigeon squabbling, peacock feathers, that's the Negro.

The Negro offers a toy *Love*;
but his (or her) death is never a toy.

The Negro is waifish, raffish, oafish.
The Negro slinks about, fishily officious.

The Negro is fiercely unfaithful.
The Negro shows furious ovaries.

"Whoever says *Sexual Assault*, says Negro."*

The Negro performs bowel-movement births;
his mama expels him from anus, not vagina.

The Negro is a dark palette.
The Negro is chocolate and ice water.

The Negro mumbles because he can't murder.
The Negro dead are instant coal.

Sunlight is Negro.
Define bitter gold likewise.

The Negro's shoes are tar.
The Negro's shirt is sludge.

The Negro gamahuches like Golliwog, stabs like Othello.
The Negress screws like Aunt Jemima, cuts like Jebezel.

---

* Cf. Fanon, unquestionable Fanon.

Wherever there is white-collar *Crime*,
a Negro will be caught red-handed.

Wherever there is blue-collar *Crime*,
a Negro will be found purple-faced.

[**Vancouver** (**British Columbia**) **25** *octobre* **mmxiv**]

"À Rimini" (1906)

à la manière de Kipling

When I to Rimini sought my *Love*,
Passing from Dante's tomb to the beach —
I mean, fleeing Ravenna to this cove —
I arrived here *True Love* to beseech....

I thought *True Love* not beyond my reach:
So I took to tramping at nightfall,
To trumpet *Desire* above recall,
Along the white foam of the strand —
Along the foam of the gold strand....

But never came Paolo to the beach —
Never did hear I his voice reach
My *Consciousness* and then command,
"Don't lie in the Duke's bed! We must stand
Erect, to feel God's outreach...."

I went to the Duke by the Via Aurelia
That runs from Rimini up to France:
I played Caesar, no, Cleopatra —
To launch a spear, deadly in *Romance*.

If only Rimini believers did know
How to separate God from *Inuendo*.
If only Rimini Christians were Christian —
Not hypocrites who wreck that *Religion* —

I could marry Duke Giovanni for
Real, and never face accusation —
The character assassination,
That names I, Francesca, "Paolo's whore."

But Duke Giovanni likes a slave —
And I was his wife, nay, *Property* —
He held without having. To the grave,
I'd be his just in name — never free
To love; but Paolo was better
Husband than brother, better lover
Than proxy, unwilling to fetter
His heart, his flesh, what did mine cover.

To the Duke by the Via Aurelia
Went I, to wife, but not to his bed,
Went I to his bed, but not to *Love*,
Went I to his brother — Paolo — instead.

Not alone as a woman to suffer —
To be spurned — for spite, or *Policy*;
To be a proxy, offered as proffer,
To stave off *War* but brave *Slavery*.

But I came to Rimini for *Love*.
I went from Dante's tomb to the beach;
I left Ravenna for the broad cove:
I didn't think *True Love* beyond reach.

Though the Duke is dull, he isn't fair:
His morals pale, his politics pall.
Sly, he makes slain Paolo appear
Black and himself white — that bleached, limp doll.

[Barcelona (Spain) 14 & 15 *février* mmxv]

Considering John Brown (1909)

By W.E.B. Du Bois*

I.

Yes, Ol' Cloudsplitter was
twitchy as a whip;

knew himself commanded to loose psychotic,
Old Testament, "God-told-me-to" bullet holes.

The man produced homely crimes;
Caucasian historians eye him with cold *Disgust*

because he preached "Black" *Liberation*
was *Prophecy* as irrefutable as sunlight.

So, John Brown earned repulsive *Prestige*:
He canted against a Federal army

as ridiculously as Don Quixote
assaulted Spanish windmills.

He got cut down, right with his boys,
because he couldn't knock down everything

and bury everyone
backing *Slavery*.

---

* W.E.B. Du Bois (1868–1965) was the #1, African-American intellectual of the 20th
Century.

II.

Still, his Harpers Ferry raid was
nothing so vile as *Frivolity*.

His failed onslaught was no *Kindergarten*
travesty

of cadavers bitten into, gnawed, mauled,
sprawled, broken like toddlers' crayons.

Brown saw *Stagnation*, *Malaise*;
The refusal to advance *Emancipation*

was, surely, he believed, *Malice*.
His murders were not for *Murder*'s sake.

While others could *Slavery* condone;
John Brown sought to see it long gone.

III.

Yes, he wanted to touch off Civil War—
voluntary, state *Cannibalism*—

and sought out "liberators" as energetic
as the gluttonous guillotines Robespierre oversaw.

They prepared in shade-equipped woods
under garlands of sun or moon.

He could see through even starless trees.
He had svelte pamphlets, a stout Bible.

IV.

Yes, his was a private "firing upon,"
but for Republican *Purpose*;

his very sons now wear sooty shirts,
crimson in spots.

Someone had to tender
tinder and dynamite;

it was he.
He got dragged to the gallows

and hanged in the wind;
now we drag ballads up

for a man
hanging so, so, so, close to *Heaven*.

[**London (Ontario)** 13 *novembre* **mmxiv**]

Witnessing "Jazz" (1910)

By W.E.B. Du Bois
(Exclusive to *The Crisis*)

The pianists sound disputatious as cannon,
while drummers brawl taps, knell cymbals;
bassists thread leaden webs of ebbing notes,
wiring auditoria with sounds as evanescent as *Thought*.
The banjo enthusiasts work strings
as if they're gears,
growling cranky into place.
Lewd trumpets, farting trombones, squealing cornets,
echo squadrons of strumpets, crones, "nymphets"....

The "performance" is convulsive *Ceremony*.
Each dark face is saturnine; mercurial sound their mouths.

The rhythm paces illogical,
but is never, on reflection,
incorrect.

In the brothels (regrettably), in the bars,
where Buddy Bolden leads,
his combo immolates —
yes, decapitates *de capo* —
th' European metronome,
so that a style African, primal,
audibly bloody,
screeching *Warfare*,
overtakes and ravages (ravishes)
Melody.

"Dulcet tones"
turn rancid, running to bone;
"*sweetness*" goes seedy.

Corruption stews in Storyville's
soupy, smoky sinks.

Each player's got a rum cask for a brain,
a casket for a heart;
easy to hear banjo strings—
as lynchers' braying ropes.

The jazzers deploy their instruments
like cheerful bombardiers,
but congress mid the crisscrossing notes
and beats,
at successful rendezvous—
as special as cannon shot striking each other
in mid-air.

In those "Naw Leens" bordellos
(so I've heard it said),
the awkward tunes slap ears
like adversarial gusts,
splash boisterous murk,
until th'auditor's engirdled
in intolerable swirls
of espaliered funk—
rococo siroccos.

In the bars I've attended—
(bleak like jail-cell bars)—
the black-soul musicians—
gargoyles in the gloom,
look down, leer at one,
from their cathedral-high perches of airs,
jittering melodies that imaginably imitate
concussive calamities in clammy beds.

That's the Negro purchase on Caucasian arias:
To orchestrate how they arise from the tom-tom heartbeat
of bump-n-grind *l'amour.*

Anyway, jazzers loom aristocratic in their *Triumph*:
The piano crackles fire;
drums snap out pompous musketry.

The *Ragtime* exponents—
like Scott Joplin—

entangle one's ears in *"lagniappe"*—
"a little something extra"—
like artillery freed to frolic.

Our sable musicians conduct flippant rodomontade,
trumpet *Effrontery*,
as they divvy up European scales
like decks of cards.

These imponderable artisans launch our ears
on an Odyssey of *Debauchery*,

as effective—
or detouring—
or destroying—
as the songs of Circe—
or the Sirens....

The jazzers bay and hooray
as kosher as the Devil.

I hear abortive canticles,
mortified epiphanies.

Some critics name this attitude "jive."
Nay, I say it's the shadow of *Justice*,

and this jittering in the music of the State
warns us, as Plato observes,

an earthquake is startling the foundations.

[New Orleans (Louisiana) **22** *juin* **mmxiv**]

Eyeing Bellocq[*]

Bellocq's *mal occhio*, his camera *Sluttery*,
"dresses" each 1/8 Negress
as some Ivy-League, *Ivory (Soap) Lady*,
no lapis lazuli in her labia, no septic
or suspect tint in her sepia tone,

and whose *Algebra* is *Gymnastics*,
and whose *frou-frou* physiques enable serpentine monkeyshines.

The Barnum & Bailey of black magic,
Bellocq parades, yes, profitable femmes —
fair ladies actually unfathomably black:

Each exotic aspect hints at the hyacinthine darkness
percolating subtly neath superficial ivory.

Bellocq models Storyville "Hostesses,"
those who decorate every hotel window, pledging,
"GIRLS, GIRLS, GIRLS!
COCKTAILS & COCKTAILS![**]
FUN! FUN! FUN!"

Such belles balance *Negress* and *Venus:*
Athens becomes an African invention.

---

[*] Cf. N. Trethewey.
[**] Negroni, Vodka Martini, Bellini, Manhattan, Sazarac....

Still, occasional *Imperfection*
intrudes on Bellocq's "masterpieces." He adjusts
his tripod, gets his opiate *Chemistry* right;
is set to immortalize a starlet in light,
when, inexcusably, a cockroach scuttles
across her tits, or scurries across her thighs,
pausing at her crotch, just long enough
to snatch a bit of dried sperm off the *chatte* hairs
and crunch it down.

[Ottawa (Ontario) 25/12/13]

Bellocq Snaps Ophelia*

I.

Guitar notes, piano notes, part, tumble, lift—
imitating curtains.

Under beautiful lamps, leaning—
almost invisibly *Physical*—

men slant toward their ladies
with ambiguous *Camber*,

or a female head graces a male shoulder,
as some lips deceive by *Compliment*,

some hands deceive by coins,
and throughout the cathouse,

drastic smoking sears and suffocates.
Now, a charitable trumpet brays,

clearing space for the piano's
cascading pizzicato,

what's *Ragtime*, its moneyed scales,
if not Americanization of the French *Can-Can*?

II.

Vodka gets to the point;
shoots straight from throat to guts to bowels;

---

* Cf. N. Trethewey (descendant of Three Mile Plains, NS).

or, merged with orange juice,
brings on hyperventilating *Hysteria*:

The brothel is the acid test of *Marriage*.
Husbands either begrudge the grip of wives;

or, tamed by the repulsive honours of whores,
deplete their gold,

and fantasize cutting the throats
of their own children.

III.

The jazzers' unfrugal playing
accents the fugues playing out

in beds, where *Jazz* issues luminous
in incidental *Darkness*,

becomes the frayed daylight
unfurled in hurled-back sheets.

IV.

Now, Ophelia opes her long legs
and exposes her tan, sporty breasts

to bad boys whose suits are robes
and to bastards raking in tens of thousands,

per annum, the confidential *Rich*,
who like to party in smog and scum.

The curs like to snag a custom slut,
and bitch, bitch, bitch!

A chilly Madonna, despising *Euphoria*,
Ophelia treads the pine staircase:

No creaking in her wake;
she's as level-headed as a prowling cat.

V.

White pearls against pale, violet skin:
The camera digests her, gathers fog.

Slender, immaculate as a gem,
she's been a sex toy since *Kindergarten*.

"I put *Innocence* aside,
for that's how clouds wipe out light."

True: Ophelia came sideways out the womb,
butchering her mother,

and half-strangling her own self.
Hers is a downfall lesson:

To go to bed a wild thing,
contriving *Filth* and *Plague*—

the Nana of Naw Leens—
with incomparable snowy skin—

garmented only in sunlight
and/or cigarette smoke—

but lips and tongue kept cat-clean
by licking toilet seats and bowls.

VI.

I spy in her *Malevolence*
camouflaged as *Indolence,*

her vagina incubating razors.
She awards me a sunburst smile,

But she's as deferential
and as arrogant as worms.

She is a successful tart—
a prize octoroon—

unless she be caught with a black crow
affixed, jerking, in her white, pussy jaws.

[Fort Lauderdale (Florida) 28 *avril* / *Nisan* mmxv]

Ophelia Answers Bellocq[*]

"**H**arlots" help husbands; we dispatch boys home—
To act hale hubbies, pleasing their plain wives,
For each's nailed a "Negress" whose skin is chrome—
Blackness gone *candidus* (silver). Our lives

As New Orleans "octoroons," shadowy
As *History*, set us tumbling before
Husky drunkards—or straplings—willowy,
Wanting to wanton with a black-white "whore."

Also glimmering in Bellocq's portraits,
We are catastrophic ladies, throbbing
Before his lens; each face, silver-nitrates-
Splattered, shattering the *Race* he's daubing.

(Whoever else could have been the result
Once a Jesus lookalike's loins did thrust
Into a slave Madonna's black-fringe pelt,
Save ourselves? Acid-bleached bloodlines; each cussed!)

The bedroom backdrop is always chocolate,
But we're posed with mirrors for face-to-face,
Lewd looks: Ass-up; knees crushing velvet:
But it's Bellocq's gaze that pictures *Disgrace*.

[Whitehorse (Yukon Territory) 19 *janvier* mmxvii]

---

* Cf. N. Trethewey.

Du Bois Critiques Scott Joplin's Treemonisha* *(1915)*

Whatever word, antique, is exhaled,
is new.
The Negro *Genius*—
is, yep, to refurbish.

Europe threw to our slave fathers, mothers—
cracked fiddles, dented valves, brass toys, junked *Music*;
but folks conjoined drumming rhythms—
African "syncopation": *Copacetic*!

Our forebears finagled instruments—
the comic banjo, the minstrel piano—
either one sounding like a crippled frog:
a loping rumble fretting strings.

Charismatic is the boogaloo,
but also tawdry. Gold-fingered
and black-bottomed be the players,
a pack of backwoods rhapsodes.

Ornery horns shimmy in *Exhibition*;
Hear merry-making—jerry-rigged—as in a brothel:
Discordant formations of backbones
meld in hectic *Melancholy*.

See: Nothing "hush-hush" suits Negroes:
Trumpet rumbles, trombone mumbles.
Indignant shrieks break from church pews:
Every true saint collapses, yelling.

---

* *Treemonisha* (1910), an opera by Ragtime genius Scott Joplin (1867–1917), was
published in 1911 and performed in Harlem (New York) in 1915.

If you're in the right kind of congregation,
you hear the angry energy of fingers
exploding along a keyboard:
A piano sounds a windfall of hammers.

Or you hear violins squealing, while
a soloist, her voice all *Affliction* and *Anarchy*,
avalanches sobs, upswelling
to the precise commotion of applause.

Uneasy, but undulant, the black-lung soul singer
projects a left-over lament, and the choir's
qualitative mournfulness
is nothing placid.

Scott Joplin knows all that I speak of,
and yet his ragged time —
his jigaboo doll, Golliwog rhythm —
exudes *Turbulence* Negroes can ill afford.

(I hear *Tremonisha*, and I can see
Nat Turner's black axe
slicing deep into whiteness.
There's peril in Joplin's klaxon opera.)

Maybe the rustic antics
afforded *Treemonisha*
are not unpopular coinage.
But I sniff Dixie's weathered perfumes.

The brisk, whisking notes —
never so sluggish as honey —
the non-ostentatious chit-chat
in the voodoo-besotted lyrics —

possess a strange *Splendour*. But
Joplin's parade —
no, cascade —
of half-yellow, hoochie-coochie gals,

each half-undressed,
and each with a squeaky voice,
leaking air like a farting balloon—
spoils his overtures.

Treemonisha is either bawdy—
or a fraud.
Surely, it's a sweaty trifle—
a lot of copy-cat horseplay—

ceaseless mugging, extravagant trills.
But nothing of the above
salvages the humdrum love story,
nor saves the disappointing repartee.

Treemonisha constitutes
an amiable nightmare—
like ballerinas put to bayonets.
Accuse me of being a dictionary

intellectual,
a critic wielding a hatchet of ink.
No! I've no obsessive *Malevolence*;
nor do I indulge in teasing.

I will refute all Negro composers—
and poets—
who think orchestrated jiggling
and scrambled jive—

or stable whinnies, pig-sty grunts, zoo-cage groans—
amount to *Art*:
Negro *Art* must be a lot less fleshy,
and a lot more bloody.

[**Ottawa (Ontario)** 23 *Nisan* / *avril* **mmxiii**]

Du Bois Screens Birth of a Nation *(1915)*

Guffaw at Sambo with his watermelon in one hand,
a banjo in the other?
Damn well cringe, then, at Nat Turner entrenching his sword
in the rump-split of a whey-face wench!

Eye the memorably Sodom-style incineration of Richmond,
putting Prez Davis to flight and on notice—
despite his elephantine braid and medals.

Note the boinging of his cannonballs
boomeranging back at his ships and trains....

(The flick means to show Davis heroic,
but he's a country-club hoodlum,
who should've been scythed at the heels.)

Griffiths does picture Lincoln as lovingly withered.
His dying enacts the lynching of a stallion,
his hind hooves still pawing the grass,
but with his head contorted,
hanging from a noose,
looped over a branch almost snapping
from his majestic heft.

Next, spy Gus, the sepulchral, silver Mulatto—
as successfully secretive as a lizard—
slithering after vanilla-cream virgins
to offer em a heaving black storm—
and leave lace-edged foam
upon their alabaster-splattered, denuded bellies.

Naturally, he croaks—
a cockroach cracked open by cackling gunfire.
But first he plays wolfshead* to a giglet's** cunny.

[Helsinki (Finland) 11 *octobre* mmxv]

---

* Outlaw.
** A giggling girl's.

From the Diary of William Andrew White, à Lajoux, Jura, France, décembre 1917

I.

A powerful rain
dins down these mountains,
rinses peak snow into hellish streams,
floods gully and pitfall.
Graves yawn open now everywhere.

(Some Christmas....
A *Somme* Christmas....

I'm down to the last crumb of cake—
and no wine—
never wine.)

We dark men are sent to—
are meant to—
stand under this inundation,
this dark, hard-driving wet,
and sweat hard, axing logs,
our drenching making harder the drudgery,
but also making slippery the axes,
so that it's harder to make a dent
in the liquefying woods,

and easier to make a dent in your own legs—
or a friend's—

or in a friend's lagging head.

II.

Aye, we're at loggerheads
with dunderheads—
our Christian brethren Canucks,
here in France, but nigh Geneva—

the Christmas crèches and chocolates—
in the milk-topped, neutral,
unconquerable, Swiss Alps.

We're here because of a battering ram
of *Right*
that let us butt our way
into the White Man's War—
belligerent clans and bellicose states—
to feel the privilege of perishing
to preserve George V,
but also so we can see ourselves stand tall
in our sons' eyes.

I'm here so that Coloured Christian Canucks
are not destitute of a down-home preacher.

I serve the King Eternal—
His fiery Crown,
His blazing Cross.

I have relinquished *Domesticity*
to live fully at ordered *Liberty*,
advancing my *Ministry*,

to even minister to wounds
and ills—

gashes and pleurisy,
pneumonia and tuberculosis—

what kill us —

Canadian Forestry Corps infantry —
the No. 2 Construction troop —

far from the Huns' bullets,
barbed-wire, bombs, bayonets.

III.

But our poor lungs are spent
in the duty to lop forests —
to splinter wood for rail ties —
so porridge-faced *poilu* can choo-choo to the Front
and take potshots at the Krauts

after beer and bacon,
tea and tobacco,
wine and whores.

Irony: We serve where Hannibal romped
and ramped elephants upon Rome —
and where Dictator Napoléon
tamped down Haiti's insurgent L'Ouverture....
But glacial *History* freezes us out.

IV.

The Western Front is due north
of us,
so the bad news trickles south.

I hear it's a mishmash of *Conjectures* —
bad plans, bad commands —

hollers in dirty horse French (*joual*)
or hoarse, hacking Cockney —

so, in a day, thousands prove
incarnately incarnadine—

bomb-blast-earthquake-overthrown,

toppled into mud pits—
curious tombs—

to be chewed open by rats' teeth.

Utmost scarlet brims each trench.

Still holding half a brow,
half a jaw,
one eye,
an abortive helmet sprawls,

or a fragment of a boot
(a shredded sock, some toes attached),

but is multiplied thousandly.

Or one sees gas-poisoned saints stagger,
with bandages for eyes.

Or the half-dead stroll like Zombies,
eyes rigid in sighting an invisible horizon,
heedless of gun flash,
likely shot-deafened,
either courageous fools,
or displaying nerves never sham.

Still, angry grey storms of lead
scatter headless homicides

in Antichrist's charnel-house church—

the ruddy meal of the battlefield—

the narcotic, necrotic feast,
ideal for vermin, *racailles*.

I've heard that shells thud the earth so hard,
corpses jiggle with the shock,

and skeletons protrude suddenly
where earthy fires flue smoke —

and flames limp, sprint, hop, skip —

in a darkling sky;

or the ghastly *merde* of chlorine harries,
worries,
those alive enough to breathe and fall,
wriggling in mire,
facing *Death*'s temporary *Cataclysm*.

All about rampage Vickers guns,
and nervous horses stamping every inch of turf
with shank-spurting gore,

while blasts and detonations
boom and boom and boom....

V.

Imported — as if conquerors — to France,
we black men decamped to this war
with drums barking, bagpipes braying,

first disciplined
by lynch-mob threats and KKK frets,

only to discover our old-new discipline is *Toil*—
unreneged Negro *Slavery*—
to roustabout mid thrusting thorns
and muscle down trees,
pulsing sweat flooding
our backs, our faces.

Until light-bodied mosquitoes
bear us lightly away.

Verily, it's *Disease* that slaughters us:

A brother goes droolingly rabid;
his face springs curving tears;
he lisps prayers and spiels curses;
then succumbs, in fits, urine spasms,
after a rattling whisper.

With mine own tears,
I try to warm his cold, drying bloodstream—
his chilling body—
the wax treasure becoming a cadaver.

(It's good that,
among soldiers,
Tenderness is legal.)

As the African chaplain,
as the single Coloured Officer (thus far)
among the male millions
the British Army fields,

it is my task to prepare us black men

to be *Christian* soldiers,

and deliver *Death* to the Kaiser's kin
and expire, kinless, ourselves,

if so's our *Fate*.

VI.

Today's sky is a vault of water —
and the earth is unfathomable mire;

our dark shadows, flashing more-or-less fasces,
slash the rain.

When it ends, we see the mountains breathe
white clouds and snow,

and as the sun sets like the lit end
of a cigarette,

clouds lap up its light
with grey *Finality*.

Still, I've enough left to write —
this inky candle-light —

such as what lit up Christ,
weeping at Gethsemane,

and soon thereafter
illuminating the Apostles' quills.

Now, we see through a glass, darkly,

until *Death* smashes that blood-stained window
hiding Heaven from us.

[**Kelowna (British Columbia)** 30 *septembre* — *2 octobre* **mmxiv**]

Red Summer Incident, Washington, DC, July 19, 1919

Crucificated upon a park bench,
his body sprawled, decussate in formation.
His head was trivial, vivid, exploded,
due to a freak bullet —
or a deliberate *coup de grâce*,
that punishing kindness.
Morbid and vile were the bleached faces
jostling, impinging upon unhinged *Homicide*
(if possible), infringing upon the black
ex-Doughboy, impertinently,
but pertinently to this set-piece *Annihilation*.
Unsmooth eruptions scattered spittle,
cusses, fists, kicks,
and black body fluids weltered up as weird lather,
or infamous, congealed slather,
in sight of the Washington Monument
and the Lincoln Memorial (its purview),
as the adjacent park re-opened as a balitorium,*
now full of menstruating grass —
red, moist, earthen weather —
where the accused, post-coital darky was now x'd,
his mouth wide open
and his pants pulled down.
The mob addressed him in unrepentant swarms:

Urged on by the Love Police —
rapists with badges, lynchers in officialdom's blue threads —
shades of the now-born *Nation*,
liking to garrote "Big-Black-Cock Golliwogs."

---

* Site of bonfire-lit orgies.

Indeed, the veteran victim had been too violently adult—
his moistures spicing his white lover's sheets,
    her knees folded over the threshold of his shoulders,
or her tits cantering upon his chest,
    this mademoiselle with the larynx of a minx
and the sex of a sphinx,
    his lolling with her in his Great War uniform,
squeezing very pleasing, very shiny breasts.
    (Infinite seemed her pale breasts;
definite his lips upon both.)

    If only he'd not become her lover—
craving always to crowbar open her *queynte*—
    and summon her benign, happy distress,
tonguing her buttery, juicy jellyroll.
    But heroes generally slouch in sluts' beds—
couch and savour this bedroom Vaudeville—
    bawdy;
after all their drastic exertions of the ordered-to-murder body....

    Our sable martyr here in America's white-marble city,
rejecting a burnt-cork Harlem Renaissance—
    any pretence of playing a eunuch Harlequin—
instead, chose to suck whiskey,
    and nice, Caucasian titties;
and so he was carelessly favoured
    to be lugged off a streetcar,
his pants tugged down,
    and uncertain confessions
translated from his gutting shrieks, caterwauling howls,
    and banshee grunts;
to render the Washington Mall
    a delicious morgue—
to join a throng of corpses (charcoal).

Quick! A rope whispered over tree limbs,
then buzzed about his stammering throat;
    his ankles whimpered where grass sighed.
Penitential is the smoke as it nears
    celestial (presidential — if flagging) stars;
and fire comes on roaring as sparks lisp,
    and the pallid, United Statesian soul ebbs from ebon flesh
to navigate aeons of darkmens* sky,
    and the distraught skin disintegrates
to red maggoty embers that soon go grey-white.

    Thus, he's died into the Puritan's only *Truth*:
Horror is Calvinist; *Eros* is catholic.

[**Whitehorse (Yukon Territory) 19 & 20** *janvier* **mmxvii**]

---

* Night.

Saint-John Perse Ponders Antillean Slavery (1924)

The cat-o-nine tails,
that tremendous tarantula,
scuttled, seratching, biting,

over every bony, bonny,
ebony back, or it scrabbled,
tickling a sable fetus,

trickling gore directly
o'er the womb, where huddles
the fresh slavelet — cutlet —

while its sire toils royally
in a sea, a Sargasso,
of sugar cane, pressing out

gold pulp muck-thick;
or dives low to crush cocoa,
to manufacture black sunlight

for the Blakean-dour mills
of Liverpool, Paris, Chicago,
to sweeten the bitter *Despair*

of coal-dusted, white urchins
in *Das Kapital* citadels,
gunpowder-black with police,

where acute *Lying* heaps up lucre.
Tis better to have black serfs*
than dead white kiddos....

---

* "Unkillable," sayeth Pound.

Ugly to the ultimo, masters
be factory bosses now,
elaborately hideous.

Yet, our "Standard of Living" —
is our *Gold Standard* —
a dewy manure pile of greasy cash,

the booty got from helter-skelter
homicides, the salty *Comedy*
of assembly-line, up-skirt *Gropings*....

Each shambling, palm-tree Midas —
selects suggestive tools
to dig out an eye,

to pincer a dead babe out a twat,
to rip up a backside so bad,
it looks a manic sheet of *Ragtime* notes.

I bet that whips poured down in waves,
scrawling an Apocalypse opus
where blood came crooked, twinkling,

and black-robed patricians took balm —
the homely *Treasure*
of the open-policy *Sex*.

View each plantation as once a dainty,
if painterly *Hell*,
echoing the hissing, alabaster lays

of Athens and Rome,
save with the provincialism of suburbs.
The baroque fact is,

every plantation was a dramatic cash-register
(with gimcrack sobs molesting conversation
slave gabble trifling with *Grammar*).

Each sugar-cane field was, I wager,
a petulant *Paradise*,
wafting the perfumes of Capri

and the acrid bull-stench of Arles,
and branding each pallid visage
with disgusting rust stains,

or plumping guts on an unloved menu
of rum and tears,
so that black babes and elders

drowned in internal piss puddles,
amid the septic silence
of yam-patch graveyards....

Should I enumerate the slaves
turned grimy phantasms, skinny relics,
in exquisite scraps of burlap,

moaning as they sweep blades gainst cane?
Should I catalogue *Catastrophe*,
or write up the hyacinth bastion

that is a gibbet or a guillotine,
viewed at twilight?
Slavery is a sunken ship,

not worth dredging up.
Anyway, the macabre teamsters —
with all their suspect *Frivolity* —

are also disappeared now,
like the erotic jottings of Austen,
or the scrofulous squibs of Pushkin;

but chalk children hold the *Profit*
in safe-deposit boxes
and make casinos out of banks.

But, such is *History*:
A scythe that gives no warning cough
as it downsizes slaves to *Capital*.

[Aeropuerto Internacional de Cancún (Mexico) 10 *septembre* mmxv]

T.S. Eliot Translates Saint-John Perse (1924)

The ocean's grave temper retorts immortally sordid,
whether tides surge at us with heady roaring
or their whining echoes dinning mosquitoes.

The Caucasian, cotton-soft masses —
the crumbling brilliant clods of cloud —
lurk ephemeral and irregular as smoke.

They are the true livestock, slave cargo,
adrft in the universal vacuum that constitutes the *Sea*
or *History*, that sound thunderous, vacuous *Theology*.

The talk of *Equality* this and *Equality* that,
so that Golliwog can bed Marie Antoinette
is a trifling parley that renders our *Supremacy*

—rich, white, blueblood, male—*Kaputt!*
If Darwin is the modern Plato, we must
shutter the grisly *Comedy* that is every *Revolt*.

[Montréal (Québec) 12 *septembre* mmxv]

T.S. Eliot se traduce San Juan Perse (1924)*

El mal genio del océano está inmortalmente sórdido,
sea que las mareas nos agitan con un fuerte rugido
o sus estruendosos ecos gimoteando zancudos.

Las caucásicas, masas suaves de algodón—
los brillantes terrones desmenuzados de nube—
son efímero e irregular como el humo.

Ellos son el ganado verdadero, cargamento esclavo,
gastado en el vacío universal que es el *Mar*
o *Historia*. De qué sirve la *Teología* atronadora.

El habla de la *Igualdad* este y la *Igualdad* aquella,
para que Golliwog puede estar con Marie Antoinette
es una conversación sin importancia que hace nuestra *Supremacía*

¿—rico, blanco, sangre azul, varón—*Arruinado*?
Darwin es el Plato moderno, y debemos
prohibir la comedia espeluznante que está en cada *Motín*.

[Montréal (Québec) 12 *septiembre* mmxv]

---

* Trans. James Eugene Lindsey.

Colette: Interview Re: "Willy" (1928)

I.

Not shy at 14, I was a black-haired girl
with a rambunctious mouth,

and I was milky in flat, child belly,
and creamy in nymphet breasts

(two petite tits like neoclassical domes
with nipples like melted crucifixes).

So, when 30-year-old Willy leered,
"Don't splay half-dressed dolls about,

"for it hints at naughty doings,"
I hissed, "Piss off, *stronzo*, or kiss me!"

See: I never expected *Romance*—
to frolic amid lilies and toadstools

like a fey, Pre-Raphaelite *faerie*.
My métier was *Theatre*, that scruffy

showcase—the strokes, titters, jiggles,
of a Moulin-Rouge "Venus Hottentot,"

and I had, congenitally, a genteel
passion for man-pleasing, female *Vice*.

I've never been one to hesitate.
My adolescent fingers fumbled

to get his erection in my jaws:
but the *Achieve is* "the thing."*

(His scrotum was like bulging, ivory tiles
craquelure-scored;

his "faucet" was creamy silver.)
Neutrality is for corpses:

I let him take me down, master me:
He fucked me like a cop fucks a cheerleader.

II.

After his initial, disgorged whiteness,
Willy's sex assumed a gruesome softness.

I figured his male wilting was *Malice*,
but I didn't yet grovel for a "bull-dyke" Sappho.

I desired savage postures, a humid bed,
sheets as clammy as slime.

But Willy was a man made buxom by fat—
an obesity also internal, muddy, congestive.

His finicky "tea-spout," going limp,
set him slobbering, depressed at this *Collapse*.

Yet, he was still very charming,
if physically dissatisfying,

and I was extremely beautiful,
though extremely slender,

---

* Cf. G.M. Hopkins.

and so we arranged an alliance wherein
he took credit—thus monetizing—my pen,

as if he had gone into convents and hiked
schoolgirls' skirts and licked their cunnies.

But his white-glove *Trade* was opium,
and Willy lived for showbiz *Gentility*,

so he jubilated in salting away my sugar—
as soon as I got any—

to splurge on stretched-out horses at races
or on a saucy *macédoine* of vineyards.

He did command top sums for my pharmacy
Virginity, the papered-over, pubescent pudenda,

re-broken in every new saga that got sold.
Our sales parley was sneers slid through smiles.

III.

But our *Love* grew as tiresome as a crucifixation.
His treacly sweat hurt me as bad as acid.

Willy took on the consistency of a moist crust.
I began to resent our *garçonnière*.

Our marriage became my feminine tomb—
chilly with the sulky muteness of the dead.

I could no longer tolerate Willy's pretense
of authoring a juvenile's pornography.

I was extraordinarily miserable.
But his showy penmanship was lionized.

No better than an ornery, senile voyeur,
his breath rattled like the leaves of *Mein Kampf*;

his whisper-lisping breath vented
a heart most natural to a snake-pit.

I could not carry any further
that absurdly toxic bacillus.

Better that I slough him off—into the grave,
Let him lounge there a putrid sore.

[Halifax (Nova Scotia) 18 *septembre* mmxv
& Enfield (Nova Scotia) 19 *septembre* mmxv]

Garcia Lorca, Harlemite (1929)

I pass through wallpaper-peeling pubs,
pass out in speakeasy Bohemia
(Harlem's Charleston-themed ruckus),

where onyx whores croon spirituals
twixt *Trigonometry* of gin
and chocolate-charring tongues.

My pillow summons *Unconsciousness*—
refuge from expense-account luncheons
with pensive mobsters,

a High Society of racketeers,
those pitiful, white-collar thugs—
Wall Street's suicidal trumpeters

who crowd each mackerel-scent brothel
with pepper-pungent tommy-guns
and coltish, jolting cusses.

Do I treasure the burnt-coffee aroma
of whisky and sperm and twat?
This be Harlem, the off-beat

sanctuary of on-the-beat Negroes—
the jazzers, the prissy punks;
Hughes' world is here:

A tangle of bitches
in a bath of ale;
that race of smutty sluts

whose staccato guffaws puff out smoke.
Mr. Langston Hughes is the Negro poet,
and a Commie faggot,

as I am the Gypsy poet
and an anti-Fascist faggot....
Our pens are best bayonets, not scalpels.

Whatever morals *Christianity*
pumps into us, *Machismo* dumps out.
Hughes is peculiar eyes

and a puffy body.
No one looks like us—
neither in eyes nor cheekbones;

nor does sex like us—
like a critic penetrating an author.
Our *Poesy*'s cut to pieces

by censors' scissors.
A drastic successor to Whitman,
Hughes overdrinks in his black beret

as he denounces Munich beer vapours,
that fastidiously *louche* moustache....
No humdrum typewriter is his.

He casts both Roosevelts
as reptilian swine,
snapping at twinkling, gold-dusted meals—

their grandiose *Consumption*
of plasma-sullied cocktails, rattail meat chunks;
and he i.d.'s cops as human hyenas,

those credited with bullet wounds
that mirror buttons—
flesh unlocked and closed up,

opening up, scarlet again,
either upon entry at a blind pig
or exit at a morgue.

He jingles: No broken-down poet
in a broken-up school.
His Harlem's a jungly-vicious, Jungian nymph,

some gum-chewin harlot soon stuffed in a palace;*
an unusually undulant woman
who digs *hombres* huffin at her privates.

We tire of wronged poets — spawn
of a failing Negroid Renaissance, sepulchral,
Harlem become the hustler's Athens.

[**Tulum (Mexico) 8 & 9** *septembre* **mmxv**]

---

* Cf. Edward VIII & Mrs. Simpson.

Apropos *Nancy Cunard (ca. 1929)*

I.

Wind twangs through rigging, sifts through hair,
thwacks through canvas topping lifeboats.
Smoke, dark and silver, smacks against iron stars,
smirches a tawdry moon.

The ocean groans like a train.
(All roots are sea routes —
the roots and routes of rain.)

I can smell the bow slinging brine
as the liner jackknifes currents,
this sable Atlantic whose ballast is lumps —
clumps —
of ice that seem to swoop up at us outta fog.

(Vast, silvery explosions of churn
at the stern.)

Cap'n must exercise *Caution,*
if we're not to be spiked by broken glaciers,
downcast in murk,
slid down to sea-bottom silt,
like doomed, damned *Titanic.*

II.

As Samuel Cunard's granddaughter —
heiress to a shipping-line fortune,
it'd be a right, ironic headline,
were I to plunge fathoms down th'Ethiopian Ocean.

But though I ship often from U.K.
(oh, the *Grief* that is England's shoreline)
to U.S. and back,
yet never pausing in Halifax,* Nova Scotia,
whence Grampy Sammy hailed,
out that damp, clammy climate,

"Decadent," I'm no welcome descendant.

III.

The scandal is: I've been, I am,
engorged with *Blackness*....

My grandee clan protests my "incisive filth."
But our *Wealth* is an embalming miasma.

My *Abundance* is Henry—
Hank—Crowder—
Negro saxophonist,
jazzman,
whose laughter burps claps of *Joy!*

His chalk-white "concubine"
(as you may denominate me)—
I find nothing iffy about us.

Exasperatingly sensual,
Hank is built like a god.
A voluntary "Negress,"
I feel guiltless, faultless *Exhilaration*.

---

* In Haligonian cemeteries, *the Titanic* graves—
so miniscule—
multitudinous marbles—
still are laid out like store-shelf items—
lots of dainties for earthworms' palates.

(*Treason* of *Love* is *Loneliness*.
Porn is *Comedy* of *Selfishness*.)

My peers cruise the rosé Mediterranean,
snap every amber horizon,

but I love it when I suddenly experience
a moth-like, uneven fluttering,
and Hank spills me down in silk,
then kindly parts my spindly gams,
and feeds his "ebony aristocrat"
into my "ivory guillotine,"
and so we enter a bluesy, earthy Zion.

Aye, I feel like Lady Chatterley,
when Hank's fingers scurry over me,
and I yield instinctively,
while he, black groom, snorts,
trampling down his white bride.

We pale ladies are told to cling to
lanky, cinematic boys,
as wan as light.
But I prefer "unpardonable *Carnality*."

Why should I back my clan's Krugerrand *Apartheid*?

IV.

High up now, a star strikes down.
We barge through squalling, brawling wet—
salty perfume all about.

I've known the salons of Paris—
the saloons of Paris (Texas),
the swishy pricks of London,
the irritatingly greedy insurance agents of London (Ontario)—
all as heartless as a helmet.

I thank heaven for a dark man
who approves my proud *Patrimony*:
Rutting!

Now I traverse the pewter slew,
awaiting the moon-purging sun,
and to leave the curvaceous ocean
and cleave unto a different bucking

as Henry's "Harlem honey."

Lo! The see-through "dusk of dawn"!

[**Edmonton (Alberta) 28** *septembre* **mmxii**]

Nicolás Guillén: The Poetics *(1930)*

*C*omposition is only white *Silence*—
Speech impediments—til black ink hisses,
Sighing language Castiglione-sweet,
And eye and tongue meet on black latitudes,

The lines traversing, versifying blank
Fields, that background gleam—like sunlight sprinkling
A sea. The furrowed sheets where ink congeals
Forward a dynasty—waves—convulsive,

Words now as incarnate as flesh, tiding,
Riding vision and/or *Articulation*,
Advancing in stepping ranks, impressive,
Blackly infiltrating chrome-plated

Space, an open book, its leaves spread, eyes-wide.

[Montréal (Québec) Halloween mmxv]

Nicolás Guillén: la poetica (1930)*

La scrittura è solo *Silenzio* bianco –
Impedimento al linguaggio—finché il nero
Inchiostro sibila, lingua dei sospiri dolce afrodisiaco,
E lingua ed occhio s'incontrano a latitudini nere.

Versi in moto, che scavano la vacuità
Dei campi, quel lontano bagliore—come il sole che spruzza
Un mare. I fogli solcati su cui si rapprende l'inchiostro
spingono avanti una dinastia—ondate—convulse,

Le parole, ora, fattesi carne, ebullienti,
Visione al galoppo e/o *Articolazione*,
Incedono inquietanti nel ronzio dei ranghi,
E nere penetrano lo spazio placcato al cromo,

Un libro aperto, squadernato, con gli occhi sgranati.

[Montréal (Québec) Halloween mmxv]

---

* Trans. Fausto Ciompi.

Jean Toomer Seduces Georgia O'Keeffe (1930)

A troglodyte *Art*—unwomanly, animal—
    your primal inklings—
white bones, gold light, the loaf of a skull,
    the coal gleam of buzzard feathers—
this diorama of discards:
    This is your *Aesthetic*, or *Addiction*,
a poisonous *Passion*—
    to pencil *disjecta membra*,
materials that have suffered a jinx—
    such as being half this, a quarter that,
or an eighth of one colour, and a sixteenth of Negro
    (my textbook *Dilemma*—
how to divvy up my identities)....
    Am I more poet than platypus,
or a monster mongrel, Georgia,
    less pure than a sun-blanched bone?
I signal (preacheth Spengler)
    The [seminal] *Decline of the West*....

Georgia, I'd like wine all the time—
    nothing but wine—
to spit at Spengler and spite Gurdjieff:
    to live so that *Poetry* births *Poetry*,
just as grapes birth wine.
    I'd like our sheets—pages, canvas,
bedsheets (!)*—to reek of wine and spilled milk,
    while you'd waft the tequila aroma
of Tex-Mex cacti desserts,
    the mescal scent of the grub
and the cactus,
    while forgetting the pinched face

---

* This exclamatory sign represents the penis broaching the vagina.

of photog Stieglitz
     (more *sty* than *glitz*)—
all his patchwork snaps of George-Steeves-style, severe nudes
     (a *khuligan** harem),
their half-smoky, unmerited beauty,
     such indelicate ladies, used to manure,
and his pointy gaze
     coloured by his *Schadenfreude*,
his Gothic ethic.
     His are engravings to gravely injure—
all his Medusas with malicious teeth,
     the involuntary ugliness of their trysts.
His *Art* is a shroud for skeletons;
     or it is stuffing for cut-open statues.

Don't think me as dark and brutish
     as Aaron, Caliban, or Othello.
I have a whole, different *Interior*.
     In our syphilitic era of yapping-dog Hitler
(that fulfillment of Spengler,
     that antithesis of Gurdjieff),
our lovemaking could conjure
     a ribald, rabid, sodden *Innocence*,
an astonishing juncture of skin, hair,
     follicles, breath, pulsations,
akin to the unapologetic *Eroticism*
     you locate in a skull
infested by desert sun.
     Why not?
Romance is just a preface to *Rape*;
     Love is misspelled *Lust*,
misplaced *Lust*....
     It's not *Love* that'll embed us;
not *Romance*, but Cro-Magnon crud,
     the drives of predators,
remorseless, pitilessly nihilistic,
     that sets me greedy for *Penetration*,

---

* Russian: Hooligan.

Georgia, primitive; the thought
    of thrusting excites my *Appetite*:
To use our body parts to squeeze out
    Euphoria,
while I'm as iron-hard as a pimp,
    and you're as plastic as a prostitute —
quite capacious (I'm sure), flexible,
    in pose, posture,
your ivory skin mating my ochre-tinged accents,
    as we lurch — like apes — gainst each other.

I tell you: Your chalk-tint rump's
    a gold mine for a black man,
a platinum *Treasury*: You're such a hottie!
    I'll daub your hair-fringed cunt with semen.
I'll glug black coffee
    whilst ogling your ivory sheen,
then I'll milk your sex vehemently,
    then spunk glop upon your face,
so that you taste my *Alienation*
    in the somber, sobering kiss,
we'll share, holed up in hotel rooms,
    as I drill you hard, just for *Fun*.
It'll be theologically repugnant, maybe,
    but artistically expedient, eh?
To be enthroned martially upon you —
    Georgia —
after having been taunted in Georgia
    (for trying to teach — *liberate* — Negroes) —
is necessary; to see your face
    become immediate debris
as our orgasm shatters home,
    and you loll like an emptied paint tube —
like one of Stieglitz's squalid nudes —
    in my vulpine, copulating *Vengeance*,
being an octoroon, just one-eighth "black,"
    really, by any objective measure,

for whom *Schandung,**
　　staged against white females,
makes good sense, given that white males
　　have *carte blanche* to defile black ladies.

Drinking is demonized presently,
　　under the Constitution,
and that's okay, for I'm seldom totally sloshed;
　　I know it's possible
to develop *Love* and not brook *Brutality,*
　　for, Georgia, you've an awkward *Elegance,*
like a ballerina in a pig sty;
　　and you crave to play out *Treason*
against your slyly sleazy husband,
　　and reveal your jumbled-up,
tumble-down *Love* for me,
　　whose face is *Anonymous*
and whose *Fate* is amnesia,
　　though I insist that all our significant feelings
are inherited from *Art,*
　　and are not inherent in our hearts.

Poetry is always unspeakable explicit, anyway:
　　A visceral tongue in a ruthless mouth.

[Halifax (Nova Scotia) 7 *décembre* **mmxv**
& Funchal (Madeira) 14 décembre mmxv]

---

* German: Rape.

To All Historians (or "The Bastille Concerto"*)

By Julien Benda (1933)

Y̲ou rank the alabaster statues of bandits—
Caucasoid cannibals—
Rasputin-like Caligulas, bad clerks, mad kings—
as untroubled, as untroubling....

But tethered to every white throne
withers a coffle of black slaves
(or blacks stacked like cordwood—
accumulated kindling to fuel *Profit*)....

If we're honest intellectuals,
we'll strip Elizabeth I of her spurious *Virginity*,
her hymen that's a cannibal's "cherry on top,"
her purple robes daubing floors mauve, bloody....

Factual Shakespeare and scientific Spengler is Dante.

Historians, our *Age* persecutes us,
for you refuse to remember
how the King's velvet robes
got purchased *via* the toddler's buggery,

or how "Liberal" Constitutions—
got from sausage-making parliaments—

all emerge fecal-stained
and gore-smeared
and reek like garbage—
due to black gold turned greenbacks.

---

* Cf. X.

Too often, you stroke your own tongues,
to avoid facing up to ass-backward *Carnage.*

The result?
Musso, Huey Long, Adolf—scoffing, guffawing.

[**Funchal (Madeira) 18** *décembre* **mmxv**]

Nancy Cunard's Love Poem (1934)

Now, Henry—Hank—snaketh unto
my jellied labyrinth;

his turgid *Négritude*
jets chalk throughout, infusing

sunlight-naked quarters—
the urgent guts of this taut, learnèd bitch.

We'd be horrid, wedded:
Spiteful quibbles would render useless
my *Beauty*—
as if I had a dried-up slot;
and/or unwelcome jealousies
would issue in unfamiliar vomit—

a hot, white sauce—
il miele del diavolo—
to desecrate my clean, angelic belly.

What is our lava value?
Does he insinuate honey
or only I?

Make me a proxy wife—
to be sexually demeaned, destroyed,
in feats of intense *Integration*.

[**Buffalo** (**New York**) 3–14–15 (π)]

El Poema de Amor de Nancy Cunard (1934)*

Ahora, Enrique — Rique — deslizando hasta
mi laberinto de gelatina;

su turgente *Negrura*
chorrea gis en todo, infundiendo

cámaras desnudas de rayos del sol —
las agallas urgentes de esta ramera, tensa y aprendida.

Seriamos horribles, casados:
Problemillas malévolos harían inútil
mi *Hermosura* —
como si tuviera un espacio seco;
y/o celos desagradables
emitiría un vomito no familiar

una salsa blanca, caliente —
la miel del diablo —
para profanar mi barriga limpia y angelical.

¿Qué es nuestro valor de lava?
¿Se insinúa la miel
o solamente yo?

Hazme una esposa apoderada —
para ser sexualmente degradada, destruida,
en actos de *Integración* intensa.

[Buffalo (Nueva York) 3–14–15 (π)]

---

* Trans. James Eugene Lindsey.

À Tempio Malatestiano (Rimini)

By W.E.B. Du Bois

I.

The blood-shitting habit of Sigismondo
(*World Protector*)—
his intestine-wrenching lust for *War*—
maketh me cringe.

Maniacal, the Renaissance rebel
who did radically slap down a pope
forecasts Mussolini,

this larger-than-life gangster—
his brain a machine-gun mechanism.

II.

Th'adolescent Bishop cometh unto him
to threaten *Damnation*,
but Sigismondo offered his own *Salvation*:

Ostentatious, public *Buggery*—
to lampoon the lad
with a human harpoon....

His troop cheered on the frivolous *Violation*,
jeering at the bent over, bottom-fouled Bishop—

jeered as the lad whimpered....

III.

Malatesta (Evil-head) plotted to post
his own denominated pontiff
on St. Peter's throne:

A paid peon to license his
ejecting red fluid from enemy necks,
projecting vanilla milk onto ladies' faces,

to show off the Papacy
as a common *Commodity.*

Raunchy, touchy, a normal "madman,"
he'd be happy to swallow whole a pope —

to enact his prophetic, black-shirt seizure of Rome.

IV.

S.M. (Sado-Maso)
ain't one of the kneeling faction,

but is obscenely spleenful:
Plying *Rape* and supplying *Reaction*
be Sigismondo's *Scripture*
(S.S.) —

to mould flesh into bug cake,
to be as irreligious as a tiger....

V.

Not to like his face?
Who don't like his face?

Oil, nickel, guns, coffee, chocolate, tobacco,
be pumpin out soon—

The prevailing momentum of Europe's *History*—
from peasants vs. popes
to clerics vs. kings—
is,

to cannibalize every culture
that got no cannon—

gut every *Civilization*
that got no gunpowder.

[**Rimini** (**Italy**) **8** *novembre* **mmxiv**]

Ezra Pound @ Rimini, 1935

I.

Now, a black cat ogles me —
a "crypto-Fascist" poet —
or merely an Americo-Italo poet —
as democratic as is Jefferson
(and/or Mussolini?)....

Well, the cat remains blackly opaque
in its oblique *Recognition*....

(But stashed in an ecclesiastical corner,
forging a well-fed shadow,
eyeballing the Fascist altar
for Italy's African slain,
there's the rotund, *Niggerati* inmate —
the profoundly well-rounded Du Bois —
bracingly cerebral —
who, like me, conjured a squib
for Nancy Cunard's seven-seas-spanning encyclopedia,
Negro [1934].

I cast my hat brim below my brow.
If he i.d.'s me, that darkie, aristocratic Commie
will scowl and berate —

play the upper-crust "Harvahd" man —
shades of Ol' Possum* —
underrating
a no-name-college Master of Arts.)

---

* T.S. Eliot.

II.

Sigismundo—"Sidge"—
was Caesar enough—
man o' war enough—
to steal Pletho's bones outta Greece

and crook em in a marble crypt
on the temple's right
(as ye enter),
so the prayerful philosopher
could have his remaining *Constitution*—

the bony alphabet of his corpus—

persist among a people—
the Riminese—

as free as the sea's insurgent waves.

III.

And how else would Ixotta
not be an unknown bed-warmer,
if *not* for Sidge's bankrolling of portraits?

Who else to divulge (Ixotta
as quixotic)
Venus,
if not divine Apollo's heir?

IV.

Sidge's jaunty suffering prefaces
Le Grand Guerre and Muss's services—
surviving the trench holocaust,
the miniature clouds suffocating
or blistering lungs
in *Obeisance*
to Great Power machinations....

It taketh a Great Man to break free
of "free" press (*Propaganda*)
and "free" enterprise (*Fraud*) —
the warmongers and high-finance punks —

and refute the nightly *Fear*
of tomorrow!

V.

I laud Muss as a breathing *Principle* —
as commandeering and as domineering
as Moors running Europe
(after overrunning Spain)....

Surely, he dishes *State* enemies
tureens of castor oil,

or baptizes em in gasoline
and lets fire canonize em;

or he chops em into poxy fragments;
or torches their redoubts to ash....

VI.

Sidge was the righteous precedent
for Muss, his successor:

To abort moochers —
sugarcoat their peppery or salty *Irreligion* —

and broadcast their mobster screams,
their epic whining.

Si, to preserve the world for Renaissances
(plural),
arms traders must be castrated —
interest-rate buggerer-uppers must be strung up —

through processes as exhaustive
and stringent
as any *Divorce.*

VII.

To be rid of lice!
To be rid of slimy parvenus!
To be rid of plutocrat-bought "democrats"!

A citizen dreams of a boss of undoubted *Sovereignty*;
whose popular business is mass *Happiness*;
whose glamorous *Sensibility*
echoes Confucius;
and whose occasions of *Artifice*
are correctly punitive

(thus the *Majesty* of executions).

Regard how all Italy eats out of Muss's hand;
that right hand that delivers wheat seeds, lemon acreages,
meaty oxen, plus disorienting wine, vineyard milk,
destabilizing honey, silvery-sequined fish,

and people's automobile crafting even
(by *fiat*).

Regard how gilded foes
get packed into black trenches
and coffined in lye:
Their last sight is dirt.

Sidge / Muss:
These are agile identities.

VIII.

Riminese, as my *Opera Omnia* opens
to *History*,
I exalt Sidge as the first
Romagnolo man got from garden-springing muck,

who rendered bishops bum-boys
and fertilized nuns,

who intuited that Venus, Cleopatra, Bathsheba,
are vivid goddesses

and attests that each such vamp —
reborn in Calabria —
is *settimocielo.*

[Montréal (Québec) — Cornwall (Ontario), VIA train 063 — Car 6, Seat 4C:
21 *novembre* mmxiv]

Bessie Smith's Seminal Blues (ca. 1935)

Won't take no mean bull for my daddy;
Want no cock-jammed-up-his-arse fool.
No cross-eyed, crotchety bull's my daddy;
Nor no blackface, Uncle Tom fool.
Want no jailbird and no bulldog baddy.
Take a snake-hip man with a jackhammer tool!

I puff, sit and piss, and don't give a shit.
Gimme a skanky missy that's skinny.
I slug back vodka; I don't take no shit!
I like a gin-white belle who's spinny:
While her jaws be slurpin my tits,
I make her twat twist and shimmy.

"What cometh into effect forthwith"
Is pink drawers a-droppin down!
"What cometh into effect forthwith"
Be cum-soaked panties a-tuggin down!
Then apes leap atop each jigglin bitch,
And maggots be the wrigglin spawn.

No one's authorized to screw too much
Or do some backyard diggin.
It's aggravatin disappointment much
To miss out on backyard diggin.
Gimme a sweetheart chocolatiferous,
His right hard candy to get me friggin.

True: I'm an adventurous sistah—
Got a bottomless, uncanny cunt.
I's a rivetingly illicit sistah,
Starvin like a man, slobberin at a cunt.
Shame? Naw, I'm a shameless resister:
Snatch all the grinning snatch I want.

Lemme fry whorehouse sausage, oysters;
Split white rum with rat's-ass Rastus;
Want no listless kisses outta cloisters,
Just pink pussy and black-ass Rastus.
I'll have that Lesbo slurpin oysters,
While pimps clap, happy as anarchists!

Bring on *Mayhem*, V.D., Champagne —
All the vomit in the wake.
Bed buddies' keisters blaze with *Pain*:
They mistake vomit for milkshakes.
I like boys with The Grand Canyon for brains
And thighs like sidewindin rattlesnakes.

Serve me a gal, Champagne cork popped,
Her disobedient panties bubblin juice.
Bring me a gal, her lips white-sauce-slopped,
Her panties pumpin sweet, shenanigan juice:
Treat that cutie to my big-booty bebop
So she blushes and gushes blues.

[Guelph (Ontario) 1 *juillet* **mmxv]**

Du Bois Protests Italy's Assault on Ethiopia (1935)

"Negroes [suffer] from *Nothingness*."
— Gertrude Stein

I.

To see ugliness in Sade,
to feel ugliness in Eliot,
to hear ugliness in Pound,

vis-à-vis the ceaselessly droning, Latin quarters —
The Vatican, The Sorbonne —
is to understand how arose

black-heart, black-shirt government
in a white-marble state.

Frost is bleak, Eliot frosty —
a fool gabbling Kitchen Dutch,*
prematurely ejaculating whimpers
about "the world's end" —
i.e., the extinction of *Albion*'s axiomatic, albescent *Supremacy*.

That's what Mussolini and Hitler symbolize.

So, Italians, agitated, shake swords at Selassie,

and now phalanxes go into abbatoirs —
where scythes (half mandibles)
swing with the pendulum gravity
of Poe-*louche*, Poe-designed, horizontal guillotines.

---

* Pidgin English.

The sky over Ethiopia is burnt-cork
because Musso's bomblets—
cluster-clouds of poison gas—
as radioactive as God's visage—

blaze the dry-grass huts
and incinerate sleeping numbers—
charred characters—
all human characteristics erased.

Skin goes to boiling; it sloughs off the bones.

Deer-coloured Abyssinians—
tawny, chestnut-tint Abyssinians—
die, but fight,
as indignant as pepper,

launching spears *contra* machine-guns.

Partial *Blame* for these pogroms?
Pound! Yeats? Pound!

& Eliot, though he's inapprehensible—
an obscure War Criminal,
camouflaged as an affable banker,

Ol' Possum, obscenely smirking
as *History* advances its obituary
for the final, free, African state.

(No, I don't count Liberia as sovereign.)

This clan of poets backs tacitly the Ku Klux Klan,
hopelessly lisping Christian irrelevancies,
or lustfully barking anthems.

I could give up Shakespeare.
I've given up on Pound.
I give away Eliot.

Indifferent to killing,
they license indifferent killing,
croon unintelligible Eliot's asinine *Grief*,
his fear that Spengler is Socrates.

II.

Oh, the cruelty of the modern poets—
to edit *History*,
black-up or white-out consitutions,
paper over dark-dark hearts,
italicize the globe as Europe's property,
and, in all, act as chaste as corpses!

Well, joint by joint,
this is how the current monsters
got pieced together:
all those elegies decrying
Caucasian *Decay, Devolution, Decadence,*
the downward trajectory of post-Darwin,
animalistic *Theology,*
the tantrums of anthems—

all became instruction manuals

for surplus police stations,
Judas legislatures,
arsonist parliaments,
the actual wreckage of Versailles
and the castration of the League of Nations,

and *Poetry* gone to *Odium* and *Ordure,*

with Sadean governors
constructing Machiavellian prison-camps,
Rasputin palaces,

and according fresh maiming,
new *Mayhem*,
to Africa.

III.

Plunge into the dark abyss of the Occidental classroom,
where chalk eclipses *Blackness*,
squawking,
and *Reason* vanishes
into either foggy *Erasure*
or swirls of smudged figures,
squealing.

Here's where scribblers, in training for *Music*,
get torn up,
trying to score *Deutschland*
Dixieland.

IV.

I recall 1929 —
the routine swarm of bankers
leaping out Manhattan skyscrapers —

to make a big splash,
bellyflops, ruddy —
after turning investment portfolios
into sieves of red ink.

Economic History is *Ado* and *fuss* —
Adolf versus Dreyfuss —
the 20th century bled into by the 19th.

Indeed, Victoria mothered an Empire of Rippers —
imperialists, promiscuous capitalists —
permitting child labour as a form of sex-work.

No wonder the theologians can't explain
Versailles or Ethiopia:
They are still investigating Golgotha—
and the unanswerable torching of Alexandria's Library.

I am sure of this:

Musso and Adolf will die
to get swallowed up
in the glittering enigma
of Napoléon's sarcophagus—

for there's no other hiding place for their ilk—
nor for their Lilliputian legislators—
not even in opaque smoke.

Besides, they believe they will mirror
Napoléon's baroque failure—

if not Caesar's conquests.

[Ottawa (Ontario) 15 *janvier* mmxvii
& Whitehorse (Yukon Territory) 18 *janvier* mmxvii]

Ellington Tours Africville, Nova Scotia (1936)

There's a plain white clapboard church—
Seaview—
boasting an oil of a fat Mary and a skinny Christ—
a black Christ silhouetted in gold leaf—
each flanked by double-gold angels upthrusting spears;
and the Negro King of the Orient sports
gold braid and an orange halo;
and the white pine cross centring the church
is topped with a gold crown....

At my *amoureuse* Mildred Dixon's cradle,
always some buddy hoists a sax,
serenades the muddy shore outdoors,
that salty shore Nova Scotia—
fringed by seaweed as ochre as shoe polish,

while gals—
nice, round, and brown—
these allocated nymphs—
flock about,
in foggy dawns that bird song clears.

Nigh the Dixon folks,
find a boat gone to pure ribs and rust;
a salty lagoon;
the clandestine shock of Newfie—
or Saint-Pierre-*et*-Miquelon—
moonshine....

No matter where I wander,
there's a surcharge for each Negro breath;
and one can't sever verse
or stanza
from congregations dependent on wine;
bios that are long on *Onanism*
and loud on *Cynicism*;
tony drinks toted by anonymous mistresses.

But I pleasure in Africville:
Watch skirts tease ultra-slender gams,
see lightning splash against windows,
hear chatter, titters, giggles, guffaws.

No wonder my piano explodes in Africville!
My keyboard jumps more thoroughly jungle—
Not so much jingly or jangly;
and I excavate "Il Cielo in Una Stanza"—
from a "House of the Rising Sun"....

(My lady's a graceful, buxom, Bauhaus nude,
I gotta sit to caress.)

Listen:
Water slams a cliff;
chunks thud free—*blam!*—
a gigantic clod crashes crushingly down;
hits waves, aiiieeeees like an orgasm.

Lurching pieces of new music
irritate the sleek, slick water
of pedestrian, audience *Expectation*.

That's my shining burden:
To upset static states
("united" and/or otherwise).

To be vatic!

Let white boys stumble mid the earthquake:
My revolutionary keyboard auguring *Liberty*—
a world wherein black ants polish off sugar.

I don't sell aspirins.
My melodies ain't handshakes.
I put out sounds that gut monarchs.

I disinfect; I don't decorate.
I turn a grudge match into a top-dollar gig.

To deliver *Truth*—
a scream out a prison cell;
an operatic aria of knives.

[**Tulum (Mexico)** 7 *septembre* **mmxv**]

Mao Authors "On Contradiction" (1937)

To *Hell* with dusty priests who whine!
We want landlords shot down,
so their pink guts burst out.

When we stab open a landlord's paunch,
note his eyes's eerie, exciting whiteness
as a profane plum wine exits his mouth.

Each nauseating cockroach dies with a grimy face,
an undying stench, because

we victims suffer *Poverty* as a belt hissing,
twisting, bucking, gainst the skin,
buckling where the leathered *Pain* strikes.

(Anyway, why must China buy pricey offshore wheat,
costly offshore rice?)

So Communists decapitate capitalists,
those who shunt nations into Auschwitz —
black boots prowling for gold-star innocents —
black scythes sighing as yellow stars fall....

Besides: Ain't no *Amnesty* for *Ugliness!*

Imperialists treasure *Genocide;*
it yields Canadas of plunder.
Their spades pan for gold
among jumbled skulls
and shattered teeth.

We hear the satanic clank of their armies—
their clinking shovels tootling up boodle.

We scamper em; caper em like capons....

Religion is a whore;
Finance is a whore:
Every chapel is a whitewashed toilet.

[**Windsor (Ontario)** 4 *mars* **mmxvi**]

Paul Robeson Salutes the U.S.S.R. (1937)

I.

Dat "Ol Man River,"
bridging Abe Lincoln and Mark Twain—
the Mississippi, turgidly sluggish
with lynchees' dissolving flesh,
and/or pernennially ruddy with tobacco juice,
sable ichor,
and apple brandy,

explains why "Missouri Tom Idiot,"
implants a garbage-shored Thames
in his *Waste Land*?

Nothin squeamish about the Dixie/Midwest river:
Confed corpses slopped up there,
slampy,* befriending *Fiendishness*—
like the cadavers of Klan pogroms—
suddenly revived and crooning in *Show Boat* comic-guise.

America is a star-empty night—
and backward, pervert, peevish, can't-do whites—
as feudal as More's *Utopia*.

Leaves of Gress gets inked over as Dante's *Inferno*.

---

* Gooey.

The Yanks are wily brutes—
obeisant to the immemorial *Fraud*
of their religions,
for they think *Salvation*
ballyhoos "Old Mr. Gory"—
Gold—
not "Old Glory,"
and credit themselves citizens
as august as sugar,
but their *History* is *Theft*.

II.

Even if my applause is lonely,
I salute the Soviets;
They're Caucasians who like to throw off chains
and set ballets to the verses of the ingenious Pushkin, *Negro!*

Against the U.S.A.'s worn-out light,
I set the colossal *Glory*
of the U.S.S.R.,
where peasants gorge on obese potatoes, icy vodka,
while conscientiously murderous generals
trust to advance *History*.

Thanks to Lenin, Stalin,
workers rusticate in the ancient Senate
that's the tavern,
and swallow *il vino dei poeti*,
savouring that favoured *Life*.

And they give Ku Klux killers
civilian headstones—
yellow-watered boulders.

Impromptu *Spendour*: The U.S.S.R.!

III.

Buttoned-down murderers: The U.S.A.!

Regard the Bug House that is the White House!
Mad Dog Roosevelt and his Pretty Boy clique!
It's a feces jungle....

Study a warren of hoods, gangstas,
FBI spooks, democratic *Savagery!*

Survey high crimes from low-down bandits—
grimy as Wall Street,
slimy as 42nd Street!

[**Whitehorse (Yukon Territory) 20** *janvier* **mmxvii**]

Louis vs. Schmeling (1938)

By Langston Hughes

Joe's blows arrive from vesuvian depths.
I watch Max's shoes verge on falling —
like feet having a heart attack.
Joey's punches are black coins

slamming a soda counter's
pearl-white dampness.
I observe men's hatted heads
jump and jerk like violin bows

pursuing a swinging jazz score.
Joe's "hooks" grab; his jabs "grope."
Dude emerges as a sassy-ass assassin
set to wallop "infuriatingly"

yet one more "Great White Hope,"
that diplomat shat outta the asshole
of Berlin —
the dopey, Chaplinesque Fascist —

with his flaming tapestries of Nuremburg.
But now comes the breach in the snow:
April! Schmeling squats down like a hen.
Carpet bombings occupy that pale visage;

the goof is sinking in white spirals;
he seems lame, then tumbling, just-so —
like a ripped-apart swan.
Reds spurted in disconcerting flashes.

Now, chattering Segregationists fall mute;
the white canvas becomes a wet, scarlet litter,
bearing up
a thudded down, beaten-nigh-to-death "warhorse."

[**Hull-Gatineau (Québec)** 26 *décembre* **mmxv**]

Harlem Pamphlet (1943)

By Langston Hughes

That skull-gaunt cops presume *Privilege*
To *Murder*, as mourners allege —

To shoot down black boys, not white toughs,
But *kids* (wrists too skinny for handcuffs),

Warns us that white police perceive
Emancipation as a sieve,

Setting too many Negroes free
From slavers' plantations. Cops see

Our *Suppression* as their *Mission*:
Police repeal *Abolition*.

Every shot dead Negro attests
To *Anti-Liberty*'s *Success*.

Every cop who slays a "nigger,"
Rapes *Justice* with gun-snout vigour.

[Ottawa (Ontario) 12 *avril* / *Nisan* mmxv]

Auschwitz II, or Birkenau: A Survey

Incandescent buttercups, deceitful milkweed—
babe-stuffed cattle-cars, hypodermic bullets—
gore-dappled dust, horizonless train tracks—
charred clover, skull-smashed-in heather—
chain-gang cigarette butts, pebble-large tears—
shredded corpses, ground-up rats—
suitcase garbage, sawed-open brains, jailed eyeglasses....

350 acres of *Gehenna*,
300 barracks of troughs and truncheons:

80–90,000 prisoners at any one time,
sometimes exceeding 100,000,

all ranked for flames,

letting Kraut docs finger—
wholesale or piecemeal—

who was to be ash,
who was to first sweat unto *Death*.

(Some carcasses got trundled into woods
and incendiaried there.)

No air in the cattle cars.
(Not an error.)

The Selection Road raced right alongside the rails.
And the outdoor cesspool,

trenchant trenches.

Excrement was exclamation,
unspeakable as maggots.

(Those sick with diarrhea were laid to defecate
on bunks above the healthy.

The bathhouse was bolted, locked.
Always a brand new padlock.
To forbid corporeal *Sanitation*.)

Zakaz Wchodzenia Na Ruiny![*]

Spanish gabled roofs rattled raindrops.

Les Hitlèriens set up slave pens like stockyards.

At *Libération*, the rouge-bearded Red Army
found 7,000 souls,
clad in pyjamas,
shoeless in blizzards.

One Commie whited a black rock, "sloganeering":
Dass Auschwitz nie wieder sei!^{**}

Barbed-wire sifts mosquitoes.
White butterfly traverses steel-mesh fence.

[Birkenau (Poland) 12 *mai* mmxv
& Montréal (Québec) 25 *décembre* mmxvi]

---

* Polish: Keep the fuck off the ruins!
** German: Auschwitz must never happen again!

Addendum to "Pisan Canto" for St. Louis Till

By Ezra Pound

Riddle: St. Till* put on spectacles;
he'd not don any....
Now, he's a spectacular spider

lynched from hemp string.
Campari had metamorphosed he to boar.
He tusked through black rags,

grey undies, to bust open
a trio of Italo cherry-pink slits —
but left one nude, mucky,

and buckled in a tub;
white towels wrung red:
The W.C. looked afflicted

with *Ebola*.
The assault was grisly business:
Forking became stabbing.

Gulps of *aperitif* brought on bile,
and the dark Yank
jammed his oar into the grouse,

up to the hip,
so he was mast to her vessel,
then screwed down scum in her privates.

---

* Cf. Canto LXXVII.

Till made veal of that elderessa;
sank his sap where she stuck soap;
so gore smeared her, besmirching.

The tub was a bog, a sty;
even her old baggy tits
dribbled blood;

lard was her limbs;
a musky scent pervaded panties
Till tore off as if shredding

butterfly wings,
to penetrate cod-cool loins —
Civitavecchia's bitches....

The lady got dug out the bath,
scooped out in a slop pail. So,
Till, the thug, gets a rope

to net his throat,
catch his breath — literally;
one more nigger buck, choked off,

so Pisa echoes Mississippi.
Lew floats now as flotsam
of the "Italian Liberation."

His *Carnage* was not "official."
But expletives squeal in like volume
outta brothel and battlefield.

Decidedly, St. Lew went too far:
Churned three "enemy" twats a *cigaló** tint,
but left the old maid resembling

---

* Mexican Spanish: A small, white coffee with liquor.

an extra large *Gerra de Sangria;*
her plucking must have been a bullfight.
Seriously, a razor scintillated.

Plasma ran like meltwater
from the snowbank corpse,
dissolving under a faucet.

Now, Till's gone where I'll go*.
We'll both be skeletons,
then dug-up bones,

crushed and ground to dust,
to be used to fertilize
graveyards reclaimed as vineyards.

[**Montréal (Québec)** 1 *mars* **mmxv**]

---

* Father to U.S. Civil Rights martyr, Emmett Till (1941–55), Louis Till is buried in Grave 73, Row 7, Plot E, in Oise-Aisne American Cemetery at Seringes-et-Nesles, France.

The Autobiography of "Detroit Red" (1946)

Papa, Garveyite—that staple onyx—
hosted the brunt of Klan *Maiming*—
the depressing shimmer of bony robes, scorching torches*....

And we got summoned to the spastic, casket opening
to view the cold drainage,
his saint's *ichor*—

his sliced off trunk,
limbs dirtied by slippage neath the trolley,
in the nigger-hating street;

his unhospitalized life coursing;
his closed mouth bubbling crimson
onto his ebon.

He'd been an august, robust *Threat*;
now he was positively diminished *Nature*.
A hearty *Upset*, an inversion: His *Death*.

The Life Insurance Company ruled
Papa'd played "an exaggerated suicide,"
and nixed the *Policy* dollars.

Mom's complexion mirrored a boiled egg.
She now studied white people thoroughly;
could spy the penis a Klansman

shelters behind his smile,
desiring to make her sheets his kennel,
given her husband's crushing

---

* Cf. Plath: "Black / Mind against all that white."

under icy flames and steel-wheel sparks,
his damnation to a mirage due to *Damage*.
Her prayers enunciated puke.

How could she allocate justly
our *Welfare* meal?
How could we retaliate

for Earl Little's bedraggled corpse?
Behead throats? Decapitate lungs?
Replace his dotty epitaph

with the incisive pressure of a broadsheet obituary?
I chose an ideal, Hollywood stardom:
To be a racketeer,

to transfigure Malcolm Little —
a lawyer wanna-be —
into that dropout *bandito*, "Detroit Red."

I seized on the freedom to gaze at Lake Erie waters —
as shining and fresh as April —
but do creature-pleasing, feel-good *Crime*,

while maintaining a spine of ice:
To be bitter in my *Splendour*!
To manhandle platinum dugs;

prove that a shoe helps in trampling a throat;
know how to appeal and how to appal;
stunt my "johnson" about a twat;

enjoy the pure groans of a doll's twitching.
My slang flowed vivid and acidic as graffiti.
I recognized that *Civilization* counts on *Silver*,

never a steeple, never a school.
I became as sovereign as any restaurant patron:
To be destructively digestive....

To rivals, I'd be as blunt and backward
as is a toilet, flushing:
To leave a chump as broken

and as empty as an ellipsis....
To be big on *Sex* and short on *Love*.
I knew I'd enjoy sleeping all day

and feasting, then diddling white witches all night:
To close my eyes to each ghetto's
provincial *Squalor*, eh?

At my height, I boasted a machine-gun,
and I was trigger-happy, dapper,
no jigaboo bugaboo:

"Detroit Red." The moniker
allies me with Mao and Red China:
Commies also can't stand to hear the *Gospel*

rolled out with guitars and pig guts.
How could I not be authentically
drastic, given self-taught rationales for *Hate*?

My mama's in a madhouse,
accepting antiquated lobotomies;
and brothers have gone so insane

with "nationalized" Islam,
they think themselves Negro Mormon
squares: same shoes, shirts, suits, undies.

(I snatched up a Qu'ran in a liquor store:
That is either a sign—
or it's *Dissonance*.)

I had a hair-trigger temper:
I got into the rackets by osmosis.
Met up with a raunchy, foul-mouth hustler—

Shorty,
whose *Obscenity* be his up-front *Freedom.*
Next, I fell in with Sophia—

slutty beauty,
a glistening, tight-cunt *putain*—
a pussy afire, a snatch ablaze:

She be surreally sexy—
a big-titted, big-butt belle—
my white rubber doll—

my locked-down whore.
Sophia plied *Sex* currency for me,
Her nipples erect under the bossy fluorescence

of streetlamps.
I felt unyielding, unclean, unforgiving.
She was humid, a groaning anchor

to those who got purchase,
mastered her bones,
as marble white as *Death,*

or tried her Virgin Mary-miraculous *vagine.*
She was no glamour-puss *pute*
with a cigarette sobbing smoke,

so easily thrown down, spread-eagled, drilled.
Took us off to "Sweet Home" Harlem
and pursued West Indian Archie's

inner-city antics.
My fists love *Warfare.*
Pimps and drug dealers were at odds,

all dutifully nasty and putridly obscene.
Archie was dangerously flush with vinegar
and bile;

he had a chilling aura.
I helped rough-up Sicilians
tryin to scuffle into

our "numbers" truffles.
Ya know, gangsters must be soldiers,
never civilians:

No place for niceties.
We'd tear out intestines as if ropes
from a crimson pulley;

and then cram a nun with members,
digits, tongues, all over her.
West Indian Archie made wops resemble

canoes—
skinned alive and disemboweled.
Faces looked like crushed crabs.

Only stench could be "heard"
in that unfamiliar funk that is heart-pumped fluid,
seething, until collected up in buckets.

(One mobster got so sliced and diced,
a happy dog jumped upon him,
gobbled the man's stumped, spurting cock.)

But quick I had to ditch this abattoir life.
It got real easy when Archie suffered
a gear-shifting, self-hypnosis—

an obliterating neuroses—
asserting I'd taken cash that was his.
His hit men would've whacked me hard!

Nervous, I made Sophia's hot bed
a dominion of bites.
I was lost in an archipelago of pincers....

Arch knew all our man-to-man secrets;
he'd locate me; set unsoiled shovels digging;
treat me to mortal lounging in a hole.

I'd be primitivized.
High time to vamoose from Manhattan—
escape the anthropological slime;

decamp to Boston with Sophia,
and find crooks with a hard-on
for a blonde wig and a boob job.

We got to Harvard, as undaunted as clouds;
set up a purring shop of thieves
to revive the flavour of Batman's "Gotham"—

sordid.
Cast off crummy duds; acted snooty;
not a *paisano* from gutters;

applied A-1 credit to cigarettes, reefers, slop.
Cambridge was a morbid refuge—
ghetto and Harvard, both awkward labyrinths.

Shorty was unhealthy, usually;
his drugs kept him eyeing
a machinery of spooks,

not only the cops, bursting with *Malice*
and Irish brogue,
who we were supposed to obey and smile at.

Anyway, we rummaged damagingly
every property Sophia conned open.
It was sinful to be empty of cash.

There was also gilt *Lust* for white skin;
the seeds of bullet holes
socked into doorways,

as presumptuous as sweat.
My archives can't be washed out,
bleached, rinsed clean.

Caught, Sophia was, to the judge,
dreaded white trash,
but could be married off

to a whey-visaged, milksop clerk
to win suburban *Respectability*.
Shorty almost short-circuited

when he heard our sentence:
He mistook "concurrently" for "cumulatively,"
and shouted he'd prefer

to have a big dinner
and fry in the lectric chair
and taste distasteful dust,

than live on, shrivelling up, in the pen.
I drink ice water and nutmeg in the brig;
steal the moniker and strike the attitude of "Satan,"

but I'm schoolin my noggin in Latin.
I peruse the magazines: Bunny Yeager
is snapping Betty Page; Chuck Yeager

is hogging aerospace.
Mao's kickin the white boys outta China.
Impeccably sinister, as I must become.

[Detroit (Michigan) 30 *novembre* mmxv
& Halifax (Nova Scotia) 6 *décembre* mmxv]

III. The Fire Sermon

[**Waste Land** German translation by Paul Celan (1947)]

Herr Hitler Himmler, the two-backed, two-faced beast,
hissing ss-ss-ss-ss-ss,
whelps skeletons....

His photos show burnt-faces, charred-faces,
fish-mouths thirsty,
hooked by a snagging fist, a gagging blade,

or one spots babies stuffed down toilets.

Nymphs exit the boudoir, but dying,
slutted, slit open.

The word-smog shrouding Hitler Himmler—
a tyranny of *GIFTGAS*—
floats the comedy of the "dirty, inhuman horde"

(sweet Baltic Sea, flow softly, till I end my song)—

provokes scissor-torn-up penises, wrenched off limbs,
flesh spastic with rot, bubbling with maggots,
under the Third Reich Big Top,

where fat thumbs thrust out Jews' eyes,
pudgy fingers vise our throats to gasping,
or we're sawn in half by clown-masked butchers.

Nymphs exit the boudoir, but dying,
slutted, slit open, to birth humungous rats....

By the waters of the Black Sea, I sat down and wept.

(Each bullet dashes slick as water,
gashes keen as an axe.)

Hear the grisly bragging of smokestacks:
"I've devoured a poet, a rabbi, a probable Nobel Laureate";
"I've heaped ash in a soprano's lungs."
The furnaces gorge, belch, glut, and bolt.

(Sweet North Sea, flow softly, till I end my song)—

The wedding ceremonies of knives and raw meat
eat up nights, wherein searchlights sledgehammer eyes,
Tomorrow's headlines= bloodlines blotted out.

Sly quislings push corpse-laden wheelbarrows
to the furnaces, but first hatchet open faces
to get at teeth, the gold and silver in a jawbone.

(Sweet Mediterranean, flow softly, till I end my song)—

The smell of the industrious smokestacks!
Each belch, non-stop, is another person
disappeared into ash.

So that an entire, European map—
peoples—
gets put to the torch....

So, thousands, millions, got processed—
to be able to sift through
needles' eyes....

(We Jewry above all—
melted down like precious-metal jewellery,
in a disposal as liquid as gold....)

Physicists are gutted,
their bellies made rugs;
brains light up as lampshades.

Fillings get torn from teeth
so as to gold-back buzz-bombs;
fat is scooped up for soap.

Railroads lug scalped wigs, wobbly crutches, hydrochloric acid
brandy, sadistic bottles, gutted suitcases, eyes-stuck-to-eyeglasses,
prosthetic axes, chopped-open teeth, false-bottom Bibles, maggot
cutlery, ant crockery,

gold rings, gold earrings, gold necklaces,
to "Canada," that warehouse of loot.
Bones ship to Strasbourg's Institute of Human Anatomy.

Here's a volcano of torn off baby shoes
and toddler clothes (unbuttoned),
a landslide of brushes,

and piles of glum shoe polish tins,
tobacco tins, *GIFTGAS!*
gay tins of the poison, a ton....

So bad's the *Butchery*, the colour red
mutinies against itself,
preferring black.

So, at my whip-clawed back, the nattering
I hear, is a machine-gun, chattering.

Later, guards sprawl naked as unsheathed daggers;
beauties get mishmashed as gristle, bone, ash—
anything easily defiled.

"Tweet, tweet, tweet, tweet
Jug jug jug jug jug jug jug jug
Jugular veins sweet
Chug chug chug chug chug chug chug"

Such screams crept by me upon the waters.

Unreal *History*=
Oppression.

To whit:

"Tituba" the Salem, Massachusetts, Negroid "witch" alleged—
circa 1692—

"Puritans horrify cos they're so flinty—
as narrow as knives:
To them, the Crucifix itself is *Witchery*,
and so their muskets cough.

"These white boys take Negresses
relentlessly, back of flour mill
or wine press, or church (of course),
to suss out virgins and sluice their slits.

"The decorative *phalloi* show *rouge*-embellished inches
winching out a wench's
'conspiratorially gnawing sex,' or plunging therein
like nails thudding into blessèd *Corpus Christi*....

"I know the body is incorrigibly animal—
nimbly and biblically bestial.
So, colonial *Political Economy*
is fleshed-out, demonic scenes

"mimicking Milton's *Paradise Lost*....
The Governor's administration
unfolds endless circuses of *Scandal*;
yet, only 'fallen' gals fall from gallows.

"About us 'witches'? I'm happy
with our fates. No innuendo.
I accept that your entire canon
of *Law* derives from *Devilry*.

"That one man throttles, mauls, another,
to steal his *Treasury*
or that the State
conspires to sever tender necks—

"to wrench lads from ladies—
is simply average *Savagery*.
But know that you're also bound for dust.
And a thousand wastes is every Crusade."

Hi de ho.

To Cernăuți then I came

Helpless helpless helpless helpless
before *History*, mortified by *History*....

O Lord, what is the soundest prayer?
Skin—like paper—has ascended as incense.

Burning has undone so many.
Burning has undone so much.

The Good News?
None of the martyrs outlived *Love*.
       Weialala leia
       Wallala leialala

[Oswiecim (Poland) 12 *mai* mmxv
& Krakow (Poland) 13 *mai* mmxv
& Halifax (Nova Scotia) 23 *mai* mmxv
& Aeropuerto Barcelona—BCN (Spain) 16 *juillet* mmxv
& Escaldes-Engordany (Andorra) 18 & 19 *juillet* mmxv
& Smiths Cove (Nova Scotia) 19 *août* mmxv]

Passages to India (1947)

Rudyard Kipling was a skinflint poet with a skinny booklet
of tinny, schoolboy rhymes—
including scrawny haiku scratched by a scraggly hand,
but also laid open sonnets in long-gone volumes,
besotted by opium,
slurring anthems—paeans to *Imperial Power*—
at soothing, narcotizing volumes,
that preached to Winston Churchill the necessity
of keeping Britain "Great" by keeping India

a brown WASTE
(White-Anglo-Saxon-Terrorized-Exploited)
province....

*

The Brits were as fickle as gods
outta the abominable "Vatican" that's Whitehall

(the tweedy directors of finances
in reedy continents, finding relevance
in shrimps cut down to size—
headless, tailless,
plus unfailing gin-and-cucumber and quinine
cocktails to spritz up every capital enterprise)

and were wantons in their walled-off cantons,
adjacent to Indian urbanity,

from whom they gleaned rice pudding and polo,
and the poetry of the monsoon rains
rhythmically polishing
(if also patiently corroding)
stolid, but paralyzed, marble statues....

*

Mahatma Gandhi was unusual, "unmanly," undulant,
wiry, a wayfarer-seeming, staff-wielding, expert "interferer,"
expert at the *coddiwomple*—
i.e., to move purposefully toward a vague destination,

albeit *Utopia*.
Maybe he faked the appearance of being perpetually peripheral,
but he was *not* the sovereign gangster....

⋆

No: That *WANTED* poster suits the *Baas*—
his grim, dour demeanour—
who ensured Kipling's "white man's burden" got borne
by African porters and Indian servants
through all his industriously sooty "possessions"
("land-grabs");
whose imperial map showed crimson splotches
wherever brown and black people could be "raw materials";
whose Union Jack sun rays that—
unlike the Japanese Empire's equally dagger-shaped beams—
injected *Christ* and *Commerce*
into jungle, forest, desert, and ice-cap;
and who demanded rubies big as eggs;
elephant testicles which, distilled and drunk, could keep
an *eminence grise* erect for joyous hours
(cf. Yeats);
plus all the ginger, indigo, pepper, cinnamon, silk,
sugar, cotton, rubber, ink, and tiger skins
that could be toted, shipped, barged, and dumped—
all on Thames' docks
at a healthy—if unholy—200% interest
(*CONTRA NATURAM*, sayeth "£")—
all profits to be paid out in gold bullion *only*. Quite—

so that the pirate could launder —
gold shower — himself
into a prime ministership, if never princehood;

while his sons could aspire to be civil servants —
simple serpents —
soldier-clerks with India ink, indelible,
plus indefatigable erasers —
whose trunks were fashioned from elephant trunks.

And their mates were debonair *memsahibs*,
journeyed to India to police their men's eyes
and loins,
preserve them from the pure persuasion
of all that multitudinous — and mutinous —
Pulchritude.

*

Because Gandhi said, "Nyet,"
to *White Supremacy* in South Africa,

Freedom — that *Juggernaut* — jaunted eastward,
due (overdue) South,
jolting two — and more — hemispheres,

though Churchill denies the Indies,
and thinks Gandhi looks as elegant, in his robes,
as sloughed skin.

*

Jawaharlal Nehru had been politic,
maybe a playboy, browsing a tumult
of soggy bottom ladies,
while Louis Mountbatten had warred
(Secondly) for Burma, through steady summers,
against "Japs" and malaria;
a bunch of sickening, Rah-Rah, Yahoo campaigns
(including the Canuck-sacrificial, Dieppe raid he fucked up);
but now he'd shutter the Raj
via enlisting Rhodes scholars
(formerly drunk and scuzzy in beleaguered Rodos);
but with Vicereine Edwina—
the pill-popping *poupée*—
aiding his liberation of 400,000,000 human beings,
thanks to (allegedly) trilateral pillow-talk....

*

No one knows whether Edwina's white-lace-gloved hand
gripped a whip in the Viceroy's bedroom,
or whether Nehru was a dirty mentor in loveplay;
or whether her quinine-tonic'd breath pelted
and petted the pundit's perfect, no-pitfall face;
or whether documented quantities of *Touching*
flaunted actual, unquantifiable passions;
or whether their *Coitus*—if any—purred
not like a Catholic mass, but roared
like elephants intercoursing with lions;
or whether Nehru groused as he rowed Edwina's icy crack;
or whether sheets wrinkled where they wrangled,
her *Lust* rankling him as their ankles grazed, bounced....

[Niagara-on-the-Lake (Ontario) 1 & 2 *mars* mmxvii
& Regina (Saskatchewan) 5 *mars* mmxvii]

Mao Reads Pound (1948)

To solve out *Crisis* upon *Crisis*—

express high dudgeon—
Umbrage—
at the accursed circus
of *Inflation* and *Depression*,

this Yank crank, Pound, enacts
gorgeous shitting,
incandescent pissing,
emitting inky characters
that succoured Italy's castor-oil crooners,
its bottoms-up Fascists.

Venice is a dump of lilies—
that marsh, as is Pisa,
as is Washington, D.C.

Under the becalmed wings of bedraggled birds,
imprisoned in storm-pregnant air—

the poet's as frail—
pale—
as a parliamentary page.

His breath is as shivering
and as stealthy as spider webs.

Bet his ink contains
untarnished graces?

[San Michele/Cimitero, Venezia (Italia) 16/5/16]

Mao Reacts to the Holocaust (1948)

Auschwitz? The Brown Shirts' Eden.
Logically patholological.

Grandiose geniuses
got crushed to ash in crematoria.

Everybody disappeared—
every-which-way,

every Jewish body,
eviscerated by everyday depletions

(deletions),

everywhere in Europe.
Survivors are as sporadic

as sunlight in a Canuck April.
Peoples must heed *Nature*'s command:

To survive, struggle!
Oppression= Death.

Thus, the People's Liberation Army
ramps, insuperable, unstoppable.

We're earthquakes incarnate.
Just ask Kai-shek, falling!

(An earthquake struggles briefly
with a citadel until all concrete yields,

and tinkling glass applauds.)
I captain an ocean—*The People*—

and helm—navigate—the *Future*,
charting what is otherwise unfathomable.

If only to breathe!

[**Whitehorse (Yukon Territory) 19** *janvier* **mmxvii**]

Mao Approaches Nanking

I.

Shanghai is factory smelters, smoke, pitch,
bellies aborting fetuses,
gore curving against sidewalks....

Thus, I stir up *The People*
so their blades hack down landlords—
and make hash of bankers—
with torrid result.

I love seeing the slain plutocrats stretched out
like mackerel slanting from fish-hooks.

II.

Through winter shadows, overlapping cool—
rippling frostiness of mountain snow—

through labyrinths of freezing white
or dull, winter sleet—

some of us wearing horses—

we move like startled wings:

To tack over iced rivers—
those crackling fissures—

to rescue the carcass of Nanking....

III.

No longer rats ground down in rubble—
we're guerilla nomads—
pace The Long March on short rations—

inching toward incomparable *Light*

despite cannibalism of our horses—
whenever necessary .

or elucidation of *Trauma*
(*Theory*)—
whenever mandatory.

(Nothing is as occult as *Eternity*.)

J'avance—
a sombre hombre, an umber hombre—
a Chinese bronze, khaki-clad Buddha—
as intrusive and as intensive
as a tidal wave. .

IV.

The mountain snow appears a sugar'd threshold—
after the deserts of dust-gilded flies.

I'm no devotee of *Doubt*—
and no chainsaw dictator—
no ghastly bureaucrat—
but will besiege and sack Beijing—

tolerate gunfight scorings—
romantic *Carnage*—

be a bull thundering like a locomotive.

There's no other way to propitiate *History!*

V.

We've weathered *Sorrow* after *Sorrow*:
Gilded deserts, unaccounted-for hunger,
icy plights, sandpaper thirst, scuttling scorpions,
rounds of fatal *Encirclement*, fire swamps,
and bullet ballets,
and leave our far-flung dead
decorating hysterical maps.

Our victories are aching stories.
We win only as we succumb to bleeding—
and only as th'*Enemy* is finally drained by bleeding—
and flits toward asylum (Formosa).

(Kai-Shek's hogs must be electrocuted:
The meddler must die—nauseatingly—like Himmler!)

VI.

After my troops have taken grass for bed,
or chewed daisies by the roots,
or slogged through furious sunlight,
or died, drowned in dozens, in bulldozing avalanches,
or reached, at last, shadow-embalmed,
the groaning sea,
we are now the pacific governors....

What has our foe wrought?

Blown-up *Kindergartens* and char-broiled infants—
atrocities for the gullet,
plus the insane whoopee of machine-gun.

Sight bullet-gored horses strewn across the plain.

The New China—
the People's Republic—
is founded upon

the fathomless otherness
of the endless, useless dead.*

[**Miami Beach** (Florida) **21** & **22** *février* **mmxvi**]

---

* Cf. Any prospectus of *Aerarium Regale Canadianse.*

Mao @ Nanking

I.

As divisive as a thousand incisions,
sunlight slicks through needling peaks,
timber-ready trees, to surf leaves —
the divorced air —
then spotlight coppery coins,

the scarlet tears of the Koumintang dripping
out nearsighted "slit eyes" bayonet'd into bellies
or out holes drilled by far-sighted bullets.

I don't balk at taking
rebarbative swords
to horse-faced, pig-headed, sons of bitches —
Koumintang assholes....

The Buddha knows our *Fury* is just:

it acquits us of atrocities
as it yields alluring victories.

II.

It was Japs who made Nanjing
a butcher-shop cash register,
who turned Chinese women
into feminine dirt, canine meat.

Intentionally, they churned brain chow-chow,
or trashed genitalia,
so these organs got strewn like garbage
all about gutters.

III.

I survey sun-and-wind-marbled water,
the river defining the valley;
I suffer no *Confusion*.

Alert to the dire fact of Hiroshima
I'll exterminate every Nazi stooge:

I like to hear swords sighing through bellies.

One doesn't wrest the diamond of *Liberty*
from anything but the black coal of *Struggle*.

Gotta use poison to kill fucking rats,
to force volatile *fascisti* to quaff cyanide —
to end their carousing, pillaging, scavenging.

We are guerillas who confront gorillas.
We practice *Hedonism* at gun-point....

IV.

I master the black arts of *Verse*
(*Poems*)
and traverse
("The Long March"),

and bear the bravura scars
of my repetitive storming
of white space —

whacking blades into chests,
cracking ink across pages.

V.

We will have China shimmer clean again—
like a white dove resting in snow....

We transform things
as much as a candle flame tears away darkness.

I'll propose a Ministry of Wine
(spirits dispense with *Depression*)—
wine as white as a nun's fart!

[Halifax (Nova Scotia) 13/3/16
& Niagara Falls (New York) 30 *Nisan* / *avril* mmxvi]

"Mao Inks 'The People's Liberation Army Captures Nanking'"

— a lu shih
April 1949

Seizing the mountain, this crazy, jagged
Zigzag of crags, snow cliffs, cleft, skittish rocks
Lunging toward the moon's white gravity,
I imagine dragons' wings brush my head.
I push vertically, hear the sky break,
Level the antiquated order of things.
    Below, the *State* totters. My million troops,
Their hands blood-baptized, their heads flame-haloed,
Scribe fresh *History* with bullets, grenades.
The city unscrolls, awaits our crimson
Calligraphy, brush-stroke and sword-stroke.
    Look! Snow hammers earth with leaden softness....
Ah, this world's mutable: mountains become coral reefs.

[Kitchener-Waterloo (Ontario)? *avril* / *Nisan* 1985?]

毛泽东作《七律·中国人民解放军占领南京》*

1949年四月

那些疯狂、粗糙的峭壁蜿蜒曲折，

悬崖白茫茫一片、裂开的岩石摇摇欲坠，

我站在山巅，

在白色光芒的牵引下，奔向月亮，

想象龙的羽翼拂过自己的头颅，

我垂直向上推开去，听见了天空的断裂，

旧时代一去不复返。

山下，整个国家在苦苦挣扎，

我的百万雄兵，

经历过鲜血的洗礼、在烈焰中重生，

冒着枪林弹雨去书写全新的历史。

南京城像卷轴一样舒展开来，

等待我们的笔锋和剑锋为它留下红色的印记。

看哪！轻柔的雪花重重地敲打着大地……

啊，　万事无常，再转身，已是沧海桑田。

---

* Trans. Qi Liang (綦亮) [Suzhou City (People's Republic of China) 19 *Nisan* mmxvi]

This Continuance Concludes

CANTICLES
I
(MMXVI–MMXVII)

～

La Beauté meurt de l'exhaustion.
—Benjamin Fondane, "Titanic."

This is how all beauty ends.
—Derek Walcott, *Omeros.*

*Extro: Reverie & Reveille**

Homer: A dog tried to hold up the corpse of Hector —
   lacustrine flesh, tinting black —
Once he was flung into the latrine-black Mediterranean,
   black sharks —
An infestation — swarmed. An epic poet is like that dog, upholding
Classicism and *Virtue*, despite fresh, imminent *Decay*, and tidal,
Ongoing *Decadence*. We swear into the open ears of the dying
To curse the souls of the vulgar, unheroic dead: Our poets's task.

Milton: The Black Panther partisan, Jesus Christ,
Insisting His pure Flesh be sacrificed,
Heeded never Roman joking nor Hebraic jests —
The scourging thorns, the spikes drove through his wrists
And ankles. His hummed spirituals dulled *Pain*.
He gulped vinegar like so much champagne.
A spear thudded in — budded from — His side.
But He knew His demise was sanctified —
So He'd be risen up — resurrected
In a crescendo of *Light* perfected.
He'd look as fresh as if he'd wandered
From a wedding-cake table. His speech thundered,
And His disciples flocked to the rose scent
Of His *Rose-Up Life*, His flowered Government.

Epic poets are mirror martyrs, of
Sorts, whose faithful words witness deathless *Love*.

Dante: The epic poet is like a weasel,
digging up the dead to retrieve the execrable
booty of their sanguinary, but truthful bones.

---

* I.e., *Error*.

Our Muse is Medusa, unhurt, hissing,
unable to loathe spirits. Each of us is
a scrapbook poet, not a textbook poet:

Our images aren't canvasses,
but broken, splintered, shattered, stained-glass:
The prism of the crashed-down looking-glass.

Pound: Let assistant professors, untenured,
slave over epic, the endless endnotes,
where what's original is illegible.

Walcott: The masque of *Interpretation* is what each epic
undertakes, no matter how metrically
sophisticated, bluesy—as in a Bessie Smith classic.

Such free-for-all? That's *Négritude*, metaphorically,
as we tally awfully black histories, allegorically,
wherein masters mutate to monsters, evermore: Categorically!

Auditor: I hear my forebears—
Voices from a hearse.
Biblical leaves curl
Like lips set to snarl.

Crippling are these truths—
From elders to youths.
Prevalent *Darkness*—
Sanitation-less—

Dirty as a grave—
Is what ex-slaves have.
Apollonian—
Or draconian—

Our verses must be:
Mellifluity
Bleeds no plain nectar
Or honey. Hector—

And our noble dead—
Must inspire each head,
Exemplifying—
And amplifying—

Pluto and Venus—
Beauty got from dross:
Undiluted ink
Sparkling at the brink.

[YVR (Vancouver International Airport,
Richmond, British Columbia) 24 *février* mmxvii]

Polemical "Conclusion"

No? The Atlantic's swirling, crimson whirlpools
don't preface Auschwitz ash-heaps?

No? Combative Nat Turner don't find any align
with that putative ally, Doc Albert Einstein?

Guess, too many of us exist under an inconsequential sun —
and are only "absurdly" human —

granted those unending allegations
of *Imbecility* and *Inferiority* and *Immorality*.

★

Am I Exhibit "A" in this regard?

I'm hardly "black," and am somewhat "Native,"
with a dragged-out, belly-dredging laugh,
and *Poetry* slagged, rightly, as "bombastic":
My voice be a lot of bitter roaring, eh?

Not to mention hoarse snorts
thuddin pidgin English
out ma mouth —

or inculpable coffles' whimpers
simpering in ma brain slosh....

What's the value of my first-person address,
i.e., "I"?

I'm just an inkhorn mate —
a volcano of books
spewed in abusive protrusion.

★

So, how is my Deity not "shabby,"
given the bounty of horrors
and the poverty of miracles
allotted our number,

we "blacks" with changeable names—
names that belong to comic-book heroes
("Malcolm X")—
and unchanging deaths?

★

Yet, this first draught of *Canticles*
is no poor song, no furtive litanies
(may I pray?)
as evanescent as a leap,
for I picture wounds as blunt as a door.

Sleepless before *History*,
one turns to *Poetry*.
Arrogant as *History* is *Poetry*.

★

Habeo stylum—
I have my pen (stylus) *and* my *Style*—
neither old-fashioned nor sorry,
and will not edit *Truth*.

Unchained poet as I be,
I post hardback cantos—
not ashen scribbles—
but igneous words ripping air
(or so I dream).

What is *now*, was *then*—once.

Would Occidental conquering be acknowledged—
Deformities, Decimations, Dooms—
our vulgar *Innocence*
would be rectified.

Concluding in Madeira,
diagonal to Zanzibar,
I can say that Africa mirrors still
the refined *Hell* that's Europe

and its overseas offshoots....

A scum of bacteria plaquing (plaguing) wine....

[**Funchal (Madeira) 20** *décembre* **mmxv**]

TABLE OF VERSES

*(published — or accepted [or not],
in order of appearance)*

~~~

"'Prophet' Nat Turner on his Southampton Insurrection (1831)."

"Nat Turner Confessing All: By Thomas Grey."

"Rum: A Metaphysical Disquisition": *Freefall.* 24.3 (Fall 2014): 8–12.

"An Introduction to the Late Revolution in 'Haiti': By Abraham Lincoln (1834)": *Arc.* 2016. http://arcpoetry.ca/2016/04/27/george-elliott-clarke-an-introduction-to-the-late-revolution-in-haiti-by-abraham-lincoln-1834/

"A Russian Aristocrat Complains of Pushkin": *The Nashwaak Review.* 30/31.1 (Summer/Fall 2013): 12–13.

"A Prospect of Bahia (January 1835): By Vitório Sule": *Existere.* 33.2 (Spring/Summer 2014): 20–21.

"The Liberation of Bahia Has Begun! (ca. 1835): By Vitório Sule": *Freefall.* 24.3 (Fall 2014): 13.

"At Pompey Square": *Vancouver Island University.* https://www2.viu.ca/gustafson/ 2015.

"Audubon's Observations (1835)": *In/Words Magazine.* 15.3 (2016): 30–32.

"Audubon's Observations: Gloss."

"Pushkin Acts Byronic": *The Dalhousie Review.* 95.3 (Fall 2015): 334.

"The Death of Alexander Pushkin": *Vallum.* 14.1 [Forthcoming]

"*La Muerte de Alexander Pushkin*": [Mexican] Trans. James Eugene Lindsey. Otober 2016.

"A Passage from *Les Cenelles: Choix de poésies indigènes* (1845)."

"Declaration of the Independence of Liberia (1847)": *Scrivener Creative Review.* 41 (April 2016): 54–59.

"Elizabeth Barrett Browning Recalls Robert Browning's Wooing (ca. 1847)": *Central European Journal of Canadian Studies.* 9 (2014): 17–20.

"Bobby & Betty: Anatomy of a Marriage." *In-Between: Liminal Spaces in Canadian Literature and Culture.* Ed. Stefan L. Brandt. Peter Lang: Frankfurt am Main, 2017. [Forthcoming]

"The Port of Bordeaux: *Des détails*": *Scrivener Creative Review.* 41 (April 2016): 66–67.

"Follow Martin, Follow Moses!: By Daniele Manin": *Soglie.* [Pisa, Italy] Fall 2016.

"Fai come Martin, fai come Moses!: di Daniele Manin": [Italian] Trans. Fausto Ciompi. *Soglie.* [Pisa, Italy] Fall 2016.

"The Head Slave Drafts His Valentine": *The Capilano Review.* 3.27 (Fall 2015): 67–68.

"To Brother Tuppam." *In-Between: Liminal Spaces in Canadian Literature and Culture.* Ed. Stefan L. Brandt. Peter Lang: Frankfurt am Main, 2017. [Forthcoming]

"Transit to Spring."

"Transit to Spring": *Canadar Somokalin Kobita.* [Bangla] Trans. Parvez Chowdhury. Dhaka, Bangladesh: Farid Ahmed Somoy Prakashan, 2016. 29.

"The Confession of Celia: A Missouri Slave, 1850": *Riddle Fence.* 17 (Spring 2014): 37–41.

"Escape to th'Escarpment!" *Poem.* 1.3 (Autumn 2013): 39–41.

"*Voice of the Fugitive* (1851): By Henry Bibb": Dodd & Kimber. *From Far and Wide: Stories of Refugees and Migrants in Canada*. [Forthcoming]

"Harriet Tubman Proceeds": *The Rusty Toque*. Issue 6. May 30, 2014. http://us4.campaign-archive1.com/?u=bf79f14a81cbbcb3771cdcaa7&id =0f6c885aa0&e=51249f1a50

"Marathon": *In/Words Magazine*. 15.3 (2016): 28–29.

"Letter from Mary Ann Shadd (1853)": Dodd & Kimber. *From Far and Wide: Stories of Refugees and Migrants in Canada*. [Forthcoming]

"Salutations to 'General Moses'": *Portal*. 25 (2016): 57.

"George Boyer Vashon Drafts 'Vincent Ogé'": *Poem*. 3.2 (June 2015): 148–149.

"*The New York Times* Uncovers Arson": *Grain*. 41.2 (Winter 2014): 63–66. *The Best Canadian Poetry 2015*. Ed. Jacob McArthur Mooney. Toronto: Tightrope, 2016. 16–21.

"*New York Times* deconspiră o incendiere": [Romanian] Trans. Diana Manole. LiterNet.ro. "Poezia săptămânii" (The Poem of the Week.) Web. 16 June 2015. http://atelier.liternet.ro/articol/16082/George-Elliott-Clarke-Diana-Manole/New-York-Times-deconspira-o-incendiere.html

"Harriet Tubman & Harriet Beecher Stowe: A Debate": *The Varsity*. [University of Toronto] 136.18 (29 February 2016): 14.

"Chain / Reaction": *The Prairie Journal*. 65 (2015): 19.

"Spirituals 1: 1–7": *The Poet's Quest for God*. Eds. Todd Swift, Fr. Oliver Brennan, with Kelly Davio & Cate Myddleton-Evans. London: Eyewear Publishing, 2016. 111.

"A Prologue to *Uncle Tom's Cabin*: By Josiah Henson." *In-Between: Liminal Spaces in Canadian Literature and Culture*. Ed. Stefan L. Brandt. Peter Lang: Frankfurt am Main, 2017. [Forthcoming]

"The Ecstasy of Linda Brent (a.k.a. Harriet Jacobs)": *Kola.* 24.2 (Fall 2012): 16–18.

"To Critique Edward Mitchell Bannister": *Grain.* 41.2 (Winter 2014): 61.

"Glimpse": *Selected Canticles.* Ottawa: above/ground press, 2012.

"Thomas Chandler Haliburton Regards Liverpool, 1855": Chaudière Books. April 3, 2016. http://www.chaudierebooks.blogspot.ca/2016/04/national-poetry-month-2016–george.html

"Pamphlet to the Electors of Canada West (1856): (By Judge T.C. Haliburton)": *Morel Magazine.* 2015. Erratic Press. morelmag.ca/article/canticles

"Letter from Rev. King": *Great Lakes Review.* 6 (Summer/Fall 2015): 21–22.

"The Love Song of Charles Baudelaire" (1857): *In/Words Magazine.* 15.3 (2016): 76.

"À Jeanne Duval: By Charles Baudelaire": *In/Words Magazine.* 15.3 (2016): 77–78.

"Jeanne Duval's Riposte."

"From Amherstburg, 1857": *Morel Magazine.* 2015. Erratic Press. morelmag.ca/article/canticles

"William Hall Halts the Rebellion at Lucknow, India (1857)": *Kola.* 29.1. 2017. [Forthcoming]

"Chronicle of the Triumph of William Hall, V.C., at The Relief of Lucknow, India: By Sir Richard Burton": Natalee Caple & Ronald Cummings. Eds. *"Harriet's Legacies: Race, Historical Memory and Futures in Canada."* [Forthcoming]

"'Darwin's "Natural Selection". Applied to Slaver Entertainment' (1859): By Mandingo Appolonius." *In-Between: Liminal Spaces in Canadian Literature and Culture.* Ed. Stefan L. Brandt. Peter Lang: Frankfurt am Main, 2017. [Forthcoming]

"William Hall: Citation for *Valour*: By Sir Richard Burton."

"Victoria Summons Hall (October 1859)": *The Maynard* (April 2015). http://www.themaynard.org/Vol8No1/VictoriaSummonsHall.php

"William Hall, V.C., Remembers": Natalee Caple & Ronald Cummings. Eds. *"Harriet's Legacies: Race, Historical Memory and Futures in Canada."* [Forthcoming]

"Statement on William Hall by the Rebel, Raja Jai Lal Singh, Writ in Prison Before His 1857 Execution (But Lost Until 1860)."

"Upon Commencing to Draft 'Moses: A Story of the Nile': By Frances Ellen Watkins Harper": *Existere*. 33.2 (Spring/Summer 2014): 22–25.

"Negro Inventory."

"*Inventario Negro*": *Revista El Humo*. 2016. [Mexican Spanish] Trans. Andrea Martinez. http://www.revistaelhumo.com/2016/01/george-elliott-clarke.html

"Longfellow Composes a 'Blues'": *African American Review*. 47.1 (Spring 2014): 182–183.

"Ante-Bellum, Autumn 1860: By Abraham Lincoln": *African American Review*. 45.4 (Winter 2012): 643–645.

"Douglass Anticipates Civil War": "February 2014 News & Member Spotlight." Denver: EDEN Theatrical Workshop, Inc., 2014. [2].

"The Narrative of Lincoln States [Not His Real Name]": Parts III & IV. *Upstreet*. 10 (2014): 55–57.

"Julia Ward Howe Composes 'The Battle Hymn of the Republic' (1861)": *The Walrus*. 12.10 (December 2015): 59.

"Jefferson Davis Opines."

"Upon Re-Reading Othello: By Adah Isaacs Menken": *Selected Canticles*. Ottawa: above/ground press, 2012.

"Sojourner Truth's War Measures: A Ghazal."

"Whitman Compiles His *Leaves*": *The Nashwaak Review.* 30/31.1 (Summer/Fall 2013): 8–11.

"How It Strikes a Soldier": *Great Lakes Review.* 6 (Summer/Fall 2015): 23.

"The Siege of Port Hudson, Louisiana, May 27, 1863: By Captain André Caillou": *The Harlequin.* 2016. http://www.theharlequin.org/clarke1/

"At Gettysburg (July 1–3, 1863)": *Sewer Lid.* March 2016. https://sewerlid.com/index.php/archives/sl-01/

"At Gettysburg."

"Death of a Union Soldier: By Walt Whitman": *Matrix.* 100 (Winter 2015): 8.

"Confessions of a Union Spy (or Ode to the Confederate Dead)": *Selected Canticles.* Ottawa: above/ground press, 2012.

"Whitman at the Front."

"Frederick Douglass Lauds the War": *Xavier Review.* 35.2 (Fall 2015): 73–74.

"Frederick Douglass Considers General Robert E. Lee": *African American Review.* 47.1 (Spring 2014): 184.

"Sherman Marches to the Sea": *Maple Tree Literary Supplement.* 21 (Aug–Dec 2016). http://www.mtls.ca/issue21/poetry-george-elliott-clarke/

"Lincoln Plans for Peace (*Pace* Appomattox)." *Contemporary Verse 2.* 2017. [Forthcoming]

"James Madison Bell in 'Canada' (1865)." *The Windsor Review.* [Forthcoming]

"Letter of Jourdon Anderson: 7 August 1865": *Morel Magazine.* 2015. Erratic Press. morelmag.ca/article/canticles

"Post-Bellum Negro Inventory": *The Capilano Review*. 3.27 (Fall 2015): 70–71.

"Instructions Upon Emancipation: By Frances Ellen Watkins Harper": *Great Lakes Review*. 6 (Summer/Fall 2015): 13–16.

"On Queen Victoria: By Karl Marx": *Rampike*. 21.2 (2012): 59.

"Adah Isaacs Menken's Compromises." *The Windsor Review*. [Forthcoming]

"Darwin's Editorial on East African Slavery (1868)": *Great Lakes Review*. 6 (Summer/Fall 2015): 17–20.

"Paradise (1869): By Harriet Tubman": *Portal*. 25 (2016): 56.

"*Le Bateau en état d'ébriété* (1870)": *The Argosy*. [Sackville, NB] 145.14 (February 4, 2016): 12.

"Anatomy of *La IIIe République* (1870): By Alexandre Dumas, *fils*": *Canadian Literature*. 222 (Autumn 2014): 30–33.

"Discourse on The Negro: By Charles Darwin."

"Ntshingwayo kaMahole Fits Guards to Battle Britain (1879)": *The Prairie Journal*. 65 (2015): 23–24.

"Ntshingwayo kaMahole Outlines Strategy (1879)": *ottawater*. 12 (2016): 21.

"Isandlwana (1879)": *In/Words*. 14.3 (Spring 2015): 22–23.

"Encountering Ntshingwayo kaMahole (1879)." *In-Between: Liminal Spaces in Canadian Literature and Culture*. Ed. Stefan L. Brandt. Peter Lang: Frankfurt am Main, 2017. [Forthcoming] Also in *University of Toronto Magazine*. 2017. [Forthcoming] See also *U of T Magazine*. April 2017. [Forthcoming]

"Darwin's Marginalia in More's *Utopia*."

"Rimbaud, Deposing (1884)": *Selected Canticles*. Ottawa: above/ground press, 2012.

"Whitman Pens 'The Rape of Florida' (1884)."

"Overheard at The Berlin Conference (1884–85)": *Zeitschrift für Kanada-Studien.* 36 (2016): 102–107.

"Partial Transcript of the Berlin Conference (1884–1885)": *Global Brief.* (Winter/Spring 2016): 64.

"Repressed Transcript of The Berlin Conference (1884–85)." *Maple Tree Literary Supplement.* 22 (Spring 2017). http://www.mtls.ca/issue22/poetry-george-elliott-clarke/

"Confession of a Jesuit Priest in Brazil, 1887": *Great Lakes Review.* 6 (Summer/Fall 2015): 9–12.

"*Ports Négriers Européens.*" *Maple Tree Literary Supplement.* 21 (Aug–Dec 2016). http://www.mtls.ca/issue21/poetry-george-elliott-clarke/

"Josef Korzeniowski *à* Freetown, Sierra Leone (1890)": *Anglistica Pisana.* [Pisa, Italy] Fall 2016.

"In the Congo": October 15, 2014. http://poetsatwork.org/international-poetry-forums/contemporary-canadian-poetry-a-roundtable/

"Flight from The Congo." *The Dalhousie Review.* 93.2 (2013): 179–183.

"Paul Laurence Dunbar Selects a Theme": *Existere.* 33.2 (Spring/Summer 2014): 17–19.

"Paul Laurence Dunbar on his *Lyrics of Lowly Life* (1896)": *Vancouver Isand University.* 2015. https://www2.viu.ca/gustafson/

"Papers of Edward Mitchell Bannister, Barbizonian": Natalee Caple & Ronald Cummings. Eds. "*Harriet's Legacies: Race, Historical Memory and Futures in Canada.*" [Forthcoming]

"Herbert Vivian, M.A., Publishes *Tunisia* (1899)." *In-Between: Liminal Spaces in Canadian Literature and Culture.* Ed. Stefan L. Brandt. Peter Lang: Frankfurt am Main, 2017. [Forthcoming]

"Bannister Reflects": Natalee Caple & Ronald Cummings. Eds. *Harriet's Legacies: Race, Historical Memory and Futures in Canada.*" [Forthcoming]

"Adrift, in Paris." *Humber Literary Review.* 3.1 (Spring & Summer 2016): 21.

"The Negro: An Anatomy: By Rudyard Kipling.'"*

"'À Rimini' (1906)." *Carteggi Letterari*—critica e dintorni—webmagazine di cultura, arte, musica, attualità, letteratura, poesia. Fall 2016. http://www.carteggiletterari.it/2016/11/12/le-altre-lingue-canada-le-aree-anglofone-george-elliott-clarke/

"Considering John Brown (1909): By W.E.B. Du Bois": *Global Brief.* 18 (Fall 2015): 64.

"'Witnessing "Jazz" (1910)': By W.E.B. Du Bois (Exclusive to *The Crisis*)": *The Maple Tree Literary Supplement.* 20 (Sep-Dec 2015). http://www.mtls.ca/issue20/poetry-george-elliott-clarke/

"Eyeing Bellocq": *KOLA.* 28.1 (Spring 2016): 10–12.

"Bellocq Snaps Ophelia": *Sewer Lid.* March 2016. https://sewerlid.com/index.php/archives/sl-01/

"Ophelia Answers Bellocq."

"Du Bois Critiques Scott Joplin's *Treemonisha* (1915)": *The Rusty Toque.* Issue 6. May 30, 2014. http://us4.campaign-archive1.com/?u=bf79f14a8 1cbbcb3771cdcaa7&id=0f6c885aa0&e=51249f1a50

"Du Bois Screens *Birth of a Nation* (1915)."

"From the Diary of William Andrew White, à Lajoux, Jura, France, *décembre* 1917": Mounted in "Called to Serve; An Exhibit Honouring Canada's Military Chaplains of All Faiths." St. James Cathedral, Toronto, Ontario, November 6–16, 2014. Reprinted in *In Flanders Fields: 100 Years; Writing on War, Loss, and Remembrance.* Ed. Amanda Betts. Toronto: Knopf Canada, 2015. 226–235. See also:

---

* Cf. "The Negro: An Anatomy." *Il grande incantatore per Ishmael Reed.* Ed. Giorgio Rimondi. Milano: Agenzia X, 2016. 10-15. By G.E.C. [Italian] Translation by Fabio Zucchella.

http://ottawacitizen.com/entertainment/books/in-honour-of-flanders-fields-a-poem
(Saturday, November 7, 2015) &
"The White Man's War." *The Ottawa Citizen.* (Saturday, November 7, 2015: D8

"Saint-John Perse Ponders Antillean Slavery (1924)."

"T.S. Eliot Translates Saint-John Perse (1924)."

"T.S. Eliot se traduce San Juan Perse (1924)": [Mexican Spanish] Trans. James Eugene Lindsey.

"Colette: Interview Re: 'Willy' (1928)": *Kola.* 29.1. 2017. [Forthcoming]

"Garcia Lorca, Harlemite (1929)."

"Apropos Nancy Cunard (ca. 1929)": *Maple Tree Literary Supplement.* 22 (Spring 2017). http://www.mtls.ca/issue22/poetry-george-elliott-clarke/

"Nicolás Guillén: *The Poetics* (1930)."

"Nicolás Guillén: la poetica (1930):" *Soglie.* [Pisa, Italia] Fall 2016. [Italian] Trans. Fausto Ciompi.

"Jean Toomer Seduces Georgia O'Keeffe (1930)." *The Windsor Review.* [Forthcoming]

"To All Historians (or "The Bastille Concerto"): By Julien Benda (1933): *Maple Tree Literary Supplement.* 22 (Spring 2017)." http://www.mtls.ca/issue22/poetry-george-elliott-clarke/

"Nancy Cunard's Love Poem (1934)": *Scrivener Creative Review.* 41 (April 2016): 63.

"El Poema de Amor de Nancy Cunard (1934)": [Mexican Spanish] Trans. James Eugene Lindsey.

"À Tempio Malatestiano (Rimini): By W.E.B. Du Bois": *Comparative Literature for a New Century*. Eds. Giulia de Gasperi and Joseph Pivato. McGill-Queen's University Press. 2018. [Forthcoming].

"Ezra Pound @ Rimini, 1935": *Comparative Literature for a New Century*. Eds. Giulia de Gasperi and Joseph Pivato. McGill-Queen's University Press. 2018. [Forthcoming].

"Bessie Smith's Seminal Blues (ca. 1935)": *Exile: The Literary Quarterly*. 40.1 (2016): 90–91.

"Du Bois Protests Italy's Assault on Ethiopia (1935)": *Maple Tree Literary Supplement*. 22 (Spring 2017). http://www.mtls.ca/issue22/poetry-george-elliott-clarke/

"Ellington Tours Africville, Nova Scotia (1936)."

"Mao Authors 'On Contradiction' (1937)."

"Paul Robeson Salutes the U.S.S.R. (1937)."

"Louis vs. Schmeling (1938): By Langston Hughes."

"Harlem Pamphlet (1943): By Langston Hughes": *The Varsity*. [University of Toronto] 136.18 (29 February 2016): 14.

"Auschwitz II, or Birkenau: A Survey": *The Sackville Tribune-Post*. February 10, 2016: 10.

"Addendum to 'Pisan Canto' for 'St.' Louis Till: By Ezra Pound." *The Windsor Review*. [Forthcoming]

"The Autobiography of 'Detroit Red' (1946)."

"III. The Fire Sermon [*Waste Land* German translation by Paul Celan (1947)]": *The Walrus*. April 15, 2016. http://thewalrus.ca/the-fire-sermon/

"Passages to India (1947)."

"Mao Reads Pound (1948)": *The Windsor Review*. [Forthcoming]

"Mao Reacts to the Holocaust (1948)."

"Mao Approaches Nanking": *Maple Tree Literary Supplement*. 22 (Spring 2017). http://www.mtls.ca/issue22/poetry-george-elliott-clarke/

"Mao @ Nanking": *The Windsor Review*. [Forthcoming]

"Mao Inks 'The People's Liberation Army Captures Nanking'": *Lush Dreams, Blue Exile: Fugitive Poems, 1978–1993*. By George Elliott Clarke. Lawrencetown Beach, NS: Pottersfield Press, 1994. 22.

"Mao Inks 'The People's Liberation Army Captures Nanking'": [Chinese] Trans. Qi Liang.

"Extro: Reverie & Reveille": The CBC Docs Firsthand website. March 9, 2017. http://www.cbc.ca/firsthand/features/canticles-reverie-and-reveille

"Polemical 'Conclusion.'"

ACKNOWLEDGEMENTS

The Pierre Elliott Trudeau Foundation's Fellowship Prize (2005–08) transported me to Zanzibar, Africa, where this epic began. Harvard University's William Lyon Mackenzie King Visiting Professorship in Canadian Studies jetted me to Stockholm, Cadiz, Rome, and New Orleans, and tethered me to Cambridge, Massachusetts, for one year (2013–14). The Library of Parliament's Parliamentary Poet Laureateship of Canada (2016–17) sustained me in Ottawa (ON), among other sites. A six-campus tour of Germany (Frankfurt [Johann Wolfgang Goethe-Universität], Marburg [Philipps Universität], Mainz [Johannes Gutenberg Universität], Münster [Westfälische Wilhelms Universität], Bremen [Bremer Institut für Kanada und Québec Studien]) and Austria (Graz [Karl-Franzens Universität]) in December 2016, organized by Prof. Katja Sarkowsky of Westfälische Wilhelms Universität (Münster) and Ms. Giovanna Riccio of Toronto, brought me time and space for some editing. Dr. Sonia Labatt, Ph.D., and Victoria University (*via* The E.J. Pratt Professorship at the University of Toronto), sent me packing everywhere else, from Paris to Puumala, from London (ON) to Liverpool (UK), and from Florianopolis to Funchal, *et cetera*. If my verses deserve curses, cuss me out. If my pressings seem blessings, laud my benefactors.

The standard suspects — *The* John Fraser, Riitta Tuohiniemi, Paul Zemokhol — backed (and eyed) my poetics. My editors were Stephen Brown, Michael Mirolla, and Mr. Zemokhol (perspicaciously, zestily). My now-ex allotted me a home in Nantes, France, 2008–2009.

My voluntary translators in *Canticles I* (MMXVII) were Fausto Ciompi (Italian), Parvez Chowdhury (Bangla), Qi Liang (Chinese), James Eugene Lindsey (Mexican Spanish), Diana Manole (Romanian), and Andrea Martinez (Mexican Spanish). Anticipate yet others....

Michael Mirolla welcomed this project as soon as I proposed it, way back in 2011. I'm proud to be associated with Guernica Editions, and I anticipate, with relish, the subsequent volumes of *Canticles*.

David Moratto executed the design of this book, but the titular font and interior drop caps reflect the artistry of William Clarke (1935–2005). Digitized in 2011 by Andrew Steeves of Gaspereau Press, *Bill Clarke Caps* is a font my late father drafted—with yardstick, pencil, and ink—in 1969.

Canticles I (MMXVII) was edited in Germany on Deutsche Bahn train IC 2026 (Car 7, Seat 115), Mainz-Münster; Deutsche Bahn train IC 2218 (Car 12, Seat 92), Münster-Bremen; and in Bremen. This book was also edited in Canada on Air Canada 606 (Seat 18A), YYZ (Mississauga [ON]) to YHZ (Enfield [NS]), and in Halifax (NS), Montréal (QC), Dorval (QC), Ottawa (ON), Whitehorse (YT), Erik Nielsen Whitehorse International Airport (YXY), Sydney (NS), Sydney/J.A. McCurdy Airport (YQY), Wolfville (NS), Vancouver (BC), Vancouver International Airport (YVR), Regina (SK), Kelowna (BC), and Edmonton (AB). Corrections were also enacted at Heywoods, Speightstown, St. Peter (Barbados). Work waxed, *décembre-mars* mmxvi-mmxvii.

ABOUT THE AUTHOR

The 4th Poet Laureate of Toronto (2012–15) and 7th Parliamentary Poet Laureate of Canada (2016–17), George Elliott Clarke is a revered wordsmith. He is a noted artist in song, drama, fiction, screenplay, essays, and poetry. Now teaching African-Canadian literature at the University of Toronto, Clarke has taught at Duke, McGill, the University of British Columbia, and Harvard. He holds eight honorary doctorates, plus appointments to the Order of Nova Scotia and the Order of Canada. His recognitions include the Pierre Elliott Trudeau Fellows Prize, the Governor-General's Award for Poetry, the National Magazine Gold Award for Poetry, the Premiul Poesis (Romania), the Dartmouth Book Award for Fiction, the Eric Hoffer Book Award for Poetry (US), and the Dr. Martin Luther King Jr. Achievement Award. Clarke's work is the subject of *Africadian Atlantic: Essays on George Elliott Clarke* (2012), edited by Joseph Pivato.

RECYCLED
Paper made from
recycled material
FSC® C100212

Printed in April 2017
by Gauvin Press,
Gatineau, Québec